MULTI-SECULARISM

MULTI-SECULARISM

SECULARISM
A NEW AGENDA

PAUL KURTZ

Transaction Publishers
New Brunswick (U.S.A.) and London (U.K.)

Library of Congress Catalog Number: 2010004000
ISBN: 978-1-4128-1419-5
Printed in the United States of America

Library of Congress Cataloging-in-Publication Data

Kurtz, Paul, 1925-
    Multi-secularism : a new agenda / Paul Kurtz.
        p. cm.
    Includes bibliographical references and index.
    ISBN 978-1-4128-1419-5
    1. Secular humanism. I. Title.
BL2747.6.K875 2010
211'.6–dc22

2010004000

Contents

Preface

This book presents the case for secularism and the secular society, issues that have moved to the center stage of world controversy. As usual, I seem to have been cast onto the barricades, for there are vigorous opponents of secularization. The topics discussed in *Multi-Secularism: A New Agenda* stand midway between philosophy and the social sciences and are relevant to both.

The agenda for secularism and the secular society is part of the battle for the open democratic society. Multi-secularism recognizes that if the agenda is to succeed, the forms that secularism take must be adapted to the unique socio-cultural traditions of a country or region, whether Christian, Islamic, Hindu, Shinto, Buddhist, or some other faith. The first principle of secularism is eloquently expressed in the First Amendment to the Constitution of the United States, against the establishment of a religion or the prohibition of its free exercise. Freedom of conscience and the right to believe or disbelieve in the reigning theology or ideology of a country is essential. The right to dissent is a human right and a precondition of any democratic society.

The second major contribution of secularism is to the humanization of ethics and the willingness of the state to permit alternative conceptions of righteousness and the good life. What are the principles and values of secular morality is therefore a key question.

Actually, *Multi-Secularism* is the third volume of a trilogy of my books published over a fifteen-year period by Transaction. The first was *Toward a New Enlightenment: The Philosophy of Paul Kurtz* (1994), edited by Vern L. Bullough and Timothy J. Madigan, which was a compilation of my articles by two colleagues who knew my work well. The second, *Skepticism and Humanism: the New Paradigm* (2001), was edited by myself and focused on two broad intellectual trends in the contemporary world, the skeptical methodology and the humanist outlook.

I am especially pleased that Transaction has undertaken to publish these volumes. My special gratitude goes to Irving Louis Horowitz, for

Transaction stands out as one of the great social-science publishers in the world. At a time when book publishing is under heavy stress, Transaction has brilliantly and courageously published distinguished books by independent scholars and scientists, books often against the grain. I am honored to continue as one within the stable of authors of Transaction. Many of the articles in this volume have appeared in scholarly or popular journals. Sidney Hook used to say that he was pleased when his "fugitive" essays appeared in book form. I am likewise gratified that many of these fugitive essays will be made available to a wider intellectual forum.

—Paul Kurtz

Introduction
The Battle for Secularism[1]

The battle for secularism has leaped to center stage worldwide; we find it being contested or defended everywhere. Of the world's fifty-seven Islamic countries, virtually all except Turkey and Tunisia attempt to safeguard or enact Islamic law (*sharia*) as embodied in the Koran. Radical Islamists wage *jihad* against the secular society. Pope Benedict XVI rails against secularism, portraying it as the major challenge to Roman Catholicism. There have been attempts in Eastern Europe to reestablish the Eastern Orthodox Church. In the United States, the Religious Right and its spokespersons vociferously castigate secularism. Mitt Romney claims that freedom requires religion. He says nothing about the rights of unbelievers in America and accuses them of wishing to establish "the religion of secularism." Regrettably, leading Democrats have remained silent rather than defend the secular society for fear of antagonizing religious supporters. Nevertheless, secularism is growing; it is essential for flourishing vibrant, pluralistic, democratic societies and especially important in today's developing countries.

However, secularism needs to be adapted to diverse cultural conditions if it is to gain ground. I submit that we cannot legislate secularism *uberhaupt* without recognizing the cultural traditions in which it emerges. Accordingly, *multi-secularism* seems to be the best strategy to pursue: that is, adapting secular ideas and values to the societies in which they arise.

The question that I wish to raise is: What is secularism and/or the secular society? I will focus on three main characteristics.

Separation of Church and State

First, secularism refers to *the separation of church and state*. In the United States, this means the First Amendment's provision that "Congress

1

shall make no law respecting an establishment of religion, or prohibiting the free exercise thereof." This vital principle implies that the state should be *neutral* about religion, allowing freedom of conscience and diversity of opinion, including the right to believe or not believe. All citizens are to be treated equally no matter what their religious convictions or lack of them. The state does not officially sanction any religion nor give preferential treatment to its adherents. We are very fortunate that the U.S. Constitution was written under the influence of Enlightenment thinking, and that George Washington, Thomas Jefferson, James Madison, and other Founding Fathers wished to avoid the establishment of the church as it existed in England. Indeed, the United States was the first nation to be based on the separation principle.

I should point out that some ninety-five nation-states have since enacted similar constitutional procedures providing for the separation of church (or temple or mosque) and state. These include France, Spain, Ireland, the Netherlands, Germany, Mexico, Brazil, China, South Africa, India, and Australia.[2] Separation is realized in various ways in each of these countries, and there are constant battles to defend separation and keep it from eroding.

Many challenges to the separation principle come from fundamentalist religions including Islam, conservative Hinduism, Orthodox Judaism, evangelical Protestantism, and conservative Roman Catholicism. To our dismay, the Bush administration has often affirmed such opposition—for example, by funding faith-based charities and opposing stem-cell research on moral-theological grounds. In Russia, President Vladimir Putin has sought to reestablish the Russian Orthodox Church; in Poland, the Roman Catholic Church seeks to resume its earlier, powerful position. Thus, the idea of the separation of church and state is always under threat. In France, the *Libre Penseurs* are always on the barricades defending secularism against incursions from the Roman Catholic Church or Islam. In Turkey, the army is ever ready to resist efforts to restrict Kemal Atatürk's secular constitution.

A key point to recognize is that one does not have to be an atheist or agnostic in order to defend the separation principle. In the United States, *most* Protestant denominations defend separation, as do secular Jews, liberal Roman Catholics, Unitarians, and members of other denominations. Secular humanists have many allies in this great battle. Indeed, both liberals and conservatives, believers and unbelievers, have stood firmly in support of the First Amendment.

The Secularization of Values

Second, when we talk about secularism we may also refer to societies that cultivate *secular values*; since the Renaissance, secularity in the ethical domain has been growing in influence. Secularists do not look to salvation and confirmation of the afterlife as their overriding goal, but rather focus on temporal humanist values in the here and now—happiness, self-realization, joyful exuberance, creative endeavors and excellence, the actualization of the good life—not only for the individual but for the greater community. The common moral decencies, goodwill, and altruism are widely accepted, as are the civic virtues of democracy, the right of privacy, the belief that every individual has equal dignity and value, human rights, equality, tolerance, the principles of fairness and justice, the peaceful negotiation of differences, and the willingness to compromise.

The modern age *is* basically secular. Quite independently of religious beliefs, the world's economies seek to achieve growth and increase social wealth, thus providing consumers with goods and services that everyone can enjoy. (I note that Pat Robertson and some other Religious Right ministers have not eschewed fancy cars and splendid homes.) It would be ludicrous to inject religiosity (save as a perfunctory formality) into the modern corporation. Here the tests are efficiency, productivity, quality products and services, and the bottom line. We are appalled that Islamists in the Middle East oppose charging interest because it is forbidden by the Koran, yet use every rationalization to circumvent that prohibition to tap the power of finance. The point is well recognized that no modern society can function if it does not train skilled practitioners in diverse specialties. No nation can survive unless it can master the practical arts and sciences. If I have a toothache, I want a dentist, not a priest; and if I wish to construct a building I had better be damned sure that I have competent architects to draw the plans and that the engineering is solid.

Similarly, it is widely recognized that broad-based education—cultural, historical, intellectual, scientific, and artistic—is the right of every child and that every adult must have the opportunity to expand his or her dimensions of experience and knowledge.

Not the least among secular values of course is *free inquiry* and freedom of scientific research, the very basis of science and technology. Religious censorship or limitation—such as that which intelligent-design advocates seek to impose on scientific theories of evolution—is unacceptable. The free mind is vital for the open society. If one wants to pursue scientific inquiry, then one needs to abide by methodological naturalism: objective standards of evidence, rational coherence, and experimental testing are quite independent of the Bible or Koran. Actually, secular considerations are vital in virtually all human interests, from sports and the arts to pharmacology, psychiatry, and meteorology. In these and other areas, religious doctrines are largely irrelevant.

Among the secular values that emerge today is the compelling *need to develop a new Planetary Ethics*. Because we must share the Earth, no entity can any longer be allowed to attempt to impose an exclusive, doctrinaire religious creed on every man and woman. We live in a multicultural world in which multi-secularism needs to be developed—in which different forms of secularism need to be adapted to the diverse cultural traditions and contexts of specific societies. Thus, we need secularized Christianity, secularized Judaism, secularized Hinduism, and even secularized Islam; all are requisite for societies to be able to cope with their problems. And here the question is, Can we develop a set of shared values and principles that can provide common ground for global civilization? High on the agenda, of course, should be our first responsibilities: to preserve the environment of our common planetary abode, to eliminate poverty and disease, to reach peaceful adjudication of conflicts, and to achieve prosperity for as many people as possible. These are practical problems that demand realistic, secular solutions.

Secularization and Unbelief

There is a third sense of secularism. Some recalcitrant foes of secularism insist that it is synonymous with atheism; some militant atheists agree with them. But I think that this is a mistaken view. Far from being secular, some militant atheists have sought to protect their "faith" by abusing the power of the state. Indeed, some totalitarian regimes that embraced atheism as part of their ideology, such as those in the Soviet Union and Cambodia, have persecuted—even exterminated—their religious opposition.

One thing that distinguishes those who share a secular outlook from those committed to the rule of dogma, whether it is religious or atheistic dogma, is the acceptance of freedom of conscience. Bitter experience has taught many of the religious that a secular state works best for them. Many religious denominations have suffered at the hands of *other* devout believers: Roman Catholics have persecuted Protestants (as with the suppression of the Huguenots in France), while Protestant states have likewise waged war against Catholics (as in Elizabethan England). Hence, there has been "a war of all against all," to paraphrase Thomas Hobbes. After centuries of sectarian violence in these places, a truce between contending factions was hard won, and the secular state was the result. Demands for secularity also reflect the experience of religious minorities. Jews have been hounded out of country after country by devout Christians; Sunnis and Shiites have slaughtered each other with impunity; Hindus and Muslims have engaged in bloody communal riots, as have militant Buddhists in some countries. Thus, the separation principle has been agreed to by many sects—even devout Mormons, Jehovah's Witnesses, Baptists, and Seventh-day Adventists in the United States. All have experienced persecution and have welcomed a *modus vivendi*. Thus, one does not have to be a nonbeliever to accept the separation principle.

The Enlightenment sought to liberate men and women from the stranglehold of religious morality inflicted on them by overzealous "virtue policemen" (we might call them "theo-thugs"). This long process of emancipation began with the defense of free thought in response to the persecutions of Bruno, Galileo, and Spinoza. This same impulse was intrinsic to the American Revolution, which appealed to "life, liberty, and the pursuit of happiness," and to the French Revolution, which proclaimed "liberty, equality, fraternity" and "the Rights of Man." Later, biology struggled to overcome intemperate attacks on Darwinism; in medical science, such advances as autopsy and anesthesia required defense against religious intransigence. Today stem-cell research and evolutionary theory are attacked on religious grounds. Such advances as the abolition of slavery, the recognition of women's rights, and the acceptance of sexual freedom (contraception, abortion, divorce, gay rights, etc.) were achieved only after protracted struggles. Traditional moral beliefs, enshrined in practice and sanctified by religious doctrine, had to be modified or overcome. Modern democratic societies have known long battles to allow diversity of taste and lifestyle.

These secularizing forces grew out of the democratic-humanistic revolutions of the modern world, which recognized that all citizens have equal dignity and value and that the rule of law should apply to poor persons as well as rich ones. Hence, intrinsic to modern democratic-capitalist and socialist societies is an acceptance of the civic virtues of democracy. Again, one does not have to be an atheist to accept libertarian values or the democratization of society.

Now, I grant that it may be difficult for a *very* devout person to *fully* accept secularity in ethics. For some believers, the quest for God and/or salvation may trump the pursuit of happiness or the battle for social justice. By the same token, unbelievers may have an easier time fully achieving the fullness of life and the realization of their talents and proclivities, including the satisfaction of sexual desires.

In the war waged on behalf of democratic institutions, there is an ongoing need to defend pluralistic societies that permit individuals "to do their own thing"—even as we hope this might be modified by responsible self-control. If we were to insist that, in the last analysis, secularism is equivalent to atheism, we may do a great disservice to secularism's importance in the battles for individual autonomy and the right of privacy.

The degree to which religiosity declines, brightens the prospects for secularization of values. Many who embrace such values are formally religious, but only nominally affiliated with churches, synagogues, and temples; they are more likely to be receptive to secular attitudes and humanist values and to be tolerant of personal diversity. This is especially the case if they are broadminded, reflective, and perhaps members of their denominations only because of an accident of birth or family pressures.

That is why a negative atheism that seeks simply to destroy religion, without providing a positive agenda, will not in my judgment get very far. The wider platform for human progress as part of a New Enlightenment needs, I submit, to advocate secularism in the above three senses: (1) the separation of religion from the state; (2) the humanization of values that satisfy the deeper interests and needs of human beings; and (3) the decline of religious practice, entailing the growth of the Human City in place of the City of God.

I am not suggesting that we should not critically examine religious claims, especially where they are patently false, injurious, and destructive. The secular world constantly needs to be defended against those who would undermine it, and we need to responsibly examine the transcendental and moral claims of supernaturalism and criticize its pretensions—especially when they impinge on personal freedoms. This latter form of secularism is akin to *neo-humanism*, a broader, more welcoming expression of the humanist outlook.

Accordingly, the secularization of society needs a more inclusive agenda to enlist like-minded nominal religionists to share in defending—and expanding—humanist values. But this must be applied to actual socio-cultural contexts. Long-standing preexisting customs will vary from culture to culture; deeply ingrained ethnicities should be taken into account, including the richness of diverse languages, culinary tastes, and differences in fashion, manners, and other normative conduct. We cannot simply repeal religion and/or hope to wipe it off the map; its tentacles are deeply rooted, and some religions profoundly define the identity of each adherent—even nominal ones. *Our approach should be multi-secular, adapted to existing institutions and mores.*

Christians and Jews, Mormons and Sunnis, Protestants and Buddhists, Hindus and Shiites carry culturally conditioned bundles of attitudes and values; it is a long process to reform behavior and move people's thinking onto another plane.

One of the basic ingredients of a reformation is to get a clan, sect, or denomination to transact with people of other faiths and convictions, hard as that often is. This involves dialogues and discussion, interaction and intermingling, appreciation and understanding of other points of view, as well as responsible criticism. One of the major dangers of any isolated religious system is that separation and exclusivity tend to solidify its dogmas.

The Agenda for Secularization

High on the agenda of secularization of course is *education*. We need to insist that all children have the right to appreciate and understand a wider range of cultural experiences—including the study of the sciences, the development of critical thinking, and exposure to world history, the arts, philosophy, comparative study of religions, and alternative political and economic systems. This entails recognizing the *rights of children* as human beings. Parents cannot starve, beat, or cruelly punish their children. Similarly, they should not prohibit them from receiving a full education. Indoctrination is an assault on the rights of children as persons.

The liberation of women from domination by men is also high on the secularizing agenda; women must be free to work and travel and to pursue independent careers, not be confined only to housework and menial jobs. Women have a right to an education and to pursue the roles they choose in their society's economic, political, and cultural life. They have equal dignity and value and should have equal status. This is today widely accepted in advanced democratic societies. It is rejected in most Muslim societies, and this is the Achilles heel of those societies that so badly needs to be pierced.

It follows, of course, that individuals should be permitted to marry or partner with whomever they wish, even if that means going outside their faith. Women should be accorded the same freedoms and responsibilities as men.

The secularization process is proceeding rapidly in today's world: Protestants and Catholics now intermarry in spite of earlier prohibitions; so do Jews and Christians, Asians and Anglos, blacks and whites. How encouraging that Ireland and Spain, formerly bastions of Catholic authoritarianism, have rapidly secularized and adopted humanistic values. Secular Jews likewise eschew Orthodoxy. Although they may retain some degree of ethnic loyalty, large percentages of contemporary Jews have sought mates outside their religion. They look to Spinoza and Mendelssohn, Einstein and Salk—modern Jews who heralded science and the arts—rather than to the ancient prophets of the Hebrew Bible. There is a beginning effort on the part of secularized Muslims, especially in Western democracies, to adopt the democratic ideals of liberty, equality, and fraternity and to become more tolerant of the multiplicity of faiths as they begin to study the sciences and enter secular professions.

There are perhaps one and a half billion people on the planet today who are nonreligious, and their numbers are growing. These include agnostics and atheists but also people who are simply indifferent to existing religions. As I pointed out, there are also significant numbers of nominal members of religious bodies who are skeptical and need to break the stranglehold of the so-called sacred texts. We should point out that although we may appreciate the historical, literary, and moral values that traditional religions have bequeathed to us, nonetheless we wish to focus on other sources of inspiration that are more relevant to life today: modern science and philosophy, the vast reservoir of the secular arts and literature, and the ever-expansive richness of cultural diversity. The Sermon on the Mount is beautiful, as is much in Buddhism, but neither should yoke us to the past.

The United States is an anomaly among advanced nations because of its widespread public piety. Europe is basically postreligious; only a negligible minority still practices the old-time religion. Similar phenomena prevail in Japan, China, South Korea, Australia, and elsewhere in the world.

In the United States, the number of secularists is growing. A rapidly increasing segment of the public is the *unchurched, untempled, and unmosqued*. Religion has little impact on their lives. According to a recent Barna poll, the unchurched comprise 43 percent of the population. These people belong to no church and very rarely worship or attend services. They are secular too; saying that a person is secular does not necessarily mean that he or she is an atheist or even antireligious. I submit that secularism can provide affirmative alternatives for nonreligious men and women of every kind. *Hence, we should focus on the nonreligious as our constituency.* Indeed, a large number of ordinary folks, a majority of scientists in the United States, Nobel Prize winners, and people affiliated with our research universities and colleges, artists, and poets—people from every walk of life or occupation—express a secular outlook and exemplify ethical beliefs that are thoroughly secular and humanistic in appeal. The defining characteristic of secularists is simply that they are *nonreligious*.

In the spirit of cooperation and goodwill, we need to convince our neighbors that we can lead the good life and be good citizens and devoted parents without the trappings of religion, God, or clergy. We need to demonstrate this by practicing good works.

Notes

1.   This article first appeared in *Free Inquiry* 28, no. 2 (February/March 2008), pp. 4–8.
2.   The complete list is as follows: Angola, Benin, Botswana, Burkina Faso, Burundi, Cameroon, Cape Verde, Chad, Democratic Republic of the Congo, Republic of the Congo, Ethiopia, Gabon, The Gambia, Guinea, Guinea-Bissau, Liberia, Mali, Namibia, South Africa, Tunisia, Bolivia, Brazil, Canada, Chile, Colombia, Cuba, Ecuador, Honduras, Mexico, Paraguay, Peru, Uruguay, Venezuela, United States of America, People's Republic of China, India, Indonesia, Japan, Kazakhstan, Kyrgyzstan, Mongolia, Nepal, North Korea, Philippines, Singapore, South Korea, Syria, Taiwan, Tajikistan, Thailand, Turkmenistan, Uzbekistan, Vietnam, Albania, Armenia, Austria, Azerbaijan, Belarus, Belgium, Bosnia and Herzegovina, Bulgaria, Croatia, Cyprus, Turkish Republic of Northern Cyprus, Czech Republic, Estonia, Finland, France, Georgia, Germany, Hungary, Ireland, Italy, Latvia, Lithuania, Luxembourg, Macedonia, Moldova, Montenegro, Netherlands, Poland, Portugal, Romania, Russian Federation, Serbia, Slovakia, Slovenia, Spain, Sweden, Switzerland, Turkey, Ukraine, Australia, Federated States of Micronesia, and New Zealand.

Section 1

Basic Categories

I

The Secular Humanist Prospect
in Historical Perspective[1]

Secular humanism holds great promise for the future of humankind. But disturbing changes have occurred in recent years, particularly in the United States, that make its promise harder to fulfill. The cultural wars no doubt will continue to intensify. Though we have made progress—as recent Supreme Court decisions testify—we face unremitting challenges to the secular humanist outlook.

If I can flash back more than half a century, clearly most political and intellectual leaders of that time were sympathetic to scientific natural-ism and humanism. I vividly remember John Dewey's ninetieth birthday celebrations in 1949 (Dewey was then the leading American humanist philosopher). One such event was attended by the president of Columbia University (and future president of the United States), General Dwight D. Eisenhower. I recall Eisenhower declaring in admiration: "Profes-sor Dewey, you are the philosopher of freedom, and I am the soldier of freedom." Can we even imagine a soon-to-be U.S. president so praising a humanist intellectual today?

In those days, thoughtful Americans had great confidence in the United Nations and its efforts to transcend nationalism and build a world community. We sought to develop institutions of international law and a world court, enhancing our ability to negotiate differences based on collective security. Emerging from the Second World War, Americans displayed a strong desire to go beyond ancient rivalries, accompanied by confidence in the ability of science to understand nature and to solve human problems.

In 1973, I edited a book called *The Humanist Alternative: Some Definitions of Humanism.*[2] In this book I observed that the twentieth century had been proclaimed to be the Humanist Century; many of the then-dominant philosophical schools—naturalism, phenomenology, existentialism, logical positivism, and analytic philosophy—were in a broad sense committed to the humanist outlook. The same was true of humanistic psychology and the social sciences in general. Indeed, I raised this question, "Is everyone a humanist?" For no one wanted to be known as antihumanist. I mean, who wanted to be antihuman? Heady with the momentum of Vatican II, Pope Paul VI even declared that Roman Catholicism was "a Christian humanism." The only authentic humanism, he proclaimed, "must be Christian."

Interestingly, it was also in 1973 that John D. Rockefeller, the scion of the Rockefeller family, published a book called *The Second American Revolution*.[3] For Rockefeller, the second American Revolution would be a humanist moral revolution; he declared that capitalism needed to have a human face. Similarly, noted Marxists in Eastern Europe at that time claimed that their Marxism was basically humanist.

In the early 1970s, I was invited to Washington, D.C. on more than one occasion. I recall attending a reception at Mrs. Dean Acheson's house and meeting, among others, Hubert Humphrey. I had been a strong supporter of Mr. Humphrey. I was the editor of the *Humanist* magazine at that time; Mr. Humphrey read my nametag and said to me, "Oh, Paul Kurtz! How nice to see you! Ah, the *Humanist* magazine, what a great magazine! I wish I had time to read it!" Walter Mondale, who was later to become vice president of the United States, and many other people identified approvingly with humanism.[4] Indeed, in a very real sense humanism was the dominant intellectual theme on the cultural scene. On another occasion, I was invited to Washington by Senator Edward Kennedy (who was planning to run for the presidency). I spent a weekend at Sargent Shriver's home. His wife, Eunice Shriver, was one of the Kennedys. I also visited the home of Mrs. Robert Kennedy. Everyone thought that the humanist outlook was important. And indeed, many of that era's intellectual leaders of thought and action were humanists: B.F. Skinner, Albert Ellis, Herbert Muller, A.H. Maslow, Carl Rogers, Thomas Szasz, Jonas Salk, Joseph Fletcher, Betty Friedan, Sidney Hook, Rudolf Carnap, W.V. Quine, and Ernest Nagel come to mind. Many leaders in the Black community were humanists, not ministers, such as James Farmer, Bayard Rustin, and A. Philip Randolph; they worked hard for minority rights. Humanism and modernism were considered synonymous. In one sense the 1970s marked a high point of humanism's influence—at least in the United States.

Now, I raise these points because there has been a radical shift today, particularly in the United States. Let me focus for a moment on this country, because of its enormous influence in today's world. America is undergoing a fundamental transformation, one that in my view betrays the ideals of the Founding Fathers. Jefferson, Madison, Washington, and Franklin were humanists and rationalists by the standards of their day, heavily influenced by the Enlightenment. How different is the national tone today. We hear calls for the nation to become more religious; we see unremitting attempts to breach the separation of church and state, such as the financing of faith-based charities. Since the tragedy of 9/11, the momentum of change has accelerated. The so-called PATRIOT Act and the relentless pursuit of "Homeland Security," I submit, are drastically undermining civil liberties.

The United States is the preeminent scientific, technological, economic, and political power of the world, far outstripping any other nation. Today the military budget of the United States is virtually equal to that of the rest of the world combined. Why has America's former idealism on behalf of democracy and human rights declined, to be replaced by militant chauvinism? Why has its commitment to humanism, liberal values, and the First Amendment eroded?

These changes began in the late 1970s and gathered force in the 1980s. Because of my role in the humanist movement, I was able to observe closely as the attacks on secular humanism and naturalism intensified. In my view, six factors were responsible for these inauspicious developments.

First, there was a sharp rise in beliefs in the paranormal, pseudoscience, and antiscience in the United States and throughout the world. Claims concerning psychics and astrologers, monsters of the deep, UFOs, and the like dominated the mass media and fascinated the public. Claims were everywhere, but there were virtually no criticisms of them. In 1976, I brought together many of the leading skeptics in the United States and the world and founded the Committee for the Scientific Investigation of Claims of the Paranormal (CSICOP). At CSICOP's founding conference I posed the question: "Should we assume that the scientific enlightenment will continue, and that public support of science will be ongoing?" I answered that question in the negative. We should not assume that science will prevail, I warned, for we may be overwhelmed by irrational forces that will undermine our cherished naturalistic worldview. At that time, very few people questioned scientific culture or the scientific outlook as such—there was of course fear of a possible nuclear confrontation, but science itself was not in question. Gradually, and much to the astonishment of many observers, an antiscientific attitude began to develop. In response the skeptical movement organized itself across the world; there now exist skeptical organizations in some thirty-eight countries, from China to Germany, Argentina to Australia. They publish some sixty magazines and newsletters inspired by CSICOP's flagship journal, the *Skeptical Inquirer.*

The second change that began to occur was the growth of fundamentalism and its prominence in American public life. The Moral Majority grew strong from the late 1970s to the late 1980s, in part by targeting secular humanism—not humanism per se, but secular humanism. I defined secular humanism first as "a method of critical inquiry." Religious Right leaders charged that secular humanism controlled the country. (In one sense they were correct, for as I mentioned above, a generally humanistic viewpoint dominated education, science, and the media at that time.) They called for secular humanism to be overthrown and for a revival of popular piety. Surely they achieved the latter objective. Consider that most intellectuals once thought Protestant fundamentalism to be beyond the pale and Billy Graham a marginal figure. As time went on, Graham would become known as a "statesman" and act as a confidante to several presidents of the United States. America's religious revival did not benefit only Protestant fundamentalism: conservative Roman Catholicism made great gains, eroding the reforms of Vatican II, and neoconservative Orthodox Judaism mounted an astonishing comeback. By the year 2000, public life in the United States was largely dominated by a theistic outlook. If I had declared the twentieth century the humanist century, respected conservatives such as Michael Novak, Richard John Neuhaus, and writers for *Commentary* magazine declared it an "anomaly." They said that the twenty-first century would be a century dominated not by secular humanism, but by religious and spiritual values. For them, the secular humanist outlook could not expire too soon.

The third factor that emerged to challenge free thought and the secular movement was the near-total collapse of Marxism. For a good part of the nineteenth and twentieth centuries, Marxist-humanist ideals had influenced intellectuals; with Marxism's eclipse, anticlericalism and indeed any open criticism of religion have all but disappeared.

The fourth major change that occurred was the growth of postmodernism. Postmodernism stands in opposition to the Enlightenment, humanism, the advancement of science, a concern for human progress, and the emancipation of humanity from the blindfold of authoritarian traditions. Postmodernism questions all these basic premises, especially the ideas of objective science and humanistic values, and it has gravely influenced the academy, not only in the United States, but elsewhere in the world.

The fifth factor that is so important is American triumphalism. Global free-market corporate capitalism now dominates the world. Pax Americana has many of the characteristics of a new kind of imperialism. The latest turn in American foreign policy questions ideas like deterrence and the balance of power. It maintains that American military might will police the world and defeat any "rogue states" that may challenge its hegemony. Unfortunately, this ideological posture has been accompanied by an open alliance with conservative and evangelical religious forces at home. In the bestselling book *Mind Siege*, Tim LaHaye and David Noebel provide a frightening apocalyptic agenda for evangelicals, admonishing their millions of followers in martial tones to prepare for battle against the secular humanists.[5] We had become Public Enemy Number One, though after the emergence of the armies of the *jihad* we have been temporarily demoted to Public Enemy Number Two.

This brings us to the sixth major change: the growth of Islamic fundamentalism. The War on Terrorism and its associated "conflict of civilizations," in Samuel Huntington's phrase, has put all Americans under a heightened sense of threat. But even this must be viewed in the context of a larger movement: an intense Islamic missionary effort, antiscientific at its root, that is sweeping the world. Islam is on the move in Africa, Asia, and all parts of the world. What may be most significant are the fast-growing Islamic minorities in Western Europe—France has five million Muslims, Britain and Germany two million each. And of course the United States and Canada have growing Muslim minorities.

No less portentous is the global rise of militant Christianity. The reality is that there are more missionaries spreading the Christian gospel throughout the world than at any time in history. It is projected that, by the year 2025, 67 percent of Christians will live in Asia, Africa, and Latin America. China, indeed, will have more Christians than all but six nations. This is occurring at a time when Europe is being secularized, with nonreligious minorities growing sharply and church attendance at record lows. But Christian missionaries are pouring forth from the United States—particularly Pentecostals and evangelicals, carrying with them a literal reading of Scripture that they apply freely to morality and politics.

What we are confronted with is the fact that the third world, which had been so powerfully influenced by Marxism twenty or thirty years ago, now confronts the clash of two powerful missionary forces: Islam and Christianity.

This is the new reality that we in the humanist and rationalist movement have to face. The armies of the faithful are powerful and multiple. We face continued, even escalating conflict between their intolerant religious ideologies and our naturalism.

I have offered a brief overview of a profound reversal in attitudes—from a period thirty years ago when humanism and secularism were in ascendancy, at least in the United States, to one in which they are being challenged at every turn, with vast sums of money and energy being applied to further missionary religiosity. This does not deny the positive developments associated with the triumph of democratic ideals, as Fukuyama has described. But it is the overall secular humanist prospect that I am concerned with.

Thus we have great tasks ahead of us in future decades. But I ask, what should we concentrate upon? I submit that there are three main battles. First is the battle for secularism. I think the first great challenge will be to preserve the secular democracies; namely, we need to make a stronger case for the separation of church (or mosque or temple) and state. The state should be neutral, allowing a plurality of points of view, from religious belief to nonbelief, to coexist. This means that we need to defend democracy and the open society, human rights, and the rule of law. Virtually all of the fifty-four Islamic countries are theocracies, grounded in Sharia as set forth in the Hadith and the Koran. Unfortunately, recent efforts by the Bush administration to shatter the wall between church and state in the United States portend great damage for secularism worldwide. They also place the administration in the contradictory position of calling for barriers between church and state in Iraq that it is doggedly dismantling at home.

The second battle will be for naturalism; we are committed to the application of scientific methods in testing truth claims—by the principle of appeal to evidence and reason. Scientific methodology is basic to our industrial-technological societies; therefore, American power is based not on theology, but on naturalistic premises. We are the defenders of critical thinking and skeptical inquiry as part of the process of developing tested knowledge. Leaders of industrial and technological economies understand this full well. No revival of religious fundamentalism must be permitted to erode this dedication.

We are also committed to the naturalistic cosmic outlook—that is, to the scientific perspective drawn from the frontiers of the sciences. Here we have much work to do. We reject the ancient religious ontological views rooted simply in the Bible, the Koran, the Book of Mormon, or

Buddhist and Hindu literature. We wish to explain nature in the light of empirical and experimental evidence. That is the key principle that needs to be enunciated: naturalism in contradistinction to supernaturalism. We are predominantly nonreligious nontheistic empiricists and rationalists. We have developed our views of reality by reference to the findings of the sciences. We are skeptical about claims that are untested. Science provides our most reliable knowledge of the universe, even as it leaves room for mystery and awe about areas of the universe not yet probed or explained.

Our third great battle will be for humanistic ethics. We believe that no one can deduce ethical values solely from theological premises. Those who depend on theology for morality often end up in conflict with hatred and intolerance on every side. For example, Muslims believe in polygamy, Protestants and Jews in monogamy and the right of divorce, while Roman Catholics (at least officially) do not accept divorce. The Catholic Church opposes capital punishment; Muslim fundamentalists and Baptists defend it. Thus there is a conflict between humanist ethics and the religious-moral ideologies that so dominate the world today, just as there is conflict among religious ideologies. But all of them are based upon ancient faiths, too often irrelevant to contemporary realities.

Thus, we maintain that a humanist moral revolution offers great promise for the future of humankind; for it allows humans to achieve the good life here and now, without the illusion of salvation or immortality. We wish to test moral values by evidence and reason, and we are willing to modify our ethical values in light of the consequences. Our approach is planetary, as *Humanist Manifesto 2000* emphasized—we hold that every person on the planet has equal dignity and value. Our moral commitment is to be concerned with the rights of every person in the global community and to preserve our shared habitat.

Humanistic ethics defends the autonomy of the individual, the right of privacy, human freedom, and social justice. It is concerned with the welfare of humanity as a whole.

In conclusion, I think that secular humanism has lost ground in the last three decades to religious forces, not only in America, but also in Asia, Africa, and Latin America. The United States is anomalous in comparison with Europe, which has become increasingly secularized and nonreligious. Hundreds of millions of people worldwide are secular; they do not look to the ancient faiths for guidance and believe that anyone can be moral without belief in any religion. The challenge today is especially urgent in the United States, no doubt because of the influence its immense power has given it in the world. Especially disturbing is the fact that the political leadership of the United States has grown fearful of expressing any support for agnosticism, skepticism, secular humanism, or unbelief. Moreover, the current administration uses the White House as a bully pulpit to spread religious gospel. It is possible in European democracies for politicians to publicly express nonreligious, even atheistic viewpoints—but alas, this is virtually impossible in today's United States.

We have been waging a rear-guard battle in the United States. We need to move to the front lines to defend secular humanism—to convince the public that it's possible to be a good citizen, contribute to society, be moral, and yet to be nonreligious. We need to defend the Enlightenment—whose agenda still has not been fulfilled, as philosopher Jürgen Habermas has pointed out. We need to encourage our supporters to speak out courageously. We need to engage in debate and dialogue, enunciating and defending secularism, humanism, and naturalism as meaningful alternatives to the irrationalism that increasingly dominates our age and threatens to overwhelm it.

Notes

1. This article first appeared in *Free Inquiry* 23, no. 4 (October/November 2003), pp. 5–6, 47–48.
2. Paul Kurtz, *The Humanist Alternative: Some Definitions of Humanism* (Buffalo, N.Y.: Prometheus Books; London: Pemberton, 1973).
3. John D. Rockefeller, *The Second American Revolution: Some Personal Observations* (New York: Harper and Row, 1973).
4. Walter Mondale's brother, Lester, was a signer of the first *Humanist Manifesto* (1933). He wrote about his memories of *Manifesto I* in "The Lingering *Humanist Manifesto I*," *Free Inquiry* 6, no. 4 (Fall 1996): 28–29.
5. *Mind Siege: The Battle for Truth in the New Millennium* (Nashville, Tenn.: Thomas Nelson Co., 2000). It is noteworthy that LaHaye is also America's number-one selling author of fiction because of his wildly successful, apocalyptic *Left Behind* novels.

II

Naturalism and the Future[1]

Naturalism has been the dominant voice in American philosophy for most of the twentieth century. Beginning with pragmatism in the early part of the century and cresting with John Dewey in the latter half, it has included philosophers such as W.V. Quine, Sidney Hook, Ernest Nagel, Hilary Putnam, Richard Rorty, Donald Davidson, and Adolf Grünbaum, among others. Today, naturalism is being challenged by religious, antisecular, and antihumanist forces, although it still plays a commanding role.

Naturalism in one sense is synonymous with modernism and secular humanism, beginning with the Renaissance, with its new emphasis on humanist values instead of religious piety. Naturalism continued with the growth of modern science and the scientific temper. It reached a crescendo in the eighteenth century with the Enlightenment and the democratic revolutions in France and the United States. The progressive ideals of Condorcet and *les philosophes* helped to crystallize a conviction that science, education, democracy, human rights, and the secularization of morality would liberate human beings from *les anciens régimes*. Founders of the American republic such as Thomas Jefferson and James Madison shared this optimistic outlook.

Today strident voices bleat, opposing the Enlightenment within the academy. Following the postmodernist disciples of Martin Heidegger and Jacques Derrida, they denigrate the objectivity of science and the agenda of liberation humanism. Exacerbating the challenge is the sudden recrudescence of fundamentalist Islam, Hinduism, and evangelical Christianity; the reappearance of the Orthodox Church in Eastern Europe; and rising conversions to Christianity and Islam in Asia and Africa.

Naturalism is too narrowly construed if it is defined *only* by its opposition to supernaturalism. Recently, the term *New Atheism* has been

21

introduced to denote the battle against theistic religion. But this definition of naturalism is too limited; it has been criticized by conservative theists and liberals alike for its negativity.

This indictment overlooks the fact that naturalism has had a *positive* impact. For naturalism does not begin with God as a myth left over from a prescientific age to be debunked or refuted but rather with *nature itself, directly experienced*, with *the primordial world of diversity and plenitude that humans encounter in living and interacting,* and with *their attempts to understand and cope with it.* As such, naturalism has been enormously beneficial for modern civilization, which, freed from the constraints of repressive theology, has a constructive agenda for the future.

There are three normative principles of naturalism that provide an effective alternative to religion and that are continuing to transform our world. By improving the human condition, they provide, I submit, promising opportunities for humankind.

The first is *methodological naturalism*, which is the bedrock of all scientific inquiry and the secret of its unparalleled success. The use of scientific methods of inquiry—broadly conceived—is the most effective way of attaining reliable knowledge. Scientific inquiry makes every effort to be impartial in evaluating, testing, and validating claims to knowledge. This entails theoretical and mathematical coherence, an appeal to evidence, and the use of experimental prediction. The grounds for accepting a claim to knowledge are that it must be corroborated (or replicated) by competent inquirers in the field under study. It does not depend on subjective caprice or arbitrary authority. Unlike religious claims, scientific knowledge is open to revision in the light of new discoveries or theories. It is fallible, following Peirce, for some skepticism is intrinsic to the very process of scientific inquiry; yet it continues to advance the frontiers of knowledge, whereas other methods do not.

Many naturalists take the natural sciences as the exemplar of knowledge. This presupposes that occult causes are inadmissible in science, and that only natural entities and processes exist and/or are dependent on physical causal processes. Here, the physicalist model is the guide. My caveat is that the methods of justification should not be too narrowly construed; the strategies of investigation and confirmation may vary from field to field, depending on the context under inquiry. The natural sciences—physics, astronomy, chemistry, geology, etc.—surely stand as an ideal model of applying a physicalist framework. The biological sciences, however, provide new concepts and theories not entirely reducible to their physical-chemical substrata. Similarly, the behavioral sciences of psychology and the social sciences, such as economics, political science, and sociology, introduce new constructs and theories, and their modes of confirmation may not be as precise as those in the natural sciences. This implies letting each science gain practical confirmation in its own way. This leads to scientific pluralism instead of physicalist reductionism.

What is especially important is the practical need to educate students and the general public to think critically—an extended sense of the application of scientific methods. This should be applied to all fields of human interest, including religion, morality, politics, and ordinary life. Scientific methods grow out of the practical ways that people cope with the world and solve problems: as Dewey pointed out, they are continuous with common sense. In the final analysis, methodological naturalism provides a powerful set of prescriptive rules that are tested by their pragmatic consequences.

Indeed, the application of the methods of science has radically transformed human civilization. In particular, the positive effects of technology have been incalculable. Technology led to the industrial and information revolutions and the ability of humans to travel, communicate rapidly, and engage in commerce on a global scale. It has increased the food supply, and improved sanitation and medical care. It has expanded the sheer quantity of manufactured goods and services, which have improved quality of life and elevated standards of living everywhere. It has opened up opportunities for education, reducing illiteracy and enhancing cultural enrichment. It has contributed to human leisure and happiness—the enjoyment of the good life by more and more people. It has solved practical problems that heretofore were the bane of human existence, built highways and bridges, and launched humans into space. It has for the first time in human history made possible the realization of the humanistic ideal that each person on the planet is equal in dignity and value.

Scientific inquiry has expanded the horizons of our understanding of the universe and the place of the human species within it without myth or fantasy; the frontiers of research are pushed forward by dramatic discoveries every day. This has led to a steady increase in the amount of knowledge that we have amassed about the universe. Unfortunately, not everyone appreciates the significance of the new scientific conceptions of the cosmos.

The second form of naturalism is *scientific naturalism*. This is very important today, for it supplants traditional supernatural and mystical theories of reality. It is essential that naturalists attempt to describe and explain what has been learned about the universe; we need to interpret the body of scientific knowledge of our time for the general public. This requires generalists who are skilled in uncovering interdisciplinary generalizations, common concepts and theories, shared assumptions and presuppositions. Philosophers working closely with scientists can help in this important task. The eventual goal of scientific inquiry is to achieve, if possible, consilience: theories that cohere/coduct together. We need to try to work out a synoptic understanding of nature.

What should concern us is the abysmal lack of information possessed by the general public, and indeed by scientific specialists themselves, about the import of contemporary scientific discoveries. Scientific illiteracy is rampant. That is why we need to provide general outlines of our knowledge of the universe insofar as we can. Most often it is scientists rather than philosophers—popularizers such as Carl Sagan, Isaac Asimov, or E.O. Wilson—who contribute most profoundly to the public understanding of science. I submit that it is important to develop a generalized view of the universe at this moment in history.[2]

We may ask, what are the implications of scientific naturalism to life as presently lived? It presents us with a universe in which "the God delusion" (Richard Dawkins's term) has been refuted and religion is often seen as destructive ("poison," in Christopher Hitchens's term), a universe that is without divine purpose and indifferent to human fears and hopes of salvation. It just *is*.

Nevertheless, the universe is a scene of natural events, and the human species is an integral part of nature. In this universe, humans are capable of marshalling their own powers of intelligence, endurance, and goodwill in order to develop better lives of enjoyment and enrichment for themselves and others, no matter what the social or cultural context. Today, for the first time in human history, humans can be liberated from bondage to ancient mythologies; morality can be refashioned to better fit our scientific understanding of humankind and our desires, interests, needs, and values. Humankind has every reason to welcome its place in nature, for nature can be hospitable to human life. Countless generations of men and women, young and old, have achieved happiness by pursuing their multifarious plans and projects.

The point needs to be made loud and clear that human life need not be a vale of turbulence or sorrow; the good life is achievable by humans without the illusion of divine governance or redemption.

This leads to the third form of naturalism, *ethical naturalism*, which focuses on human values and comes to fruition with secular humanism.

If the universe has no special place for humans, how shall we assert our own significance? Human life is an audacious expression of how we choose to become what we want. What is the relevance of nature to our decisions?

We cannot deduce what we *ought* to do from what *is* the case; we cannot draw our values solely from the facts. Nonetheless, the facts of the case *are* relevant to our moral values and principles. We need to take them into account in decision making. Science thus can serve ethics, enabling us to make wise choices. We need, however, to understand the limits and constraints, the possibilities and opportunities, of the environments in which we live. We need to understand the circumstances and facts that surround us within the contexts of choice. Understanding the consequences of our choices may better enable us to modify them; our expanding power over the means at our disposal and the creation of new ones help us to refashion our ends. These considerations are relevant to the things we hold, cherish, and esteem. It is clear that we can make reasonable value judgments in the light of inquiry.[3] Accordingly, naturalism has direct relevance to the decisions we make and the values we prize. Hence, there is an intermediary relationship between values and facts, an "act-ductive," if not deductive or inductive, relationship of facts and values to actions.

Theists complain that a person cannot be good without God; they charge that secular ethics is groundless and, hence, unreliable. On the contrary, there is considerable scientific evidence that human beings are potentially moral—caring, empathetic, compassionate, and altruistic—and that with education and social development they can behave morally. In any case, methodological and scientific naturalism have profound implications for a meaningful life. This depends on the flexible application of the naturalistic method and outlook to life. Naturalism in the future must be prepared to *reconstruct* the morality of the past so that it more adequately serves human needs and values in the present. Philosophy can be a stepping-stone to a new naturalistic ethics, but it needs to be transformed directly into *eupraxsophy*. As I view it, eupraxsophers are those skilled in the art of living, and their recommendations have behavioral implications for the practical life.

Naturalistic secular humanists need to advocate ethical positions in the *agora* of life as lived, and to *intellectually and passionately propose and defend them*. We need to minister to the passional needs of ordinary people, students, colleagues, coworkers, and citizens in the communities in which we live, and to strangers and aliens in the wider community of humankind. We need *eupraxsopher-practitioners in the art and science and poetry of living*. And we need to apply this insight to social institutions as well.

Ranged against naturalism and dealing in illusion and delusion, fantasy and nonsense, are the priests and mullahs, rabbis and ministers, who are burdened with ancient mythologies. They seek to intrude, cajole, persuade, and convert others to their archaic worldviews, and have no qualms about doing so.

As ethical naturalists (i.e., secular humanists), we need to be forthright about our deeply held convictions and apply them to the world in concrete terms. This is central if we are to continue to advance naturalism in the future. Indeed, I submit that the new frontier for naturalism is *applying normative ethics to better enable us to lead more reasonable and satisfying lives* on the scale of individuals, communities, and the planetary civilization that has emerged.

Notes

1.   This article first appeared in *Free Inquiry* 28, no. 1 (December 2007/January 2008), pp. 4–7.
2.   A good book in this regard is Natalie Angiers's *The Canon: A Whirligig Tour of the Beautiful Basics of Science* (Houghton Mifflin, 2007).
3.   In my writings I have listed a whole number of normative principles, virtues, and values to which naturalistic humanists are committed. These belong in the *valuation base*: the common moral decencies (integrity, trustworthiness, benevolence, fairness); excellences (health, self-control, self-respect, high motivation, the capacity for love, caring for others, beloved causes, *joie de vivre*, achievement motive, creativity, exuberance); altruism, impartial ethical rationality, human rights and responsibilities, the aphorisms of a good will, etc.

III

Naturalism, Secularism, and Humanism[1]

A provocative book by physicist and astronomer Victor J. Stenger, *God: The Failed Hypothesis*[2] reviews the scientific evidence for the existence of God and concludes that it is totally inadequate. Stenger has authored several books rejecting theism and supernaturalism. In his latest book, he considers the scientific case *for* God, including fine-tuning intelligent design and other forms of "evidence," and arrives instead at the null hypothesis.

No doubt Stenger will be labeled an "evangelical atheist," a generic term of denigration used to describe scientific critics of the God hypothesis. To invoke a colorful phrase from an earlier era (coined by William Safire for Spiro Agnew), theists believe that we are "nabobs of negativity." Quite the contrary, we affirm that, however imperfect, we are paragons of rationality, understanding, virtue, and excellence; or, at least, we strive to be. We are interested in enhancing human life, not undermining it; we are not naysayers, for we wish to realize the goodness of life for ourselves and others.

No one can deny that we are skeptical of the God hypothesis; we are, because we find insufficient scientific evidence for accepting it. Still, we cannot be defined by what we are against. We do not think there is evidence for supernaturalism; we are surely *nontheists*, but that does not mean that we should be *simply* defined as atheists. We do not believe in the Tooth Fairy, or Santa Claus either, but that does not define us. We do not think that our agenda—that is, the agenda of *naturalism*—should depend on the agendas of others, least of all on the agenda of *theism*.

Scientific critics of theism, in my view, are to be *applauded* for making it clear why they cannot accept the God hypothesis and why they reject the theistic tales and parables of the past. Although those tales may have been meaningful to men and women of earlier epochs, they no longer resonate with most modern humans in the midst of our planetary civilization. Contending with planetary crises requires that we do more than simply reject theological claims: we must assert new and useful recommendations concerning the human condition. I concede, of course, that we are atheists—but the key point is that *we are more than that.*

The real question for us is what we are *for.* Three terms describe our position come readily to mind: first, we are *scientific naturalists*; second, we believe in the principles of *secularism*; and third, we are committed to *humanist ethics.* Actually, we do not begin with the fact that God, as a personal being, does not exist but rather with the world and human life as we find them; we seek to describe these things and explain them in natural terms. The perspective of scientific naturalism is *nature first and foremost*, not the unknown transcendental world of the theist. We begin with actual facticity, things or events that we encounter in experience; and, there, we find order and regularity, contingency and chance, change and process. For primitive human beings, the world was mystifying, full of unexpected tragedies and conflicts, sickness and death, danger and fear. Humans in the infancy of the race attributed thunder and lightning to hidden gods and the seasons of change, birth, maturity, illness, and death to mysterious occult forces, which they considered divine and, hence, supplicated for relief and favor. They looked to what in time became an entrenched priestly class that orchestrated sacrifice, prayer, and ritual to placate the deities.

Humankind has come a long way since then. In particular, we have discovered the causes of many of the phenomena that terrified our ancestors. Naturalistic explanations of tornadoes and forest fires, famine, and epidemics have replaced occult accounts. Historically, first philosophy and later science attempted to provide cognitive tools for interpreting nature and learning how to cope with it. Illnesses had certain symptoms that could be cured; death was a natural fact of all living things, though we could reduce pain and suffering, contribute significantly to health and happiness, and even extend life. Supernaturalism was thus replaced by naturalism. More effective methods of inquiry enabled us to postulate hypotheses and develop theories to explain phenomena and confirm our theories by experimental methods and the use of logical inference.

Scientific Naturalism

Thus, we insist that we are naturalists—not atheists—*first*, because we seek to use the best available tools of critical thinking and scientific inquiry to account for what we encounter in nature. We do not think that the concept of God (or gods) is helpful any longer. To attribute pestilence or disaster to the wrath of the gods is an oversimplification of what happens and why. We reject the ancient mind's simple invocation of hidden deities who reward or punish human behavior. We do not deny that the universe is often a scene of inexplicable events. Yet, in part because we have learned to explain so much, we are willing to suspend judgment about that which we still do not know. We approach these matters in the position of equipoise, as an agnostic, with an open mind—though not an open sink into which any wild anthropocentric, speculative fantasy can fall and be accepted as true. I have called this principle the "new skepticism." Doubt is part and parcel of scientific inquiry; under the principle of fallibilism (formulated by Charles Peirce), we recognize that we may be mistaken. Hence, we should be ever ready to modify our conceptions of nature in the light of new evidence, confirming our hypotheses and theories by reference to the data of human experience and rational inference, not faith or fear, mystery or superstition.

What matters is that we begin by opening the "Book of Nature," not ancient books of scripture, such as the Bible or the Koran—testaments of early human civilizations that were prescientific and prephilosophical. Thus, we say we are naturalists, using scientific inquiry to develop reliable knowledge.

That is why I have resisted the efforts of our critics to label us solely as atheists, although our method of inquiry does lead most of us to atheism or agnosticism. On the contrary, we begin with an open mind, a process of investigation and inquiry, research and exploration, dialogue and debate, and we insist on applying the best methods of objectivity, corroboration, and replication to work out explanations of what we find in nature.

We are skeptical of both the belief that God is a person who communicated with a limited number of specially chosen prophets at some remote time in history and that faith in God is the only solution to life's quandaries. This seems to us to be an anthropomorphic imposition of human hopes and fears into nature, an attempt to bypass this life by yearning for salvation in the next. Life may cause the bitter tears of tragedy to fall, as doubtlessly it did for so many of our ancient forebears. But, today, it can provide abundant opportunities for achieving the good life and creating the conditions in which we can achieve some measure of harmonious social justice. We need to cope with the disappointments, adversities, and infirmities of life, if and when they occur, by summoning our best resources to cope with them and endure in spite of them.

I reiterate that we are *naturalists* because we begin with the world as we find it; we do not seek to leap beyond it, even while we strive to understand it fully, in all its most mysterious complexity. We maintain that humans are capable of developing a critical understanding of how nature works and why. We are committed to the use of science and reason, and we wish to educate the public about it. This does not qualify us as evangelists, only as *educators*.

Humanist Moral Values and Principles

A second charge hurled at us today is the claim that naturalists lack any grounds for morality. This overlooks the fact that human civilization has developed powerful moral principles and values rooted in human experience and reason, not in God. Witness Confucianism in ancient China, philosophers such as Socrates and Aristotle in Hellenic civilization, and the long march of secularization in the modern world, in which the principles of democracy and toleration, negotiation and compromise, reason and inquiry have replaced reliance on the faith and authority of theologically moral creeds.

That is why secular humanism is virtually synonymous with modernism. That is why we say we are secularists, seeking the realization of autonomous human values, independent of theology. That is also why we are committed to the separation of church—or mosque or temple—and state, and why we consider political liberties so vital and theocracy so dangerous. This demands some confidence in human reason and our ability to create a better world.

In short, *secular humanists are committed to realizing the best that we are capable of as human beings*; we wish to use our creative powers to develop the arts as well as the sciences, to fulfill our potentialities, and to enhance human freedom in a just world. We deplore supernaturalists' attempts to flee from reason and freedom. We say that life is, or can be, intrinsically good in its own terms, without looking outward for deliverance. Countless generations of humans have, indeed, found it meaningful, a source of enrichment and enjoyment.

The Need for Community

Another likely reason there has been so much opposition to naturalism and its Enlightenment agenda is because believers fear that we will take away from them the support that religion had provided in the past. Religious institutions may have endured so long because they offer comfort to those buffeted by the vicissitudes of life: fortune or ruin, pleasure or pain, the unpredictable but inescapable coming of disease, defeat, and, finally, death. Perhaps that is why devout religionists hate and fear "blasphemers," as we are sometimes called. They view us as threatening to whisk away the props that sustain them. This is an understandable fear but an unnecessary one all the same. It is as foolish to believe that, if most people stopped believing in God, all moral standards would collapse as it is to think that gravity will someday no longer press our feet to the floor when we get out of bed in the morning. Indeed, secular moral standards often predated Judeo-Christian values.

This raises an existential-psychological question. The books of Abraham present the mythic figures of Moses (an imposing, patriarchal figure, offering the Promised Land to God's "chosen people"); Jesus (a bisexual, androgynous Son, sacrificed by God so that true believers can achieve "Rapture"); and Muhammad (a harsh prophet threatening hellfire, torture, and violence to those who do not submit to Allah but promising paradise to those who do). Can naturalists create secular communities of equal strength and support to help those burdened by the vicissitudes of fortune?

In his insightful new book defending Darwin, *Living with Darwin: Evolution, Design, and the Future of Faith* (Oxford University Press, 2007), Philip Kitcher, the John Dewey Professor at Columbia University, argues that secularists should not seek to destroy the existential-psychological forms of solace and comfort that many religions offer *unless* they are prepared to provide *new* foundations—new sources of community and comfort that can provide the aesthetic and moral dimensions for new forms of "spirituality" realized in naturalistic terms.

Not everyone feels this way. Some libertarian secularists are so relieved to be emancipated from the stranglehold of orthodox religious communities that they do not wish to enter new humanist communities. Yet all too many individuals in contemporary, affluent societies feel alienated and lost. They are surrounded by a banal consumer culture; a competitive free-market economy where to the winner go the spoils; a vulgar mass media saturated with advertising, sensationalism, fear-mongering, violence, and mayhem. They ask how they can find deeper meaning and motivation in the fast-paced culture in which we live *without* drawing on Jesus, Muhammad, Buddha, or the Kabbalah.

Given that the mythic system of ancient beliefs has been undermined by the scientific outlook, can we create new symbols appropriate to the Age of Science, new metaphors for human possibility, new sources of inspiration and hope, and a new resolve to go on living in spite of adversity?

No doubt, our commitment to truth comes first, but we cannot overlook the power of affection and love in enriching our lives. Caring for other persons as they care for us can soothe the aching heart in times of grief and open it up to laughter and joy, devotion and creativity. The love shared between parents and children, sisters and brothers, companions and partners, friends and colleagues builds supportive bonds of shared experience. We learn to develop an attitude of goodwill toward others in our face-to-face communities of interaction and also, in time, to transcend local and parochial interests for the wider community of humankind. We do not need to believe in God to extend sympathy and altruism beyond our ethnic and racial groupings—and ultimately to all human beings on the planet Earth.

Thus, the challenge we face is whether we can create alternative institutions that satisfy the hunger for meaning, that satisfy our ideals, that support sympathetic communities, that are able to provide comfort in times of stress. We need alternative institutions that will support us in appreciating the majestic reality of the universe, in forging our determination to enter into nature, to understand how it operates, and, ultimately, to build a better world—to bring about a more creatively joyful life for ourselves and others in the new planetary civilization that is emerging.

We say "Yes" to the rational and passionate dimensions of life and "Yes" to the affirmative principles of humanist ethics. We *can* discover and luxuriate in the boundless potentialities of the good life. This, I submit, is the bountiful existential-psychological fountain from which we need to draw in order to supplant the God hypothesis. We need to affirm our commitment to the possibilities of achieving the fullness of life. Let us eat both of the "fruit of the tree of knowledge of good and evil" and of the "fruit of the tree of life!" We need to cultivate ethical wisdom and to appreciate the intrinsic value of life for its own sake.

Notes

1.   This article first appeared in *Free Inquiry* 27, no. 3 (April/May 2007), pp. 4–7.
2.   Victor J. Stenger, *God: The Failed Hypothesis*, Prometheus Books, Amherst, N.Y.: 2007.

Section 2

Secular Morality

IV

The Ethics of Secularism[1]

The secular humanist is often challenged thusly: "If you do not base your ethics on religious foundations, then in what sense can you be good?" The ethics of secularism has a long history in human culture. In the following, I wish to present four contemporary aspects of the ethics of secular humanism: liberation, enlightened self-interest, altruism, and goodwill. These principles are grounded in human experience and are thus natural. They are herein delineated in answer to the charge that the "new atheists," with whom secular humanists are often conflated by public opinion, lack an ethical outlook. On the contrary, one can be a secularist and also be a good person.

Liberation

Historically, secularism has been an ethic of liberation for those revolting against repressive institutions of society, such as those originating with the Puritans, the Victorians, and the Catholic Church. Secularists wished to realize happiness here and now rather than focus on alleged divine rewards in the afterlife. They objected strenuously to the barriers to this pursuit laid down by authoritarian-theological dogmas. Intimate relationships outside of marriage, the termination of unhappy or even abusive marriages, birth control, interracial marriage and miscegenation, homosexuality—in most countries, these were forbidden by church and state. Similarly, alcohol consumption and activities like gambling, which can be pleasurable if done in moderation, were often condemned as sinful vices.

Paradoxically, the upper classes were allowed to enjoy themselves, while the poor were considered debauched if they pursued similar activities. Often, the enforcement of the standards was hypocritical; the elites used them to hold the lower classes in check. More often than not, religious morality became the instrument for maintaining the social order.

Libertarian ethics emerged with the rise of democratic liberties. Freedom *from* repression became the battle cry of generations of liberal secularists and humanists. Thus *the right of privacy* became a central moral ideal and still is; with this came the demand for toleration of diversity in tastes and lifestyles. This led to the conviction that society should not seek to legislate adult moral behavior so long as it does not harm others.

Today, the battle over same-sex marriages illustrates this issue. Although progressives now champion equal rights for homosexuals, gays and lesbians, many authoritarians still remain adamantly opposed.

The recent ruling by the California Supreme Court that the denial of marriage to gays, lesbians, and transgendered persons was unconstitutional is a welcome development for secular libertarians. California now joins Massachusetts in this regard. The Council for Secular Humanism filed an *amicus curiae* brief (drafted by Edward Tabash, chairman of the First Amendment Task Force), which pointed out that much opposition to same-sex marriage is based in religion and as such is a violation of the First Amendment. The California Supreme Court chose not to use this argument but instead focused on other issues, such as equal protection of the laws. What is at stake is fairness in the application of tax and inheritance laws, eligibility for healthcare coverage and retirement benefits, access to loved ones and input into decisions about their care in medical settings, equal considerations of applications for the adoption of children, and other rights enjoyed by heterosexuals but generally denied to same-sex relationships. Then there is the fundamental right to marriage itself, which many believe strengthens the commitment between two persons who have freely chosen to tie their lives together.

In many countries, same-sex marriage is already recognized—Belgium, the Netherlands, Spain, Canada, and South Africa. In other countries and in some U.S. states (Connecticut, Vermont, New Jersey), civil unions or domestic partnerships are recognized, allowing homosexuals many of the same privileges and rights as heterosexual couples.

A key argument used by the California Supreme Court is that laws prohibiting same-sex marriage are similar to those that prohibited interracial marriages and miscegenation in the United States sixty years ago. At that time, twenty-nine states had restrictions against interracial marriage. The California Supreme Court's decision notes that California was the first state (in 1948) to repeal this law. Today, no states in the U.S. prohibit interracial marriage.

By contrast, forty-four states now prohibit same-sex marriage or define marriage as the union of a man and woman; twenty-seven have already enacted similar amendments to their state constitutions. Indeed, in California such an amendment is on the November ballot—an estimated 1.2 million names were gathered by petition. If enacted, it would overturn the California Court's decision.

Parenthetically, it would be regrettable if the liberation of gay people from discrimination were to engender a new and bitter phase in the impending elections in the United States. There are too many other important issues that ought to be at the top of the political and social agenda, not a *Kulturkrieg* against moral freedom.

Enlightened Self-Interest

Implicit in the democratic revolutions of modern times is the realization that the pursuit of happiness is an essential secular goal. This is true for all men and women no matter what their station in society. Intrinsic to this is the concept of self-interest. It is not wicked or evil to be concerned with one's own good. This has high priority on the secular ethical agenda. Each individual has but one life to live, and in the last analysis every person is responsible for his or her own well-being. Neither the church nor the state should dictate how a person is allowed to live. Although each person is dependent on others—on parents during the formative years of nurture and growth, on teachers during the period of education and development, on society and the economy for income and providing jobs—*the* project of every person is that he or she is in some sense autonomous and that what a person becomes depends on the personal choices that are made. These decisions concern our attitudes toward others, our selection of sexual partners and degree of commitment, our career paths—intellectual, emotional, social, political, educational, medical, and moral choices are made every day. Hence, every person needs to be *self*-interested. He or she should not abdicate his or her right to personal freedom to others. A person's sense of self is at the center of his or her existential world; it identifies a person's needs and shapes dreams, plans, and projects, values and ideals. Thus, self-interest is the crux of how a person lives and determines whether he or she merely survives or thrives by realizing the fullness of life.

There is a whole constellation of needs that a person must satisfy if he or she is to flourish. First of course are the basic biological needs for food, water, shelter, and protection needed to satisfy the built-in homoeostatic conditions necessary to live and function. Beyond that are the sociogenic needs that emerge in every community—the family, tribe, town, society, or nation at large. There are psychogenic needs as well: the capacity to relate to others, to love and be loved, to develop rationality, to exercise creativity and achieve some degree of realization of one's own unique talents and aspirations. Individuals exist both in a sociocultural setting and a geographical location. Each person is conditioned by vast impersonal forces—yet each has some measure of freedom of choice that is real.

I have written so much about this in my books and articles that I hesitate to elaborate further other than to say that a person's potential goals are multifarious and depend on who he or she is and where he or she lives at a particular time in history. For every person, the first challenge of life is to *live*, and the second is to *live well* and achieve some measure of happiness—or as I have described it, a meaningful and enriched life overflowing with the possibility of creativity, joy, and exuberance.

It is, of course, essential to recognize that our lives are interjoined with other human beings, and so among our noblest values are those we share with others. Secular humanists, whatever the cultural context, have extolled *enlightened* self-interest, not solely egoistic or selfish behavior but a life in which persons can relate to each other and enjoy consummatory experiences together.

Accordingly, self-interest *is* central, but *enlightened* self-interest emphasizes personal *excellence* and the qualities of a life well lived. Excellence depends on proper nutrition and health, self-discipline and self-restraint, the capacity to love and be loved; some measure of rationality, some aesthetic appreciation, and some fulfillment of one's talents. Included in a good life is the development of moral relationships with others.

Altruism

Although secular humanists have heroically defended the rights of individuals to pursue their own interests, altruism, I submit, is also intrinsic to the good life—though some radical libertarians have denied that anyone is capable of genuine altruistic behavior. I do not think that human motivation is simply based on egoism or selfishness, for there is abundant evidence of altruism in human conduct. Some libertarians have been accused of being indiscriminate fleshpots (for whom "anything goes") or ruthless Machiavellians to achieve their aims. This need not be the case. *Moral* libertarians have internalized principles of self-control and have a compassionate regard for the needs of others. Therefore, I see no contradiction in espousing both self-interest *and* altruism as concomitant in a full life well lived.

Such self-interest may be said to be *enlightened* when we take into account the interests of others in addition to or instead of our own. Such altruism is justified in two senses: on utilitarian grounds because of the positive consequences of assisting people who need help, and intrinsically because altruism is praiseworthy for its own sake. "Why should we be concerned with the good of others?" asks the egoist or cynic—to which I respond: we should be concerned with the good of others because that helps other persons in need *and* it bestows upon persons who perform such altruistic acts a quality of experience and a deep sense of right. Examples of altruistic behavior in relationships are abundant: it occurs between parents and children, teachers and pupils, medical professionals and patients, lovers and loved ones, siblings, colleagues, and friends. It is the bond of a friendship that especially illustrates this moral quality, for it ties people together and implies recognition that one person is willing to perform favors and make sacrifices for another and exceed the normal obligations of a relationship. This is based on a sincere sense of caring.

The real test of altruism arises when we encounter strangers in our midst to whom we voluntarily offer a lending hand, although we are not required to do so. The helping professions minister to those in need every day. This is their job and a source of income, of course, and they perform what is expected of them. But their actions have a moral dimension and are often rooted in empathy. For the average person, altruistic concerns may awaken a sense that if I *can*, I *should* help another, not simply out of self-interest but because I have a moral sense that I *ought* to deep within my being, even if I am reluctant to do so because it is inconvenient or demanding. A deed can be an eloquent expression of our highest moral capacities—as the Old Testament recognized when it stated that we should treat aliens in our midst with some moral compassion. Kant's categorical imperatives to treat other persons as ends in themselves and not as means can be generalized, for if the maxim under which I act were flouted, it would mean a breakdown of all moral standards. These rational considerations have persuaded innumerable persons to behave altruistically. A self-interested person may calculate that it is to his or her long-range advantage to help others. But even these reasons may not be sufficient for insensitive individuals who may be selfish, lack the milk of human kindness, and are disinclined to adopt a moral frame of mind. Such a person may be motivated by ambition, wealth, sexual gratification, glory, or power and be impervious to any sense of responsibility to others, as the tyrants and despots throughout history so blatantly illustrate.

When a lack of altruism develops into a criminal mindset that causes actual harm, victims must be protected by laws. Fear is a deterrent used to maintain law and order. However, we should insist that laws be just and fairly applied.

There is still another powerful motivation for altruistic moral conduct: passion for empathy, which can be developed within children and adolescents; that is, by nourishing within the young an appreciation for the interests of other human beings within their immediate communities and the world beyond. The justification for altruism is thus a combination of rational considerations and emotions. It has, if you will, a *rational-passional* source: it draws upon both the mind and the heart, reason and emotion, cognition and caring. The best guarantee of morality is to cultivate within human beings concern for other human beings. This is the task of moral education. Social approval also exerts a powerful influence on motivation: there is disapprobation for callous deeds committed and approbation for those based on beneficence.

The question is often raised, what is the ultimate source of altruism and moral caring? Self-interest is no doubt a strong motive for many people: persons may donate to a charity because of social recognition—their names may be placed on a plaque. Or perhaps they will receive a tax deduction. Yet over and beyond that, I submit that altruism has deep sources within human nature and is valued for its own sake, considered worthwhile for both the giver and receiver. Indeed, there is a good deal of evidence that such moral conduct is a result of biological evolution. This would mean that human beings are potentially moral and that whether these tendencies come to fruition depends on the social context in which a person is nourished and cultivated. There is a moral sense implanted within humans through the long process of evolution, though sociopaths tragically may lack that sense. To be fully human, I submit, is to develop our moral sensibilities.

Goodwill

Goodwill is a key secular virtue, but it is most effective when it is based on an *affirmative attitude toward living*. Individuals who have a positive attitude are more likely to express goodwill toward other human beings.

For persons of goodwill, life is intrinsically worthwhile—indeed, it can be bountifully overflowing with zest and exuberance—and their affirming attitude has an effect on other people. By loving life, such people are able to share their sense of the good life and are considerate of others' needs and interests. This affects those they encounter—children and pets, parents and grandparents, lovers and partners, brothers and sisters, aunts and uncles and cousins, friends and colleagues, and even strangers whom they meet in the world of affairs. A person of goodwill usually has confidence in his or her capacities for enjoying the good life and self-respect. He or she is well motivated and expresses it with spontaneity and vitality.

Life presents us all with challenges: a self-reliant person can seize the opportunities and realize their promise and deal with defeats with some equanimity. For such people, life is rich with meaning and significance—there are always new plans and projects down the road.

Reflective thinking and rational behavior have vital roles to play, but this leaves room for passion and emotion. The intensity of living is thus enriched by the heart as well as the mind. Life can be interesting and exciting despite its disappointments, which must be balanced with its promises and achievements.

Alas, we are all too often surrounded by naysayers—people of bad will, the pallbearers of the world. They spread doom and gloom, negativity and despair. They are pessimists and nihilists. Such people are profoundly ill at ease. They find little satisfaction in living, and they resent that other people are enjoying life. For them, life is a vale of tears. They leave all who meet them with a bitter taste.

No doubt everyone faces adversities. But there are also attainments. In any case, persons of goodwill endeavor to manifest constructive attitudes toward one and all. Such persons are willing to be helpful, and they express amiability, especially when the occasion arises. They endeavor to be polite and do not knowingly insult other people and are sensitive to their feelings.

The person of goodwill is of good character, good-hearted, good-humored, agreeable, and honorable. He or she has internalized what I have called in my book *Forbidden Fruit* "the common moral decencies" and "excellencies."

Such people are well-intentioned and well-meaning, striving to be cooperative, beneficent, empathetic, and altruistic. They are good companions, friendly and fraternal, especially toward colleagues and acquaintances encountered during various activities. They understand that they should try to be helpful and agreeable with coworkers. In times of defeat or tragedy, they will seek to assist or console other persons who are demoralized or suffer.

Secularists do not need to look outside the world of human affairs to a transcendental source to bolster this attitude. Pivotal to goodwill is that such persons endeavor to be reasonable, rational, and sensible yet also are empathetic, sensitive, and supportive. They do not need religious commandments to tell them not to harm others and to be kind and considerate. The secular humanist, especially in an open society, recognizes that *this* life affords manifold opportunities to achieve goals and discover satisfactions not only for oneself but also for others. Persons of goodwill seek to overcome obstacles, solve problems, and ameliorate the human condition wherever he or she can; such persons are not easily demoralized or embittered. Blended with the resolve to improve life for oneself is the need to respect others and applaud their achievements. A person of goodwill is gratified if other people they know succeed. If others prosper, they prosper.

There is a stoic attitude about those situations in life that are beyond our power to repair, such as an incurable disease, crushing defeat, or an accident. One goes on in spite of suffering the blows of outrageous fortune.

A person of goodwill is a morally decent person capable of attaining some measure of excellence in life. And goodwill is among the most eloquent of human excellences. Such a person has integrity, is truthful, keeps promises, and is sincere and honest. He or she is trustworthy and shows fidelity to friends, relatives, colleagues, coworkers, and fellow citizens.

Such persons are dependable, reliable, responsible, and are prepared to help others. They hold themselves accountable for what they have or have not done but avoid vindictiveness. Persons of goodwill bear malice toward none and do not harbor hatred, envy, jealousy, animosity, or resentment. They do not carry grudges and do not blame others for their travails or misadventures.

They are thus considerate, thoughtful, caring; every effort is made to reduce suffering and pain whenever they can; not only for other human beings but other sentient beings in the biosphere. Such persons are beneficent, charitable, kind, and appreciative of the needs of the helpless, the weak, the forlorn, the disadvantaged, and the handicapped.

People of goodwill are not awed by those who wield power, seek fame, or amass wealth; they do not seek to confer favors only on the high and mighty. A person of goodwill is fair and shows gratitude and appreciation for deeds well done.

Although such people may disagree with the beliefs or predilections of someone else, they will accord them the same rights as is expected of themselves. Thus they are tolerant of diversity in tastes and lifestyles, however different they may be, provided they are not destructive to the freedom and rights of others.

Persons of goodwill will not resort to violence to achieve their aims and wherever possible will urge peaceful means to achieve shared goals and values. Ever willing to sit down and break bread with others, to forgive and forget past mistakes and misdeeds, they eschew revenge and retribution. Wherever possible, they seek to negotiate differences and work out compromises in the spirit of fair play and reasonableness, recognizing that cooperation is a virtue that enables civilizations to flourish.

Secular humanists are impressed by the magnificence of nature and are in awe of the immensity of the expanding universe—on both the macrolevel of galaxies and on the microlevel of subatomic particles—and by the teeming biosphere. The evolutionary history of the universe as revealed by the sciences is the history of humankind as well, for the human species emerged from the same natural processes that formed galaxies, stars, and planets. Each of us is composed of recycled stardust to which we will eventually return. Of the billions of seeds, sperm, spores, and eggs that appear and are wasted in the fecundity of reproduction, so very few are fertilized and survive as an individual form of life. Every living person is unique, equal in dignity and value, possessed of the potentialities of creative living.

A person of goodwill has a deep appreciation of the meaningful opportunities for finding joy in living and of excitement and thrill of achieving a full life. It is hoped that he or she has discovered that *life* is its own reward. Fortunate is the person who has actualized the bountiful satisfactions of a life well lived. He or she recognizes with some humility that human beings are fallible and that we should seek to be the best that we can become.

In the light of this, a person of goodwill is able to express a positive, accepting attitude toward oneself and others and has developed a reflective intellect and an open heart. For such a person, life can be beautiful and is to be enjoyed and adored. He or she is eager to share this attitude with others so that they too can exult in the enrichment of the full life. Such a person realizes that after all is said and done, and in spite of limitations, life—*this* life—for ourselves and other sentient beings, is a wonder to behold and appreciate. And this applies to everyone that we touch or encounter in the planetary community of humankind. Goodwill is thus an exemplary, essential humanist virtue on the path toward a New Enlightenment.

Note

1.   This article first appeared in *Free Inquiry* 28, no. 5 (August/September 2008), pp. 6–10.

V

Morality Is Natural[1]

I have been interested in moral questions for as long as I can remember. I became keenly aware of the need for social justice as an adolescent growing up during the Great Depression when so many people suffered hardship. I even flirted with utopian visions of a perfect world—though I eventually became disillusioned with this quest. I enlisted in the U.S. Army during the Second World War in order to combat fascism. I was horrified by the devastation that I witnessed—the Nazi Holocaust, Soviet tyranny, and the brutal bombing of open cities by all sides, including the Allies. As a GI in the European theater of operations, I was appalled by the nuclear destruction of Hiroshima and Nagasaki and the death of tens of thousands of innocent civilians, but I could find few soldiers who agreed with me. They cheered the allied victory and wanted to get home.

I began reading books on ethics, beginning with Plato's Republic, and was especially impressed by the Socratic quest for knowledge and virtue. Later, studying at NYU and Columbia, I was influenced by American pragmatic naturalists, John Dewey and Sidney Hook, who thought that the method of intelligence was the most reliable guide for resolving moral problems. I also read the logical positivists, whose scientific philosophy and critiques of metaphysics and theology I accepted—though I took exception to their defense of the emotive theory of ethics, which proclaimed that ethical statements were "subjective" (expressive and imperative) and could not be verified. I took a course with AJ Ayer, the leading English exponent of the emotive theory; and as a smart alec undergraduate argued with him and insisted that " the killing of innocent people was wrong;" but I was uncertain at that time about how to justify that judgment. I was so intrigued by such moral questions that I resolved to devote my life to moral philosophy. I now consider myself to be an eupraxsopher, being interested not simply in the love of wisdom (meta-ethics), but in the practice of wisdom. Philosophers from Aristotle to Kant have defended the autonomy of ethics as a field of inquiry, independent of theology. I believe that there are moral truths and that these can be drawn from ethical reflection.

I must say that I am puzzled by the mantra intoned by so many theists today that "a person cannot be moral unless one believes in God." If this is a factual claim, it is patently false; for many good people have neither gone to church nor believed in God and yet have behaved morally; and the converse is often true. Is there a necessary logical connection between the fatherhood of God and basic moral principles? I doubt that. I would rather suggest that the belief of theists that morality presupposes religious faith is grounded in the apprehension of true believers that they would not behave morally without God (or Big Brother) looking over their shoulders. The underlying premise of the theist is that human beings are born evil (stained by "original sin") and unable to do good without the fear of punishment or the promise of reward in an after life. It implies that they lack an internalized empathetic moral conscience, and that the sanctions of religion (and law) are necessary to compel obedience to moral duties.

I disagree with that dismal view of human nature. Human beings are capable of either good or evil. We are potential moral beings; how we develop depends on a complex of bio-genetic and social influences, including parental care, belonging to some community, character formation, and the cultivation of some degree of moral cognition. Thus, it is possible to develop through moral education and life experience an empathetic-cognitive appreciation for the needs of others. I do not deny that there are exceptions, such as psychopaths and sociopaths, but morality is natural to the human condition, especially as human beings have evolved in socio-cultural communities. I am here presenting a naturalistic perspective on the good life, not one rooted in vain otherworldly hopes and fears.

I submit that a kind of autonomous moral sensibility can be brought to fruition; and that belief in God is not a prerequisite for knowing moral truths or acting morally. As a matter of fact believers in God historically have often waged pitched battles on both side of moral controversies—they have been for or against capital punishment; the rights of women; slavery; monogamy, polygamy, divorce; the justification of wars; monarchy, oligarchy, democracy, or theocracy. There is of course disagreement among secularists as well, though they do not claim to derive absolute moral principles from revelations On High. The point is there is there no easy road to moral truth; and it is presumptuous of theists to claim that they have a monopoly of moral virtue—particularly in the light of religious wars of violence and hatred waged historically and still today in the name of God. Witness the killings perpetrated by Catholics and Protestants, Christians and Jews, Muslims and Hindus, and other religious denominations among themselves. The present-day slaughter of innocent Sunnis and Shiites is tragic testimony that piety is no guarantee of moral purity. Religions of course have done much good for the benefit of humankind, but they have also at times been oppressive.

Now that I have devoted my entire life to ethical inquiry, what do I infer from these observations? Well first, that a bit of humility is in order. We need to recognize that moral choices are sometimes difficult to make. Although there is a fund of moral wisdom that has been developed by humankind, life does not always present us with clear-cut good or bad, right or wrong choices. Often we are confronted with two (or more) goods or rights, both of which we cannot have (e.g., I may wish to go college full time, but I need to take care of my handicapped sister at home); or sometimes its is a choice between the lesser of two evils (e.g., voting for presidential candidates, neither of whom I really want.) One has to be sensitive to the nuances and complexities in many moral dilemmas.

Second in importance is the need for tolerance for differing life styles, particularly in pluralistic societies. Disputes about the right of privacy versus the demands for public order; the alleged sinfulness or appropriateness of various forms of sexual morality (adultery, gay marriage, celibacy, sodomy, etc.); demands for the censorship of pornography versus freedom of expression; reproductive freedom for women; euthanasia and assisted suicide; the ethics of stem-cell research, etc. has led to an intense culture war. The principle of "live and let live—so long as we do not harm others" has some merit. Hence some respect for alternative conceptions of the good life, though not immune to criticism, should be encouraged. All of this is consistent with the core virtues of our secular democracy.

Does this mean that without God "anything goes," as Dostoyevsky implied, that morality is simply a matter of taste, and that there are no ethical standards at all? On the contrary, there are some objective moral judgments that can be made and some behaviors are in principle wrong (e.g., "torturing innocent children"). Statements such as "we ought to tell the truth" or "keep our promises" are general statements that help to guide us, though how and in what sense they apply depends upon the actual existential contexts at issue. In the first case, we might consider it prudent to abandon our commitment to truth telling in time of war, as there may be a higher duty to self-defense; and in the second case, Socrates observed that if friend asked you to hold a weapon for him with the promise to give it back when he asks for it, and if in a moment of anger he demands that it be returned, you might decide justifiably to withhold the weapon until he calms down.

I should qualify my position by stating that I am a relativist—in the sense that moral principles and values are related to human (individual and social) interests, wants, desires, and needs. But at the same time I am an objectivist, since I think that these principles and values are amenable to critical examination; and if need be, they may be modified in the light of inquiry—we need to take into account the pre-existing principles and values that I (or my community) may cherish, the facts of the case, a comparative evaluation of means and ends, and the consequences of various courses of action.

I submit that there are basic moral principles that civilized communities share. I have called these "the common moral decencies." They emerge in the face-to-face interactions within a community. These are generally accepted by both theists and secularists, and they reflect the bedrock rules of civilized conduct. I do not deny that humans may differ about some of them, particularly their range of application; and thus a degree of cultural relativity may be present. Moreover, new principles may be discovered and hard-fought battles may be waged to gain recognition of them—such as the war against slavery in the United States in the nineteenth century, and the campaign for the rights of women, minorities, and gay people in the twentieth century. Nonetheless these general moral principles have evolved in human culture over a long period of time and there is a broad consensus concerning their viability; they appeal to the reflective moral conscience.

A brief catalogue of some of the common moral decencies is listed as follows:

The Common Moral Decencies

I. **Integrity**: We ought to tell the truth, keep promises, be sincere and honest.

II. **Trustworthiness**: We should show fidelity to our friends, relatives, and neighbors in the community at large; we should be dependable, reliable, and responsible toward others who depend on us.

III. **Benevolence**: We should manifest a good will toward other persons. We should avoid malfeasance, harming or injuring others (do not kill, torture, or abuse others). We should avoid malfeasance to public or private property (do not steal or destroy property that is not yours). Sexual relations should be based on mutual consent between adults. We should strive for a beneficent attitude (kindness, sympathy, compassion). We should assist where we can in alleviating another person's pain and suffering. We should help increase where we can the sum of goods for others to share.

IV. **Fairness**: We ought to show gratitude to others, be held accountable for our conduct. We should seek justice, equity. We should manifest tolerance; be cooperative, seek to negotiate any differences peacefully and work out compromises wherever possible.

The justification of the common moral decencies is first, *empirical* (having evolved in human civilization over a long period of time); second, *consequential* (no society can long survive if they are consistently flouted); and third, *principled* (they are so important that they should only be violated reluctantly, if higher goods or rights are at stake. These are *prima facie* general rules, but how they actually apply depends on the concrete moral situation at hand. The most reliable guide to action is moral intelligence able to weigh alternatives and make choices after a process of deliberation.

Thus far I have talking about our duties and obligations towards others. What about our obligations to ourselves? Again, is everything permissible within the life of desire and passion? My answer is, no and yes, depending on the individual. I am not talking about the Puritans or Taliban "virtue police" who are unhappy if other people are having a good time. They wish to ban anything that they cannot understand or enjoy. I am talking rather about standards that we ourselves discover as essential if we are to lead a life full of enrichment. Obviously, there are some limitations and constraints on personal moral freedom that a mature person herself or himself decides to adopt. There are some things that we learn that we simply cannot do. "It is illegal, immoral, it makes us fat, or it is bad for our liver," to paraphrase an old refrain. We learn that some modicum of temperance and moderation in our desires is essential if we are to lead a full life.

On the other hand we are all different as individual persons; and our idiosyncratic tastes and values are uniquely are own. As a secularist I would say that each person needs to find meaning and purpose in his or her own terms, though some persons may lack the existential courage to become what they really want. Each person's life is like a work of art; for we are constantly adding the shape form, color and tone to what we create. Life has no predetermined meaning per se; it presents us with opportunities; and the meanings that we discover depend on our own creative decisions. They are realized in the plans and projects that we unfurl every day. In one sense, each moment is intrinsically good in itself; though it needs to fit into a kaleidoscopic rendering that we constantly reinforce or remake. The significance of living is found in the educational experiences that we have had; the careers that we pursue or jobs that we endure; our partners and lovemates, friends and colleagues; the children that we have had, if we choose to have them, and their upbringing; our interests and activities; the beloved causes that we have become involved in; in sum, all of the things that we have undertaken or undergone during our lifetimes. Secular humanists have invariably emphasized the importance of *happiness* in realizing a full life. This has meant many different things to different men and women: for some it is the quest for passive withdrawal or meditation; for others maximizing hedonic pleasure, money, power, or sexual conquests; for the bourgeois sacrifice for God or country; and for still others, service for a worthy cause. This is relative to a person's own interests, talents, and predilections.

I wish to propose still another ideal of the good life, which has special meaning in free, open pluralistic and democratic societies. This I have called the achievement of the *exuberant life*. Many of the models of the good life, particularly those with strong religious overtones, emerged under social conditions that were oppressive for the average person. Aside from the ruling classes, the wealth of society was limited; all too often there was not enough to eat; disease was rampant; wild animals or marauding bands often posed threats; and life was apt to fulfill Hobbes' warning: it became "nasty, brutish and short." Today, we live in affluent consumer economies; we have the power of science and technology to cure many of the diseases and afflictions of the past, to reduce human pain and suffering, and to raise standards of living. We are at the dawn of a new era where we can extend life significantly. Here the exuberant life of the Promethean spirit assumes real power, for we can perhaps discover new knowledge and wisdom, new reservoirs of joy. I would suggest that the life of exuberance is becoming available to a widening circle of individuals. For the first time we can extend the opportunities of the creative life, of work and leisure, travel and adventure. These daring opportunities for achieving a good life also enable us to attain lives of *excellence and nobility*. It is not salvation in the next life that we search, but the exuberant life here and now.

Strikingly, for the first time in human history the potentialities for enriching life are possible, not only for individuals who live within affluent democratic societies, but for *all of humankind*. The rapid growth of the Asian economies, China, Korea, Japan and India clearly show that the possibilities of extending the promise of a good life to everyone on the planet beyond Europe and North America are real.

Here I wish to close with a new moral obligation that is both realistic and attainable. Thus we can extend our moral concern to the entire planetary community of which we are a part. Planetary ethics has emerged to capture our moral outlook and imagination. A new imperative beckons: "We should consider every person on the planet equal in dignity and value." We should attempt to do what we can to extend an empathetic concern for the entire family of humankind. The common moral decencies now have a wider range of application, and the possibility of realizing exuberant lives for everyone on the planet at least is a realistic goal. If we are to achieve this goal, then we need to transcend the ancient religious, national, racial, and ethnic barriers of the past. We need to focus on "Humanity as a Whole" as our key moral concern. Finally, we now see clearly that each of us has a responsibility to do what we can to preserve and enhance the natural ecology of our shared planetary habitat. This high ideal is not only profoundly necessary, but also appealing to a reflective moral sensibility.

Note

1. This article first appeared in *Think: Philosophy for Everyone* 15 (autumn 2007), pp. 7–14.

VI

Affirming Life[1]

Eupraxsophy Revisited

There is no word in the English language that adequately conveys the meaning of *secular humanism*. Secular humanism is *not* a religion; it represents a philosophical, scientific, and ethical outlook. I have accordingly introduced a new term, *eupraxsophy*, in order to distinguish humanistic convictions and practices from religious systems of faith and belief.

This term can be used in many languages. It is derived from Greek roots: *eu-*, *praxis*, and *sophia*.

Eu- is a prefix that means "good," "well," or "advantageous." It is found in the Greek word *eudaimonia*, which means "well-being" or "happiness," and it is also used in English terms such as *eulogy* and *euphoria*.

Praxis (or *prassein*) refers to "action, doing, or practice." *Eupraxia* means "right action" or "good conduct."

Sophia means "wisdom." This word appears in *philosophy*, combining *philos* ("love") and *sophia* ("wisdom") to mean "love of wisdom."

Eupraxsophy is designed for the public arena where ideas contend. Unlike pure philosophy, it focuses not simply on the *love* of wisdom, though this is surely implied by it, but the *practice* of wisdom. Moral philosophers should be interested in developing the capacity for critical ethical judgments. That is an eminent goal. But eupraxsophy goes further than that, for it focuses on creating a coherent ethical life stance. Moreover, it presents hypotheses and theories about nature and the cosmos that at any particular point in history were based on the best scientific knowledge of the day. Humanist eupraxsophy defends a set of criteria evaluating the testing of truth claims. It may espouse at any one time in history a particular set of political ideals. Eupraxsophy combines both

53

a *Weltanschauung* (a worldview or personal philosophy of life) and a philosophy of living. But it takes us one step further by means of commitment; based upon cognition, it is fused with passion. It entails the application of wisdom to the conduct of life.

Eupraxsophers make choices—the most reasonable ones in the light of the best available evidence—and this enables them to act. Theologians, politicians, generals, engineers, businessmen, lawyers, doctors, artists, poets, and plain men and women have beliefs upon which they act. Why deny this right to the informed eupraxsopher scientist- philosopher? It is our conviction, however, that one's beliefs should be based upon reason, critical intelligence, and wisdom. This is what the suffix -*sophy* refers to. Wisdom in the broad sense includes not only philosophical and practical judgments, but also scientific understanding.

Intrinsic to this definition is a scientific component, for wisdom includes the most reliable knowledge drawn from scientific research and scholarship in the various fields of inquiry. Theoretical research is morally neutral. The scientist is interested in developing causal hypotheses and theories that can be verified by the evidence. Scientists describe or explain how the subject under study behaves without evaluating it normatively.

Humanist eupraxsophy, on the other hand, attempts to draw the philosophical implications of the sciences to the lives of men and women. It seeks to develop a cosmic perspective that is based on the most reliable findings discovered on the frontiers of science. It recognizes that there are gaps in our current knowledge that still need to be investigated. It is keenly aware of human fallibility about what we do and do not know, yet it boldly applies practical, scientific wisdom to life.

Accordingly, the primary task of eupraxsophy is to understand nature and life and to draw concrete normative prescriptions from this knowledge. Eupraxsophy involves a double focus: a cosmic perspective and a set of normative principles and values by which we may live.

Humanists do not look upward to a heaven for a promise of divine deliverance. They have their feet planted squarely in nature, yet they have the fortitude to employ art, science, reason, sympathy, and education to create a better world for themselves and their fellow human beings.

From the standpoint of the individual, happiness is achieved not by a passive release from the world, but by the pursuit of an active life of adventure and fulfillment. There are so many opportunities for creative enjoyment that every moment can be viewed as precious; all fit together to make a full and exuberant life.

What is vital in humanist eupraxsophy is that humanists are not overwhelmed by the tragic character of the human condition; they are willing to face death, sorrow, adversity, and suffering with courage and equanimity. They have confidence in the ability of human beings to overcome alienation, solve the problems of living, and develop the capacity to share the material goods of life with others and empathize with them. The theist often has a degraded view of human beings who, beset with original sin, are incapable of solving life's problems by themselves and need to look outside of the human realm for divine succor. The humanist accepts the fact that the human species has imperfections and limitations, and that some things encountered in existence may be beyond redress or repair. Even so, he or she is convinced that the best posture is not to retreat before the unknown, but to exert intelligence and fortitude to deal with life's problems. It is only by a resolute appraisal of the human condition, based on reason and science, that the humanist's life stance seems most appropriate. The secular humanist is unwilling to bow before either the forces of nature or would-be human masters. Rather, he or she expresses the highest heroic virtues of the Promethean spirit: audacity, nobility, and developed moral sensibilities about the needs of others.

Joyful Exuberance

Humanists find exuberance to be intrinsically worthwhile for its own sake. This is usually identified with happiness. The Greeks called it *eudaimonia*, or well-being; this meant the actualization of a person's nature, with pleasure as a byproduct, not for the solitary moment, but in a complete life. This entails some moderation of a person's desires. But I add that, in joyful exuberance, there is high excitement, the intensity of living, throbbing with passion, engaging in daring activities of enterprise and adventure.

Joyful exuberance is enhanced when we not only fulfill our needs and wants, but creatively express our goals and aspirations. It denotes some degree of excellence, nobility, even perfectibility, of a person's talents and achievements. It comes to fruition for those who find life intensely worth living and at times exhilarating.

More than that, it involves a flowering of one's personality in that person's own terms. And in its highest reaches it expresses the fullness and richness of living.

This occurs when a person is able to realize his or her wants and talents, dreams and aspirations, and when a person is able to share the bountiful goods of life with others—children and parents, brothers and sisters, relatives and friends, colleagues and neighbors—within the various communities of humankind. This is most eloquently achieved when there is moral growth and development: a person is able to appreciate the needs of others; there is a genuine willingness to relate to them, to love and be loved, to share and even to make sacrifices for their benefit.

Joyful immediacies are experienced when there is a flowering of life. There are three *e*-words that describe this state: *excellence, eudaimonia,* and *exuberance.*

And there are five *c*-words that define it: *character, cognition, courage, creativity,* and *caring.*

This does not deny or ignore the pain and despair, defeat and failure, evil and tragedy that may befall a person, the unexpected contingencies of fate and fortune that may be encountered: intractable illness, premature death, betrayal, cowardice, dishonesty, or ingratitude.

The mature person has developed a reflective attitude that enables him or her to place these misadventures and setbacks, painful as they may be, in a broader context. He or she can compensate for the shortcomings of life by pointing to the times that he or she has overcome adversity; and he or she still finds life worth living because of poetry and profundity, laughter and delight, romance and love, discovery and ingenuity, enlightenment and success, and the times that he persevered and prevailed. If a person's career and life is like a work of art, then we need to appreciate its full collage, its contrasts and highlights, tones and shades, colors and forms. Marshaling some stoicism in periods of anxiety, hopefully a person will find that the good that one experiences can outbalance the bad, the positive the negative, and that optimism can master pessimism.

The affirmative person may sum up his or her life and declare that, after all is said and done, it was worth living, that though one may have some regrets for what one could have done but did not, or for what might have been but was not, all told it was good. And, ah, yes! Although there were periods of pain and sorrow, these were balanced by those of pleasure and joy. What an adventure it was—far better to have lived and experienced than not to have lived at all!

Creating Your Own Meanings

The meaning of life is not to be found in a secret formula discovered by ancient prophets or modern gurus, who withdraw from living to seek quiet contemplation and release. Life has no meaning per se; it does, however, present us with innumerable opportunities, which we can either squander and retreat from in fear or seize with exuberance.

It can be discovered by anyone and everyone who can energize an inborn zest for living. It is found within living itself, as it reaches out to create new conditions for experience.

Eating of the fruit of the Tree of Life gives us the bountiful enthusiasms for living. The ultimate value is the conviction that life can be found good in and of itself. Each moment has a kind of preciousness and attractiveness.

The so-called secret of life is an open scenario that can be deciphered by everyone. It is found in the experiences of living: the delights of a fine banquet, the strenuous exertion of hard work, the poignant melodies of a symphony, the appreciation of an altruistic deed, the excitement of an embrace of someone you love, the elegance of a mathematical proof, the invigorating adventure of a mountain climb, the satisfaction of quiet relaxation, the lusty singing of an anthem, the vigorous cheering in a sports contest, the reading of a delicate sonnet, the joys of parenthood, the pleasures of friendship, the quiet gratification of serving our fellow human beings—all of these activities and more.

It is in the present moment of experience as it is brought to fruition, as well as in the delicious memory of past experiences and the expectation of future ones, that the richness of life is exemplified and realized. The meaning of life is that it can be found to be good and beautiful and exciting on its own terms for ourselves, our loved ones, and other sentient beings. It is found in the satisfaction intrinsic to creative activities, wisdom, and righteousness. One doesn't need more than that and, hopefully, one will not settle for less.

The meaning of life is tied up intimately with our plans and projects, the goals we set for ourselves, and our dreams and the successful achievement of them.

We create our own conscious meanings; we invest the cultural and natural worlds with our own interpretations. We discover, impose upon, and add to nature.

Meaning is found in the lives of the ancient Egyptians, in their culture built around Isis and Osiris and the pyramids, or in the ruminations of the ancient prophets of the Old Testament. It is exemplified by the Athenian philosopher standing in the Acropolis deliberating about justice in the city-state. It is seen in the structure of the medieval town, built upon a rural economy, feudalism, and a Christian cultural backdrop. It is experienced by the Samurai warrior in the context of feudal Japanese culture, in the hopes and dreams of the Incas of Peru, by the native Watusi tribes in Africa, and in the Hindu and Muslim cultures of India and southern

Asia. And it is exemplified anew in modern postindustrial, technological, urban civilizations of the present-day world, which give us new cultural materials and new opportunities for adventure.

Human beings have found their meanings within the context of a historical, cultural experience, and in how they are able to live and participate within it. Life had meaning to them; only the content differs; the form and function are similar. Life, when fully lived under a variety of cultural conditions, can be euphoric and optimistic; it can be a joy to experience and a wonder to behold.

Note

1.   This article first appeared in *Free Inquiry* 24, no. 6 (October/November 2004), pp. 5–7.

VII

The Pursuit of Excellence: Raising the Level of Taste and Appreciation[1]

A heated controversy engulfing us today concerns "the right of privacy." Personal liberty is heralded by liberals, Democrats, libertarians, and conservatives alike. They say that they wish to protect individual freedom from repression, although they differ about which freedoms need to be preserved. Conservatives are especially worried about the government's intrusion into the private domain. They emphasize economic freedom, a reduction in taxes, and the deregulation of business. Liberals fear Big Brother from any source—repressive governments, powerful religious institutions, or corporate conglomerates.

The burning issue in the United States today is whether there are constitutional grounds for the right of privacy. Chief Justice John G. Roberts, Jr. implied as much at his hearings before the Judiciary Committee, inferring that many of these rights are now "settled law." Justices John Paul Stevens, Ruth Bader Ginsburg, Stephen G. Breyer, and David Souter insist that the Constitution is a living document and that the right of privacy is implicit in it. Strict constructionists deny this.

The right of privacy allows individuals to pursue their own interests and values without interference, so long as they do not harm others or prevent them from pursuing theirs. This is an ethical position, not simply a legal one, and it is intrinsic to the ethics of secular humanism. The cultural battleground over the right of privacy has been bloodied by disputes concerning its application: freedom of choice is widely defended. This entails reproductive freedom (abortion, contraception, artificial insemination, therapeutic cloning) and the right of a person to control his or her own body. The right of adults to pursue their sexual proclivities (sexual freedom, same-sex marriage, adultery, sodomy), and in general to satisfy their desires as they see fit without interference from the state (as Justice

Anthony M. Kennedy has argued) is also protected. "Informed consent" has also emerged as a vital principle governing health care (the right to die with dignity, euthanasia, assisted suicide). Most secular humanists defend all of the above. Cultural conservatives do not.

How far does the right of privacy extend? It has been said that "*De gustibus non est disputandum*" (of tastes one should not dispute), recognizing the pluralistic idiosyncratic diversity of desires and preferences: one person likes potatoes, another tomatoes. One prefers blue; another red. One relishes hot tamales and drinks beer; another prefers quiche and daiquiris. One is attracted to blondes, another to brunettes.

Archconservatives have deplored the right of privacy, since they are shocked by forms of behavior in society that they find distasteful, such as sexual promiscuity, gay marriage, marijuana use, or rap music. Libertarians are disturbed by efforts to impose the norms of a particular religious tradition, the standards of an elite class, or phobias against certain elements of popular culture on the entire society. Secular humanists in principle argue for toleration, saying that in doing so we need not necessarily condone such behaviors, and we can criticize them. Even so, we have no wish to prohibit them by law.

Both claims have some merit. Secular humanists, who defend the right of privacy and have in the past defended emancipation from extremely restrictive social standards, are fearful of oppression by the state, the economy, or the church. Conservative reactionaries are disturbed by what they view as the breakdown of the moral order, and they worry about their children coming under the influence of noxious lifestyles.

I believe we need to add a concomitant principle alongside the right of privacy—this I call (borrowing a phrase from the business literature of two decades past) "the pursuit of excellence." I submit that we *can* and *do* disagree about tastes, and that some preferences may very well be better than others; that is, educated tastes have an intrinsic appeal that underdeveloped, tastes may not. Those who proclaim the sanctity of unbridled individual freedom need to develop an appreciation for qualitatively developed pleasures. Subjectivity is not the governing rule. "Anything goes" is not blithely accepted. Some pleasures may be better than others on a comparative scale: more satisfying, more enduring, more expressive of the creative potential of developed personalities. John Stuart Mill, in his famous work, *On Liberty* (recently added to the hit list of the ten worst books by the indignant conservative publication *Human Events*), attempted to defend the view that "I would rather be a Socrates dissatisfied than a pig satisfied." This suggests a criterion of better or worse intrinsic in human realization, and it recalls Aristotle's list of actualized virtues and excellences in the *Nicomachean Ethics*.

It is often not a question of either/or, the so-called higher pleasures versus the so-called lower pleasures, but *both*. In any case, the physical-biological pleasures in moderation and with temperance, as well as the pleasures of intellect, art, and morality of a fully developed person, are important in achieving the fullness of life. We need to affirm that, as humanists, we are committed to both the sciences *and* the arts—to what Matthew Arnold called "The best that has been thought and said."

I submit that, if an open democratic society cherishes the right of privacy, at the same time it needs to encourage the cultivation of *excellence and nobility*. It should endeavor to raise levels of taste and appreciation by means of education and persuasion.

First, *moral education* is vital in developing moral character and moral reasoning and the capacity to empathize with the needs and interests of other persons—and also the capacity to govern our passions with some measure of mature self-restraint.

Second, *cultural education* is essential, including enriched cultural opportunities to elevate aesthetic appreciation and sensitivity to music, dance, poetry, literature, drama, architecture, and the other arts.

Third, the development of *intellectual talent* is central to a democracy: programs to reduce illiteracy; to learn about human nature and evolutionary history; to expand knowledge of science, the nature of the universe, and human culture; and to develop reflective and practical wisdom.

Religious schools, such as the *madrassas* of the Middle East, emphasize rote learning and indoctrination. This is contrary to the program of humanistic education, which emphasizes the development of independence and innovative thinking. We need to educate individuals so they can be open to new dimensions of experience and appreciate alternative cultural forms. Overemphasis on otherworldly religious duties may block the fulfillment of highly developed intellectual moral and aesthetic experiences.

We have called for a cultural Renaissance as part of the new Enlightenment. This involves at a minimum the development of cognitive skills, a capacity for critical and creative thinking, an understanding of the methods of scientific inquiry, and the scientific outlook. But this also involves the reformation and transformation of our values, which enable us to go beyond the banalities and vulgarities of so much of pop culture. In his book *Vulgarians at the Gate* (Prometheus Books, 2001), Steve Allen dealt critically with "raunch radio" and "trash TV." He advocated raising the standards of popular culture, and in particular he chastised those who are willing to use four-letter words at the drop of a hat. (What would he have said about *The Aristocrats*, a new film overloaded with words like *fuck* and *shit*?) Allen was criticized by civil libertarians, who feared that his ideas could be interpreted to condone censorship and play into the hands of cultural vigilantes. Allen responded that surely we should be able to criticize excessive vulgarity in the public square and attempt to improve popular taste without countenancing puritanical censorship committees.

One can deplore the excesses of popular culture. On the other hand, there are other expressions in our culture that are no less crass or vulgar. Many of these are usually ignored by archconservatives, who are primarily agitated by "sexual improprieties" and do not worry about other debasing forms of behavior. May I list some of these:

- *Violence*, for its own sake, is widespread in our culture. By this, I mean brash violence in movies and on television and in books and computer games in which murder, war, and the battering of women are glorified. These seek to arouse terror and horror. One particularly egregious example that comes to mind is the film *The Devil's Rejects,* in which brutal murders are depicted with the gore and guts of victims spilling out. Similarly, television programs are becoming excessively graphic and obscene. I don't advise censoring or forbidding the broadcast of these programs, but I would support efforts to limit young children's exposure to them. I do not wish to curtail all such dramatic portrayals, but *please*, not in primetime. I might note that the freedom to depict violence frankly for worthwhile artistic ends should be defended. We may speak out against a film like *The Devil's Rejects* while celebrating significant works like *A Clockwork Orange* or *Schindler's List.*
- *Greed:* the focus on economic gain and the ostentatious displays of wealth as typified by Donald Trump in his television series, *The Apprentice*—and by contestants who will bear any hardship or break any allegiance trying to win a million dollars on *Survivor*—are also questionable in terms of values. Programs like these glorify cutthroat competition and success at any cost. Perhaps this reflects the attitudes of advertisers, who will do virtually anything to hook viewers and entice consumers to buy their products.
- *Credit madness:* High credit-card debt continues to build up as frenzied spending balloons beyond the means of many consumers. Bankruptcies are at an all-time high, even as new legislation goes into effect making bankruptcy more difficult. Two further signs of greed: the U.S. government provides the second-lowest share of per-capita GNP of any Western nation for foreign aid (after Italy), and tax cuts for the rich still remain on the books in spite of growing deficits.

- *Gambling* has become a national passion. The growth of gambling casinos beyond Las Vegas and Atlantic City continues at a dizzying pace. Virtually every major city in the United States seeks to entice suckers to slot machines and roulette wheels. "Gaming," they say, is a form of entertainment. Unfortunately it has become more than that; rich and poor alike may become addicted to gambling, believing in "luck," as though unaware that gambling sprees have ruined lives and wrecked families. There are few public campaigns pointing out the dangers. The case is similar for the proliferation of speculative investment schemes and the boom in real estate prices. Investment in securities and property is a sensible way to earn income and ensure a comfortable retirement. Unsavory get-rich-quick schemes have been marketed by hucksters—and the public is not adequately forewarned about the excesses of speculation.

- *Sexual exploitation:* many films depict sexual brutality, sexualization of the very young, and degrading sexual behavior. Adults should have the right to read or see what they wish without censorship. There is often, however, an excessive focus on promiscuity for its own sake, and secular humanists need to point this out. It is one thing to view films in the privacy of one's own home; it is another to flout certain behaviors without consideration of standards of good taste.

- *Religious extremism* can be a problem. When adherence to a religion requires obedience, withdrawal from the world, prayer to achieve goals, and contrition, individuals may be debased and lose their ability to function in the mainstream society. Yet some who claim to be religious leaders are held above criticism, such as con artists who practice faith healing and other forms of deception and operate unchallenged by any save James Randi and a few other skeptics. Belief in miracles, Jesus and Mary sightings, and other forms of superstition need criticism in contemporary society. Joe Nickell, senior research fellow of CSICOP, today stands virtually alone in the United States in his heroic role. The distortions in Mel Gibson's film, *The Passion of the Christ*, illustrate the problem we face of religious mythology touted as true.

- *Other forms of addiction:* the frantic pace of modern culture contributes to addictive behavior. People use alcohol, cigarettes, drugs, and other forms of immediate gratification without moderation. The campaign against cigarette smoking needs to extend to alcohol and gambling. We need to address *depression,* a huge problem in contemporary society.

- *Breakdown of families:* Humanists need to concern themselves with society's high divorce rate, which often leads to children being left adrift. We need to restore an appreciation for family values, but expanded ones, including nontraditional gay and lesbian relationships. Alas, in the United States, 18 percent of children live in poverty versus 5 to 8 percent in Western European countries. Many who claim to believe in family values are indifferent to this fact.

- *Vindictive retribution:* the resort to excessive punishment is widespread. Half of all the prisoners in the world are in American jails. The United States is the only major democracy that condones capital punishment. Arguments against execution aside, some 132,000 people now languish in life imprisonment. Much of this vindictiveness springs from biblical morality, which promotes an "eye-for-an-eye" mentality.

I find many of the above behaviors—usually condoned or ignored by conservatives—to be obscene. One fact to bear in mind is that the United States is the most religious democratic country in the world. Yet our religious beliefs are often accompanied by dysfunctional values. Gregory S. Paul has shown that countries that have the highest proportion of the population who interpret the Bible (and other sacred texts) literally tend to focus on puritanical repression and have the *highest* incidences of crime, homicide, sexually transmitted diseases, teenage pregnancies, and divorce. Five of the "red" states have the largest proportion of Bible-thumping believers, and also the highest murder rates (Louisiana, Mississippi, Alabama, Georgia, and Nevada). Studies show that societies with the highest intensity of religious faith, at the same time, often have the highest incidence of violence.

Secular humanists are skeptical of religious claims. They deplore superstition and credulity. However, it is imperative that we step beyond debunking and that we provide alternatives that contribute to human enrichment. These include creative growth, human fulfillment, aesthetic enjoyment, peak experiences, cognitive skills, and moral empathy. We emphasize the opportunities for the good life that affluent society offers: abundant cultural opportunities for leisure, travel, and recreation. We also emphasize the need to build moral relationships between individuals.

Other moral principles that need defense are *the principles of fairness*. This is especially the case in a society that focuses excessively on self-aggrandizement, competitive achievement, greed, and the accumulation of wealth. *Caring* for others is essential, not only within local communities but also on the planetary scale. This does not derive its source from obedience to religious commandments, but grows out of a genuine internalized sense of *empathy*. This is an important component in the transformation of values that secular humanists seek to bring about as part of a new Enlightenment.

Note

1.   This article first appeared in *Free Inquiry* 26, no. 1 (December 2005/January 2006), pp. 4–7.

VIII

A Good Will[1]

The question is often raised, "Can a person be good without God?" Secular humanists (including freethinkers and rationalists) have been critical of that old-time-religion mind-set that would answer, "No." Not only do secular humanists *not* accept most teachings of religion, such as the creationist account of the universe, but they deeply question many of its moral admonitions. So the question is, "Are there alternative humanistic and naturalistic guidelines?" My answer, of course, has always been in the affirmative.

I have suggested in past editorials in *Free Inquiry* what a humanist morality entails. I have called this morality "eupraxsophy"—good, practical wisdom drawn from science, philosophy, and ethics. Indeed, secular humanist ethics provides a transformational matrix of aphorisms, principles, and values. Among these are the *common moral decencies* (do not lie, cheat, steal, etc.), which express the principles of moral conduct, historically developed and widely shared by diverse cultures. There is also a set of values that humanists cherish; these are called *excellences* (rationality, personal freedom, creativity, etc.). I have also acknowledged other widely recognized norms in the civilized world, such as those embodied in the United Nations' Universal Declaration of Human Rights. Humanists emphasize the importance of rational ethical inquiry to resolve moral dilemmas, and they seek to encourage growth and development in the young. Humanist ethics urge individuals to assume responsibility for their own lives and strive to achieve happiness and exuberance.

In continuing this exploration, let me suggest still another transformational principle that is basic to morality, what has been called "a Good Will." Indeed, the great German philosopher Immanuel Kant said:

> Nothing can possibly be conceived in the world, or even out of it, which can be called good without qualification, except a Good Will. ... A good will is good not because

of what it performs or affects, not by its aptness for the attainment of some proposed end, but simply by virtue of the volition, that is, it is good in itself … like a jewel, it would still shine by its own light, as a thing which has its own value in itself. … This then … must be the supreme good and the condition of every other. [*Fundamental Principles of the Metaphysic of Morals*, Immanuel Kant]

I agree with Kant about the importance of a good will, which is intrinsically good in itself, but I submit that we need to appraise it in terms of its consequences as well. For a good will is also good for *what it accomplishes, its effect upon other human beings in the communities in which they live*. We do not judge an act by its motive or intention alone, but also by its impact upon others in the world.

It is clear that human beings are dependent on other human beings, with whom they can share the joys, sorrows, values, and setbacks in life. They learn by living and doing. We cannot and should not abdicate our responsibilities to make this a better world for ourselves, our families, our friends, and other human beings within our range of contact. This means that we should use our intelligence to weigh alternatives, to balance choices, and to make prudent decisions as they relate to others. We cannot escape from the world. We live within it, and, as such, we have the challenge of improving ourselves as best we can and, if possible, reforming society and working with our fellow human beings to do so. Thus, a good will is also an instrumental good, judged by its consequences in human affairs.

I think that it is important to stress the moral difference between acting according to these principles from an internal motivation to do good because it is our moral duty, rather than from fear of repercussions or consequences if we don't. There is a qualitative moral difference between those who act according to moral principles simply because they fear certain consequences (e.g., the disdain of their peers, the vengeance of a god, or the fall of civilization) as opposed to an inward motivation to simply do the right thing.

The importance of a good will is attested to by countless generations of human beings. It cuts across diverse societies and cultures and appeals to both the religious and nonreligious, for this principle rings true throughout human experience. The person of good will is or should be cherished by the community, though his or her intentions may sometimes be misinterpreted and he or she maligned.

Being of good will means that we are not mean-spirited or surly, despairing or nihilistic, vindictive or hateful. We should try to be affirmative about what life offers, not fearful or defensive; we should be hopeful, not cynical or nasty; we should exude some realistic optimism that we can influence or mitigate evil and improve human affairs. We should strive to resolve our problems and overcome adversity. We should try to select courses of action in the light of both reason and good will. Indeed, this positive attitude is a fundamental principle to which, I submit, we each need to be committed—even if, at times, we are defeated or suffer tragic reversals. By a good will, I mean that we should strive whenever we can to *do* good. Surely, this includes an obligation to assist those who are in need, including children, the infirm, the destitute—those who suffer and need help. But more than that, we should develop a *generalized* attitude of sympathy, benevolence, and affection toward others.

Perhaps we need more precise language. A person of good will is well-intentioned and has a loving concern, an empathetic regard, a compassionate interest in other humans, and a genuine desire to do good for them. At the very least, this means to avoid harming or inflicting pain and sorrow, unjust punishment, or violence on them. But more, I submit that people of good will should try to be helpful, regardful of others, even altruistic—not for their own sake or self-interest, not for fame, glory, power, money, or approbation, but *for the sake of others.*

Perhaps the best term to describe people of good will is *caring*. We should care about what happens to other sentient beings (*all* sentient beings, not only humans) when we can—we may not always be able to do so because not everything is within our reach—but we ought to at least strive to do so. The antithesis of this is indifference, hostility, and callousness. For those within the sphere of our conduct or who are affected by it, we should avoid jealousy, envy, and resentment. We ought to have a genuine affectionate regard for them. By that, I mean that we should be happy if our friends, relatives, or acquaintances are happy.

Doing moral deeds may be a source of satisfaction in itself, and performing charitable and philanthropic work—whether the contribution is publicly acknowledged or not—is good not only for the recipients but for the givers. Many have discovered that "It is better to give than to receive."

This sentiment may sound Christian, but it is anything but that. The teachings attributed to Christ insist that belief in Him is the road to salvation; those who do not will not only be barred from the kingdom of heaven, they may be sent through the gates of hell. But I say that we should develop genuine affection for others, even if we disagree with them or if they do not accept our beliefs and values. This is consistent with the biblical injunction in the Old Testament that we should honor and respect "the aliens within our midst," as we hope that they will honor and respect us. The principle of tolerance is essential to moral conduct, and we should apply it even to those with whom we differ; the old adage is to "live and let live." But we need to state this value more positively: We prosper morally, if *they* prosper; we are exalted in *their* exaltations; we are pleased if *they* are pleased. This principle draws on the generosity of the human spirit; it is a mark of a magnanimous personality.

I realize that this attitude of good will may be difficult to apply to all our adversaries and enemies, such as to those who are hostile or commit grievous deeds against us. Every civilized community needs to deal with those who are beyond the pale of civilized conduct and behave intolerably. Yet we should, wherever we can, forgive and forget and not harbor resentment, seek revenge, or exact retribution for its own sake. We should try to negotiate our differences and compromise our own interests for the sake of harmony. We need to transform discord into accord, animosity into respect, confrontation into appreciation, and suspicion into understanding—for persons within our community and the extended community of humankind.

We should consider every human being to have some dignity and value. For those whom we believe are not deserving, we should endeavor to learn about their needs, to accept their idiosyncrasies, and try to persuade (not compel) those who differ with us to be open and outgoing, kindly and sympathetic. We need, of course, to be realistic about situations where there are conflicts, a breakdown of communication, and where our differences seem intractable, as in times of war or revolution. Yet even here, we should never abandon lightly our general disposition of good will.

In my view, we can and should love many people in life: people of good will should exemplify the open heart, the beneficent disposition, the truly charitable interest. We should avoid being malicious, spiteful, vengeful, prejudiced, or hateful. In doing good for others, we are ourselves made better; in bestowing gifts where we can, we can grow together, enhancing our lives as well as those of the recipients—our horizons as human begins are expanded along with theirs. If we behave decently, others may appreciate our gestures and behave correspondingly. The milk of human kindness—the empathetic concern for the needs of others—is the bond that enables civilization to consummate the highest virtues of which we are capable. It is the mark of human excellence and nobility. We do not need dictates or commandments from on high in order to express genuine good will. It can be developed in the human community, and it can be nourished in our children by cognitive moral education and love.

Good will not only applies to our relationships with others, but *to ourselves*. By this, I mean that each of us should try to develop a positive attitude toward his or her own life; we should hope for the best, not the worst. This means that we need to believe in our own powers, to have some confidence in our abilities to achieve some measure of what we want. Thus, each person should recognize that he or she has but one life to live and that he or she should strive mightily to make that life worth living. If we are to lead significant lives, we need to make moral choices and take responsibility for our actions. We need to consider ourselves to be equal in dignity and value to others. We should not sacrifice our will to live and enjoy. We should not be consumed by self-hatred, loathing, or low self-esteem; we should not be overwhelmed by our limitations or inadequacies, our failures or foibles. If we are battered by the blows of fortune, we should not grovel in the mud, supplicating to unknown and unseen forces, but get up and strive to move forward. For every disagreeable day, there is a new tomorrow. We should try to profit from our mistakes, learn where we went wrong, and correct ourselves. Reasonable optimism—realistic but not foolhardy—is essential if we are to create lives that are well lived.

We should avoid hedonophobia, that is, we should not fear to enjoy life or believe that we are not entitled to do so. We should likewise avoid destructive pessimism, the view that nothing will work out in the end. This is the refuge of bitter people, the haven of the sourpusses of the world. We need a friendly attitude, some wit and humor, laughter, and fun. We should accept the fact that we are not perfect but still able to overcome our errors and misdeeds and move on to a new plateaus of experience. No doubt, we need to work hard if we are to attain our goals, but we also need to take time to smell the lilacs and perfume, to taste honey and nectar. Unlike some moralists, overwhelmed by their sense of duty, I affirm that the pursuit of happiness—exuberance—is morally justifiable and personally enriching.

Accordingly, a good will should be applied not only in our attitude toward others, but in respect to our own wants and needs. Self-interest and altruism are not antagonistic, but complimentary. Under whatever sky you live, you should do the best you can, for other human beings and for yourself. You should consider every moment precious and try to live fully and decently. Thus, we need to cultivate a lust for life, attempting as best we can to realize our highest potentialities, without unnecessary recrimination or self-immolation. A good will can be continuous with the *joie de vivre,* not alien to it; it can help to consummate a life enriched with beauty and grandeur. A good will in this sense can be overflowing, for it is concerned with realizing the capacity for happiness in one's life and for others. A good will is something that we should impart to children by example and education. And it is an attitude and disposition that we should gladly share with our relatives, friends, colleagues, and fellow humans in the extended community.

How do we ensure social conditions so that well-intentioned persons of good will can be encouraged to develop? In my view, people who are unhappy are apt to be negative and niggardly. I suspect that they need to satisfy their basic needs if they are to discover the billowing fullness of life. To do so requires some satisfaction of their homeostatic, biogenic, and sociogenic needs, including the capacity to develop loving relationships with others, sexual gratification, friendship, acceptance within a community, the development of a sense of self-worth, and creative work—all of which can contribute to self-actualization. The achievement of exuberance, no doubt, is more difficult in overly repressive religious societies, for they seek to restrain our finest human impulses for freedom and achievement. It is easier in affluent, open, democratic societies.

Good will is natural for the exuberant person who has discovered the sheer love of life. Contented at the core, he or she can be deliriously joyful at moments of peak experience, glowing with the vitality of living. Such a person has overcome the corroding sense of sin and guilt that weighs down so many good people and can be released from the stranglehold of repressive religious traditions. At long last, he or she can luxuriate in the goodness of life, can love and be loved, can appreciate the needs of others, and can express the grace of a good will.

Note

1.   This article first appeared in *Free Inquiry* 25, no. 3 (April/May 2005), pp. 5–7.

IX

Neo-Humanism[1]

In the current discussion of the "new atheism," one point is often totally overlooked by most commentators: the positive dimensions of unbelief. Conservative religious critics have deplored the denigration of religion as an assault on the moral order and social fabric. They ask, "What does secular humanism have to offer?" I respond with *neo-humanism*, a new term I have introduced to highlight secular humanism's affirmative ethical principles and values.

There are various forms of unbelief in America and the world today. At one end of the spectrum stand the "evangelical atheists" (so maligned by their critics), who focus primarily on the case against God, noting the lack of evidence, the disregarded contradictions, and the atrocities committed in his name. But we need to point out, if for the umpteenth time, that the community of religious dissenters in America includes not only atheists but also agnostics, skeptics, and even a significant number of religiously affiliated individuals. The last may be only nominal members of their congregations and may attend church or temple primarily for social reasons or out of ethnic loyalty to the faiths of their forebears. This ethnic cultural fixation can be very difficult to overcome, and it may linger long after belief in a given body of doctrine has faded—sometimes for many generations. Yet such individuals, though still members of their religious denominations, are skeptical about claims.

In the middle of the spectrum stand the "humanists," and even that category has its internal distinctions. On one side, some humanists seek to appropriate the term *religious* in a metaphorical sense. Among the self-described religious humanists, we may find people identified with liberal Protestant denominations, Unitarian Universalists, secular Jews, lapsed Catholics, and even some who wish to distinguish the "religious" quality of experience from religion (following philosopher John Dewey).

Although they are naturalistic humanists rather than supernaturalists, do not believe in a transcendent God, and wish to encourage a new humanist cultural identity based primarily on ethical ideals, they call this "religious."

On the other side of this category are the *secular* humanists, who are wholly nonreligious and naturalistic. They do not consider their stance religious at all; they think that the term *religious* obfuscates matters. They draw their inspirations primarily from modern—not ancient—sources: preeminently science but also philosophy, ethics, literature, and the arts. Nonetheless, they wish to encourage the growth of secular-humanist communities in order to provide shared bonds of fraternity and friendship.

May I suggest that the term *neo-humanism* best describes a new posture, which aims to be inclusive and respond to the critics of unbelief:

1. *Neo-humanists are skeptical of traditional theism.* They may be atheists, agnostics, or even dissenting members of a church or temple. They think the traditional concept of God is an illusion. They reject such writings as the Bible, the Koran, and the Book of Mormon as divine revelations. Their skepticism of the ancient creeds reflects the light of scientific or philosophical critiques of the arguments for God—or, more recently, the scientific examination of the sources of the "sacred texts." They also criticize the moral absolutes derived from these ancient texts, viewing them as the expressions of premodern civilizations—though they may believe that some of their moral principles deserve to be appreciated in order to understand their cultural heritages. Nevertheless, they consider traditional religion's focus on salvation in the next life an abandonment of efforts to improve this life, here and now. They firmly defend the separation of religion and the state and consider freedom of conscience and the right of dissent vital. They deplore the view of the subservience of women to men, the repression of sexuality, the defense of theocracy, and the denial of democratic human rights.

2. *Distinctively, neo-humanists look to science and reason as the most reliable guide to knowledge*, and they wish to extend the methods of science to *all* areas of human endeavor. They believe that critical thinking and the methods of reflective intelligence should guide our behavior. Neo-humanists appreciate the arts as well as the sciences, and they draw upon the literature of human experience for inspiration. Neo-humanists, however, seek objective methods of corroborating truth claims, not poetic metaphor or intuition.

3. *Neo-humanists are uniquely committed to a set of humanist values and principles*, including the civic virtues of democracy and the

toleration of diverse lifestyles. They cherish individual freedom and celebrate human creativity and fulfillment, happiness and well-being, the values of the open pluralistic society, the right of privacy, and the autonomy, dignity, and value of each person. Neo-humanists are no less concerned with social justice and the common good, environmentalism, and planetary ethics. They insist that human beings are responsible for their own destinies and that they need to use intelligence and goodwill to solve problems. They attempt, wherever possible, to negotiate differences rationally and to work out compromises using science, reason, and humanist values.

Thus, to focus solely on atheism's negative posture fails to do justice to the richness of neo-humanist eupraxsophy. Neo-humanism rejects theism and affirms the secular outlook. It is broad enough to encompass atheism, agnosticism, *and* humanist ethical values. It is a large enough mansion to include both nonreligious humanists and those who consider humanism to function religiously in so far as it celebrates *human* ideals and values. Neo-humanists do not believe in God, yet they wish to do good.

Note

1. This article first appeared in *Free Inquiry* 27, no. 6 (October/November 2007), pp. 4–6.

X

A Modified Naturalistic Ethical Theory[1]

I wish to sketch a modified naturalistic ethical theory. Much of this of course will be without elaboration. I should point out that not all secular humanists will agree with the views herein outlined. Secular humanism is not an *ipse dixit*, "thus sayeth the secular humanist," and there is some diversity of views; though we generally agree that one can be good without God.

The first point that I wish to emphasize is that we need to begin with *value as the broader category, not simply moral value.* Ever since the nineteenth century, philosophers, economists, social scientists, biologists, and psychologists have focused on the problem of value. The term "value" refers to the objects that humans (and other sentient beings) prefer. The bone has value for the puppy, the worm for the bird, the commodity for the human being. Value is "the object of any interest," according to Ralph Barton Perry.[2] This is a naturalistic account relative to human interests, needs, and wants. The fact that someone wants or desires something does not necessarily make it good or right. Nevertheless preferential behavior is the bedrock of human value, which we later can and do evaluate critically.

Second, closely related to value is *valuing, a selective behavioral process* whereby a person (or organism) strives to appropriate goals. Humans like or desire, prize or cherish, many objectives; we prefer some and shun others. We engage in conative processes of acquiring, using, and consuming them. The full range of values include *instrumental values* (desired because of what they lead to, e.g., vitamins are for good health), and *intrinsic values* (good for their own sake, e.g., orgasmic pleasure). There are *economic values* sought after in the marketplace (produced, distributed, advertised, consumed), *aesthetic values* (prized because of their beauty, tone, color, shape, form), and *moral values* (e.g., decency, honesty, integrity, etc.). Human beings value a wide range of objects and activities. These often are idiosyncratic (e.g., I like potatoes, you like tomatoes, etc.). Morality seeks to grade or rank values for the individual person on a scale of desirability. Competing value systems in the community lead to a quest for adjudication of differences, finding some better or worse and in defining general principles to decide between them.

Third, here we enter into a process of *valuation* and *evaluation*, in which cognition plays a role. Human beings need to make selections between different options. How to choose among alternative values is an ongoing daily exercise. *Thus decision-making is involved in virtually all human endeavors*. Often it is a problem of better or worse on a comparative scale rather than simply good, bad, right, or wrong; and we make prudential choices.

Fourth, e*motion, passion, and feeling enters into virtually all decision-making valuation processes*, though of special significance is the relationship to cognition, thought, and reason. We need to deal with the whole person in which reason and emotion are intertwined; for what the person likes or dislikes is an essential component of his or her selective process of choosing. In one sense his or her personality traits or states of character define who or what is preferred (e.g., some people are addicted to alcohol, others like sports, religious rituals, musical concerts, or intellectual pursuits). Human societies come to emphasize and encourage some values, which take on higher moral significance, and they discourage, forbid, or enjoin others as demeaning or ignoble.

All of the above aspects of human behavior can be studied empirically. It takes "moral values" out of the abstract clouds and provides some natural bio-somatic, psychosocio-genic phenomena capable of being studied scientifically. Moral values clothed in God-talk are twice removed from flesh-and-bones, blood-and-guts human experience and behavior.

Fifth, there is a good deal of evidence from science that human beings and the social groups in which they live tend to *develop moral standards* whereby certain forms are praised and encouraged, and others denigrated and rejected. Sharing similar basic needs, humans come to reject those forms of behavior that are destructive of the social fabric and they tend to esteem those that enable the group to survive, function, and even flourish. Over the long stretch of the history of *Homo sapiens*, humans have evolved moral tendencies or potentialities that motivate them to value certain forms of conduct and to condemn those they deem harmful. These concern common human problems: the relationship between the sexes, the caring and education of children, the gathering and distribution of food and water, the search for shelter, the treatment of the sick and elderly, the relationship to other groups that are encountered, the need to defend themselves from threats from wild animals or from marauding individuals or tribes, etc. Thus many claim that there are similar cross-cultural patterns that function to satisfy basic biogenic and socio-genic needs of individuals and their social groups. We of course recognize that there is cultural relativity in the types of dress preferred, food consumed, and other cultural artifacts; nonetheless there is a core of moral standards or virtues—which I have called "the common moral decencies." These denote universal (or general) principles that people recognize that they ought to abide by, though there may be exceptions. Many thinkers have postulated a common human nature (Aristotle) and stages of moral growth and development (Piaget, Kohlberg[3]). I am here referring to empirical data. Is this the "ontology" that Craig demands? No, as I said, I am dubious of such language since I find it to be speculative. I am simply presenting a naturalistic interpretation of the human species functioning in the world; and it is based on the empirical sciences of biology, genetics, neuroscience, psychology, and the social sciences.

Sixth, general moral principles are enculturated by education, conditioned by custom and passed on from generation to generation (in the form of *memes*). They are codified by law and sanctified by religion. Every effort is made to educate character in the young so that they express socially approved virtuous conduct. These have, I submit, both biogenic and sociogenic sources.

Deontological intuitionists thought that the principles that I call "the common moral decencies" are self-evident to a rational person; and that they do not need be proved. Some scientists say that our capacity to recognize them is instinctive.[4] This would be similar to the human capacity for languages. Perhaps this is an oversimplification, for they are not recognized without some measure of education and enculturation. They are tested pragmatically by their consequences (a society that flouts them cannot function very well); they may be discovered by our cognitive faculties; but they are deeply infused by emotions—such as empathy and caring for others, and this means the capacity for altruistic acts.[5] They become in time so important that one cannot ignore them easily, so there is some sense of their obligatory appeal. Although not absolute, they are general and we have a responsibility in principle to follow them except when they conflict with other prima facie general moral principles and values. In any case, I submit that they are not God-given, but are rooted in both our biogenetic evolution and social-cultural civilizing processes.

On the contrary they are considered "sacred" because they are deemed so important. Perhaps they have their genesis in the mothering or parenting care needed to nurture the young. This distinctive behavior is found in other species: even the most ferocious wolves and lions care for their young. In humans it is extended during the long period of tutelage.[6] Granted that some individuals may lack a moral sense, they may become sociopaths or psychopaths, indifferent to the feelings of others. They have a very low MQ (moral quotient). Hence, every community needs to hold offenders of its cherished principles accountable and they are punished and/or rehabilitated. The problem with the moral sense by itself is that it competes with other powerful impulses in the human breast: the competition for sexual partners, the lust for personal power, wealth, ambition, glory. There is thus a conflict between decency (the social virtues) and self-interest. Konrad Lorenz postulates the instinct for aggression, particularly among males—and ways to overcome it by sports, the arts, and other forms of substitution and sublimation.

Secular philosophers generally developed ethical ideals for the individual, and they concentrate on maximizing good—which is related to happiness. Some have defended self-interest theories (e.g., libertarians); others hedonism (maximizing of pleasure and the avoidance of pain), and still others self-realization theories (in which the fulfillment of a person's talents are sources of the highest satisfaction).

Generally, secular naturalists have eschewed salvation in the next life as a false illusion; and they have focused on improving the human condition here and now by seeking to actualize happiness both for the individual and the social good. In regard to the individual, humanists have combined hedonism and self-realization: the good life we seek is concerned with creative fulfillment and joyful satisfaction throughout a complete life. In contemporary affluent societies this leads to *exuberance*, in which the widest range of pleasurable activities are sought. To use John Stuart Mill's language, both the higher and lower pleasures are desirable—both the biological pleasures of food, drink, sex, *and* the pleasures of intellect, art, and moral deeds. Both self-interest and altruism are essential to a fully developed person. Here the *fullness of life* is the model.

To achieve a full life the individual needs to develop certain *excellences*.[7] These include: good health (adequate nutrition and exercise); self-control and moderation; self-respect and self-esteem; high motivation; the capacity for love (orgasmic, filial, friendship, collegiality); caring for other sentient beings; commitment to a beloved cause(s); a sense of the *joi de vivre*; the achievement motive; and creativity.

One needs to balance one's commitment to others (family, children, parents, lovers, friends) in the community of face-to-face social interaction *and* the community of humankind (on the planetary scale) with one's commitment to one's self to lead a satisfying and fulfilling life. The basic principles that humanists find compelling are a generalized *good will* to others and oneself (i.e., to do the best we can); the use of *reason* (to solve problems, to overcome obstacles); the *courage* to do so without fear and trembling (the Promethean audacity to succeed); and *caring* for other human beings.

In this regard, *altruism* is essential for moral development. An altruistic act is carried out for the benefit of other person(s), without any primary expectation of reward and perhaps at some expense or sacrifice to oneself; a basic rule of ethical rationality is that we ought to mitigate human suffering and sorrow, and to increase the sum of human good and happiness, providing it is possible to do so. An impartial ethical rationality should thus apply to all human beings who have equal dignity and value. Some feelings of empathy seem essential for altruism to flower.

It is apparent that we cannot reduce morality to pure rationality alone—much as philosophers tend to do—for human beings are more than rational animals. This caveat is similar to objections voices about "economic man" i.e., the view that a rational person in the marketplace makes decisions on the basis of self-interest in order to maximize economic gain. The "hidden hand" of the free market, according to Adam Smith[8] is a dynamic model that engenders profit, productivity, and growth. Unfortunately consumers and entrepreneurs do not always behave in this way, for advertisers can condition consumers to buy what they want but do not need, and an individual entrepreneur's quest for power and glory may outweigh the desire for gain.

The economic model surely has some explanatory value, but it is not infallible, and there are many deviations from it. Similarly, the ideal "moral person" is not perfectly rational, making choices based on the overriding or strongest reason; for passions, desires, feelings, attractions, revulsions, antipathies, and lusts intervene. I know of enough cases of married philosophers, family men with children and well established careers, who fell in love with a student and abandoned everything for passion, accepting the scandal that it often provoked. (Similarly for theologians who bugger young lads.) So, where is the perfectly rational person in decision-making? I am not of course condoning such behavior, only pointing out the difficulty often of pure rationality.

That is why we need to leave room for both cognitive thoughts *and* emotional attitudes in dealing with how human beings actually function. Daniel Goleman has called this "emotional intelligence," the capacity to express, but also to moderate our competing attitudes and desires.[9] This involves both self-control and compassion. I think that some measure of objectivity is still possible within a person's emotional life, given who and what we actually are as blood-and-guts humans throbbing with feelings. I call this objective *relativism* (not objective subjectivism), for our choices are relative to the values that an individual or society cherishes. Nevertheless they are amenable to some weighing of rational interests and passionate desires and testing them by their consequences. I think that Plato's depiction of three horses pulling the chariot of the soul is rather insightful, since we need to balance desire, pleasure, and reason and it is not the case that pure reason is always the lead horse able to control the other two. Some individuals are able to express their emotions and satisfy them yet balance them rationally with other desires and needs, especially in relationship with other human beings.

One thing that is intriguing about the theists who have contributed to this volume is that I detect a strong whiff of Platonism; for God functions as "the idea of the Good," providing a model for an allegedly higher plane of an abstract Form. Packed into the idea of God are their own moral predilections. The idea of a most holy, omniscient, omnipotent, beneficent, and just being is infused with moral qualities. That is why philosophers such as Dewey[10] have recommended that we need to take account of the immediacies of experience, and the things that individuals prize, praise, enjoy, like, want, cherish, or if you will, the *prima facie given* values that you bring into a situation of choice. Values are based on our interests and desires, but valuations can modify and balance them in the light of reason. What you should decide depends on who you are, how the socio-cultural climate has conditioned your likes and dislikes; and these need to be taken into account and transformed into appraisals by cognitive inquiry. Prizing can be modified by reflective evaluation and perhaps reconstructed; although this may be difficult for many individuals who are steadfast in their proclivities and attitudes and refuse to budge. Something similar is true of the social moral patterns of a society, its customs, habits, traditions, laws—to which children have been conditioned. If we are going to get anywhere, particularly in pluralist societies where many value systems compete, we need to find common ground and the cognitive reconstruction of our values is very important. This is often difficult to achieve. But it can be and has been done by persistent argument and persuasion.

A brutal illustration comes readily to mind: why are so many young Muslims willing to wrap bombs around their torsos and blow themselves to smithereens (in Iraq, Palestine, Saudi Arabia, Lebanon, etc.). No doubt there are political reasons and resentment against Western secular cultures, but why do so many people in Islamic culture approve of their role as martyrs? A key answer is because of indoctrination in the faith, by which values are conditioned and become entrenched. This is made possible by being sent to madrassa schools, where they are required to memorize the Koran by repetition, and accept its beliefs and values without question; another explanation is because the Imam intones prayers five times a day (in large cities over loudspeakers) and men are brought together in mosques to submit in reverential acts of bowing. Women are shielded in burkas and veils conditioned to accept their lesser roles of submission to men. Apparently, sexual passion incites men to continue their dominance of passive women. Similar illustrations are the use of prayer by Orthodox Jews who are confirmed at thirteen, the catechisms of Roman Catholic children (the familiar statement is made, "Give us a child before age five and we will recruit him or her into the faith,") or the recital of the Nicene creed on Sundays, week after week, by Protestants.

One way to overturn these ancient creeds is by an appeal to reason, and/or the lure of enticing new ideals and values. Thus we must in any society confront the old with the new, established moral principles are challenged by daring new ones that may be reformist or even revolutionary in strength. The campaign against slavery was considered radical in its day as was the Suffragist Movement for equal rights for women. Today many conservatives consider "the right of privacy" a shock. It has suddenly emerged to compete with orthodox prohibitions about so many things, such as the right to euthanasia, abortion, and same-sex marriage, all of which horrify traditionalists.

*   .*   *

I have introduced the concept of a *valuation base,*[11] which I submit is relevant in any process of decision-making and can help us to decide. The valuation base is relative to an existing individual or actual society. It includes both prescriptive values, norms, standards, and principles *and* value-neutral facts, means, conditions, and consequences. What is in the base?

First, the *pre-existing prizings*, the immediacies of feelings, desires, attitudes, the well-established values, whether idiosyncratic or common, which we bring with us in any situation and which may either be reinstated or modified by a process of inquiry.

Second, the *rules, norms*, customs, or standards of the social milieu, which have been institutionalized by education, reinforced by law, sanctified by religion, encouraged by social approbation or disapprobation.

Third, the *prima facie general principles* or rules to which we are committed—"the common moral decencies"—and these compete with new principles, such as the "civic virtues of democracy," "the right of privacy," and "human dignity," which today are being extended on the planetary scale to all members of the human family. It is when there is a conflict that the common moral decencies may need to be balanced with new radicalized or revolutionary principles of ethics, such as in the battle for equal rights, which we are currently experiencing. Here we need to negotiate compromises.

Fourth, of crucial significance is the need to consider the *facts of the case*, the circumstances before us. The individual or social group needs to investigate these in order to make a wise choice.

Fifth, factual knowledge includes an exploration of scientific knowledge not only about what is the case but what are *the causes* that are relevant to the conditions that we face.

Sixth, we need to take into consideration the *goals* that we wish to achieve, as well as *the means to fulfill them*. We need to ask, what is possible and feasible as ways of realizing our ends—the expansion of technological means at our disposal in the modern world (improved travel, communications, health, longevity, etc.) has transformed human life from repeating ancient homilies to adopting dynamic new styles to fulfill new opportunities for achieving a better life.

Seventh, the importance of *moral education for children*, the need to expand their horizons, to develop and cultivate the capacities for moral thinking.[12] And every society needs to enculturate desirable traits of character and instruct children to appreciate virtue and empathy, but they also need to teach them how to be self-reliant and how to think clearly.

Eighth, an important criterion of adequacy are the *consequences* of our actions that spill out into the real world, once our choices are implemented. This enables us to modify our decisions by seeing their results, and we may generalize what we have learned for similar situations in the future.

Ninth, one further criterion that we use in appraising principles and values is their *consistency* with values and standards we already accept, particularly when we wish to extend human rights and reform inconsistency in treatment by putting it under a common principle.

Undoubtedly, there are other considerations besides those enumerated that may be relevant to a valuational base. For example, in society we need to take into account other people's attitudes in the community and recognize the difficulty often of persuading them to change. We need also to confront economic and political realities.

The choices people make are about conduct and action, not about propositions about practice on the meta level. They concern real behavior in the world. The key point that I want to suggest here is what I have called the role of *act-duction* in such reasoning. Ethical choices are a function of the unique, deeply private tastes and desires, preferences and wishes of each person. The choices we make are also related to the actual historical, social, and cultural framework in which we exist, including the social mores and laws of the society. Thus life in ancient Egypt, Palestine, Greece, or Rome differs from China and Japan, Europe and the Americas. And modern cultures are far different from their ancient precursors.

Ethical knowledge has a degree of probabilism and fallibilism attached to it. We need to recognize that there are alternative lifestyles and a wide variety of human values and norms. This presupposes some comprehension of the fragility of the human condition and some skepticism about our ultimate perfectibility. Thus, ethical wisdom recognizes that life is full of uncertainties. In one sense, it is permeated by indeterminacies.

All of the contingent differences must be put into the valuational base, and they influence the decisions we make. The choice we select is accordingly relative to the given *de facto* prizings and valuations, customs and laws, institutional constraints and demands of the times. What was a wise choice for Pericles in Athens may not be the same for Darius of Persia, Cicero in Rome, Abelard's Heloise, Queen Elizabeth in Shakespeare's England, Richelieu in France, Susan B. Anthony or Robert E. Lee in the United States. Accordingly there is an intrinsic contextuality and relativity of all choices, for they are always related to specific individuals and civilizations. The relativity of choice is *endemic* to the ethical life. Let me reiterate that there is a difference between totally subjective and capricious choices (as let us say Nero was wont to make) and those *that are informed by knowledge and selected after a careful process of reflective inquiry*. There are ethical qualities that stand out and from which we may learn and generalize. That is why we can empathize with Othello overtaken by jealousy and anger or Macbeth by the lust for power. There is a kind of eloquent reflection on the human condition as people wrestle with moral dilemmas. And there are certain courses of action that seem appropriate and others that are profoundly flawed, even tragic. It is not simply a deductive or inductive model that we use, or even abduction (used to formulate new hypotheses, according to Peirce). Undoubtedly deduction, induction, and abduction each has a role to play in the process of inquiry. But what is preeminently vital in formulating judgments and practice upon which we act is *act-duction*; namely *the course of action that I will embark upon at the conclusion of a process of inquiry*. The act plays itself out in the real world for everyone to see; it has an impact on behavioral conduct. The process of evaluation and appraisal is about the appropriateness of particular actions in a specific context or case, and in similar situations like that.

The salient point is that ethics is relative to life as lived by specific person or societies, and it is rooted in historical-social conditions and concrete behavior. Ethical principles are thus in the mid-range; they are proximate, not ultimate. We do not reason about the moral life *in abstracto* and hope to make sense of it; we always begin *here* and *now*, with *this* individual in *this* society faced with *these* choices. The basic subject matter of ethics is action and conduct.

Rarely when we engage in ethical inquiry do we begin at the beginning—except perhaps in crisis/existential situations where we are forced to examine our root values. Rather, we find ourselves in the midst of practical demands and conflicts, trying to make sense of the web of decisions and behavior in which we are entangled. And included in our nexus is the considerable fund of normative data that we bring with us; the things we cherish or esteem, or conversely detest or reject, and the principles to which we are committed. Ethical inquiry in initiated when there is some puzzle about what we should do or some conflict between competing values and norms. It is here that skeptical inquiry is vital: for it is the open mind in operation that is willing to examine our values and principles and to select those that seem approximate. The ethical inquirer in the best sense is committed to the use of reflective intelligence, in which a person is able to define and clarify one's values and principles and to search for alternative courses of action that seem most fitting within the context of inquiry.

I am afraid that the deductive model does not suffice in the real world; i.e., simply deducing obligations and therefore actions from universal principles or inflexible moral values. Nor is the inductive model adequate. We cannot generalize principles from the facts of the case, nor deduce what ought to be the case from a set of facts, though the facts are relevant in formulating valuations and actions. The position that I am here defending is a *modified form of ethical naturalism*. I do not think that this reduces us to subjective caprice, where there are no standards for evaluation. There surely are, but these need to deal with the sticky factors in the complex situations we face, the contingent, pluralistic and bizarre facts in real life which often are stranger than fiction. What I am pointing to is the need to consider a wide range of factors in formulating a decision: values, norms, rights, means-ends, facts, causes and effects.

This is sometimes criticized as "situation ethics," and people complain that therefore "anything goes." Although what we do always has a frame of reference, we nonetheless can generalize and we can and do develop reliable guides for action in similar situations. We need to make wise choices and develop knowledge relative to the situations in which we find ourselves.

I reiterate, the criterion of *consequences* provides a powerful pragmatic test that the proof of moral actions is in the eating. What constitutes fitting or appropriate results, however, may be open to dispute. The appeal to consequences in a multi-plural world does not depend just on one criterion (utilitarianism), but many. Sometimes what will ensue is totally unpredictable, and we may need to learn from our mistakes and revise our values and principles. An illustration of this concerns attitudes about capital punishment. Many people in favor of the death penalty do so because the think that it is a deterrent and will keep people from committing heinous crimes. If it turned out that it is not a deterrent, would the person who supports capital punishment be willing to change his mind? The answer is that *only* if his or her views are not encased in a hard-shell attitude resistant to modification. This especially applies to those who insist upon the "an eye for an eye" retributive principle or those who think on the contrary that "criminals should never be punished," only rehabilitated.

I have come to the conclusion that philosophers are often little help in concrete cases of disagreement, and that meta-philosophy, though useful to professors of philosophy, hardly help ordinary folks to resolve moral dilemmas. A graphic illustration of the irrelevance and insufficiency of philosophy historically is the fact that Aristotle, whom many consider the greatest mind of antiquity, had few if any temples built to honor his impressive contributions to thought. I am told—though I have never been there—that there is one small sign in Stagira, Thrace, which notes "Aristotle Born Here." His pupil Alexander the Great, who conquered empires and nations, had many cities named after him. Hume, the leading thinker of the Scottish enlightenment, similarly has no commemoration of his powerful influence in philosophy, though a statue in his honor was recently installed in Edinburgh on the main street. Compare this to Mohammad, Jesus, or even Joseph Smith, and you can see the power of philosophy versus religion; or compare it to the monuments in Washington, DC in honor of great political figures such as Washington, Jefferson, and Lincoln. Incidentally, there is nary a commemoration to Charles Peirce, William James, or John Dewey, three leading philosophers of the Golden Age of American philosophy. The apotheosis of Karl Marx and Frederick Engels by communist regimes was an effort to enshrine a philosophy, but we see the disaster that this led to when philosophy was transformed into ideological dogma.

What I conclude from this is that we either need to transform philosophy from "the love of wisdom" (read to mean "the love of meta-wisdom" in ethics)—once removed from the life of action or conduct—to the *practice* of wisdom, not simply practical *wisdom*. I have introduced a new term to designate philosophical practitioners, or if you will, *eupraxsophers*, namely those who are skilled in the "*practice* of good wisdom" and can offer competent advice.[13] This is more like competent medical practice or effective psychological therapy in clinical psychology, or a skilled teacher actually challenging students to learn in the classroom. Therefore philosophers in the public square who know about the issues firsthand, and are aware of competing values and principles, need to enter the public square and get their hands messy in concrete cases; and they must be willing to make actual recommendations. Unfortunately, philosophers in the classroom today more often than not present students with all sides of a question and leave it to the students to make up their own minds. So they often revert to their prejudices.

Yet if so, philosophy is deficient; and what we need is a new craft, practiced by *eupraxsophers*, practitioners in the art and science of decision-making, men and women with some expertise and reflective experience, able to shed light on alternative courses of action and also able to recommend (not demand, legislate, or dictate) courses of action. Thus, *act-duction* has the inquirer examine all the features of a case to recommend what appears most reasonable and attractive; and it is this kind of practical valuational wisdom that enables individuals in society to make wise choices. Again, it is not simply on the meta level, but in the normative domain of actual values and principles.

In this sense there are degrees of objectivity, and our values and principles which are submitted to scrutiny in the light of inquiry are comparatively better than those that have not passed the test of both rationality and practical experience. Thus one can be good without belief in God. And such objective inquiry, I submit, is more reasonable than appealing to the premise of the theist, grounded in the final analysis in faith.

In free societies where skinheads and racists often abound, where a drug culture runs rampant, where promiscuity, violence in the media, and wasted lives are everywhere in evidence, humanists wish to defend moral excellence and qualitative standards. Libertarianism will not work if we do not at the same time develop moral responsibility. Religious conservatives wish to regulate conduct under the aegis of the Church or the State. I question this authoritarian approach. The best alternative is to develop the civic and moral virtues by means of moral education.

Pure tolerance has its limits; it cannot succeed unless it is accompanied at the same time by a commitment to raising the level of taste and appreciation. Western capitalist and consumer-oriented societies are all too often vulgar and banal, and they lack standards of decency. Humanists have a hard task and a double battle—for moral freedom *and* for improving moral standards. Although we do not wish to legislate morality, this does not mean that we should not criticize the vulgar excesses of modern consumer-oriented culture. This should not be left to the religious conservatives railing from the pulpits. Secular humanists have an obligation to encourage the finest cultural expressions, intellectual, aesthetic, and moral appreciation.

Some degree of skepticism is a necessary antidote to all forms of moral dogmatism. We are continually surrounded by self-righteous moralists who claim to have the Absolute Truth or Moral Virtue or Piety, and they wish to impose their convictions on all others. The best antidote for this is some skepticism and a willingness to engage in ethical inquiry, not only about the moral zeal of others, but about *our own*, especially if we are tempted to translate the results of our own ethical inquiries into commandments. The epistemological theory presented here, the methodological principles of skeptical inquiry, has important moral implications. For in recognizing our own fallibility we thereby can learn to *tolerate* other human beings and to appreciate the plurality of lifestyles. If we are prepared to engage in cooperative ethical inquiry, then perhaps we are better prepared to allow other individuals and groups some measure of liberty to pursue their own preferred lifestyles. If we are able to live and let live, then this can best be achieved in a free and open democratic society. Where we differ, we should try to negotiate our divergent views and perhaps reach common ground; and if this is impractical, we should at least attempt to compromise for the sake of our common interests. The method of ethical inquiry requires some intelligent and informed examination of our own values, as well as the values of others. Here we can attempt to modify attitudes by the appeal to cognitive beliefs and to reconstruct them by an examination of the relevant evidence. Such a give-and-take of constructive criticism is essential for a harmonious society. In learning to appreciate different conceptions of the good life, we are able to expand our own dimensions of moral awareness.

We might live in a better world if *inquiry* were to replace faith; *deliberation*, passionate commitment; and *education and persuasion*, violence and force. We should be aware of the powers of intelligent behavior, but also the limitations of human beings and of the need to mitigate the cold and indifferent intellect with the empathic heart. Thus I conclude that within the ethical life we are capable of developing a body of melioristic principles and values and a method of coping with problems intelligently. There is a form of *eupraxia*, or good practice, that we can learn to appreciate and live by, and this can be infused with *sophia*. When our ethical judgments are based on ethical inquiry, they are more apt to express the highest reaches of excellence and nobility, and of civilized human conduct. Although the ethics of secular humanism developed in this paper may not satisfy those who hunger for salvation, it nonetheless has much to commend for those seeking the good life for themselves and their fellow human beings.

Notes

1.   This article first appeared in from *Is Goodness without God Good Enough?: A Debate on Faith, Secularism, and Ethics*, Robert K. Garcia and Nathan L. King (editors), (Lanham, M.D.: Rowman & Littlefield, 2008), pp. 25–46.

2.   Ralph Barton Perry, *General Theory of Value* (1925).

3.   Lawrence Kohlberg, *The Psychology of Moral Development* (New York: Harper and Row, 1982); Jean Piaget, *The Moral Judgment of the Child* (London: Kegan Paul, 1932).

4.   For example, see Mark D. Hauser, *Moral Minds: How Nature Designed our Universal Sense of Right and Wrong* (Harper-Collins, New York: 2006).

5.   There is a growing scientific literature that postulates that altruism has biological-genetic roots. See Elliott Sober and David Wilson, *Unto Others, the Evolution and Psychology of Unselfish Behavior* (Harvard University Press, Cambridge: 1998).

6.   E.O. Wilson has attempted to show these kinds of behavior in other species and the human species. See *Consilience: The Unity of Knowledge* (Alfred Knopf, New York: 1988).

7.   For a discussion of these, see Paul Kurtz, *Embracing the Power of Humanism* (Rowman & Littlefield, Latham, Mass.: 2000).

8.   Adam Smith, *The Wealth of Nations*

9.   Daniel P. Goleman, *Emotional Intelligence* (Bantam, New York: 1995).

10. John Dewey, *Theory of Valuation* (University of Chicago Press, 1939).

11. Paul Kurtz, *The New Skepticism: Inquiry and Reliable Knowledge*, chapter 9, (Prometheus Books, Amherst, N.Y.: 1992).

12. See the book by Stephen Law, *The War for Children's Minds* (Routledge, London: 2006).

13. Paul Kurtz, *Living without Religion: Eupraxsophy* (Prometheus Books, Amherst, N.Y.: 1989).

Section 3

Secularism and Religion

XI

Skeptical Inquiry and Religion[1]

What is the relationship between skepticism and religion? Can we apply the methods of skeptical inquiry to its claims? Contemporary skepticism rose out of, and is related to, scientific inquiry and is not primarily a philosophical movement, as it was in ancient Greece and Rome. Contemporary scientific skeptics have concentrated the lion's share of their attention in recent decades to the claims of the paranormal; that is, to areas of human interest which allegedly could not be dealt with in terms of the existing scientific paradigm: parapsychology, astrology, aspects of UFOlogy, alternative medicine, monsters of the deep, urban legends, communication with the dead, etc.

Charles Fort proclaimed forthrightly that there were anomalies, strange or unusual phenomena that were usually ignored by science, for they did not render easy explanation. Science focuses on uniformities, not irregularities. Skeptics were accused, improperly I think, of doubting such anomalies on *a priori* grounds as impossible or improbable, without bothering to investigate them. Such a posture indeed would be dogmatic and negative. Skepticism is a *method* of inquiry primarily, not an attitude or posture or philosophical viewpoint that denies entities or phenomena out of hand.

The skeptical critics of the paranormal attempted to use the best empirical and analytical methods of investigation. Generally they were able to provide alternative naturalistic explanations for what had seemed totally mysterious. Some paranormalists rejected these explanations. They derided Phillip J. Klass, for example, for providing possible scenarios of alleged UFO phenomena, claiming that they were contrived; and they attacked the skeptical critics of Gauquelin's so-called astrobiology, accusing them of bias. On the whole, skeptics found that paranormal phenomena, when submitted to vigorous experimental testing, could be explained by prosaic causes. Skeptics discovered that the tests designed by believers often were not rigorous, that their protocol was loose, that eyewitness testimony was unsubstantiated, that there was experimental bias, poor statistical analyses, and even outright fraud. Parapsychological inquirers benefited, I submit, from these skeptical critiques; similarly for those sympathetic to astrology and UFOlogy. For the alleged paranormal phenomena were transformed into the normal; once empirical scrutiny was applied to them, it was discovered that they could be accounted for. Scientists could claim with reason that they were skeptical, for having investigated paranormal phenomena they eventually came to doubt their veracity.

Interestingly, contemporary skeptics were reluctant to apply similar skeptical critiques to religious claims, and for a variety of reasons. For one, many of these claims are dependent upon faith, and were held for deeper psychological or sociological reasons, or even rooted in philosophical or theological arguments. The grounds for the claims were often shrouded by the sands of historical time, and the epistemological justifications for the beliefs were not easily discernible. Unlike paranormal claims the major religious creeds were institutionalized, enforced by the tradition and the power of the church and/or state. Accordingly, it became highly dangerous to make inferences about revered historical claims and to question the sacred cows. For in doing so, one was shaking at the very foundations of the social structure, and philosophers and scientists from Socrates and Spinoza, to Bruno and Galileo, encountered strong resistance from ecclesiastical and political authorities. It is entirely different to criticize astrologers, psychics, and UFOlogists, for they have little institutional power, and their claims were often relegated to the sideshow. Who cares if Champ, Bigfoot, the Bermuda Triangle, and other popular media-driven legends were true or false? It was fun and games, a form of entertainment or circus. People enjoyed listening to the proponents, for those who believed in the claims, and their opponents—especially the magicians who could duplicate their tricks. It was all part of *showbiz!*

In the last decade the skeptical movement has, in spite of the earlier disclaimers, turned to religious questions. I am referring to the reports of miracles, faith healers, visitations by angelic or demonic beings, ghosts or goblins, or contact with dearly departed friends and relatives. I have characterized these phenomena as *paranatural*, for like the paranormal they could be investigated empirically. Did people actually see a vision of the Virgin Mary in Medjugorje, Yugoslavia? Were the prophecies relayed to the children who had this vision later confirmed? Were people actually cured by miracles at Lourdes? What about the claims of faith healers? We could diagnose such claims beforehand, by examining the medical records that are available, and afterwards by follow-up studies. There are also historical artifacts that can be investigated: Was the Shroud of Turin Jesus' burial cloth? We could engage in carbon-14 dating, and the image on the shroud could be duplicated. Similarly for the alleged ossuary of James, the brother of Jesus, recently discovered and found to be a forgery. All of these used science to test their veracity.

There is, however, a range of core beliefs of religious faith that many devotees believed were immune to skeptical inquiry. Did Jesus raise Lazarus from the dead? Did he affect miraculous cures and exorcisms, as the New Testament relates? But more centrally, was Jesus himself resurrected from the dead? Were the Ten Commandments actually delivered by Moses to the children of Israel? Did Mohammed receive visitations from Gabriel, the angel of Allah? Is the Koran an accurate rendition of this divine messenger? Did Joseph Smith receive the golden plates from the Angel Moroni, as claimed in the Book of Mormon? Here of course we are dealing with the claims of revelation, which are framed in concrete empirical terms and open to examination. In this sense they likewise are paranatural, and in principle at least such revelatory reports could be examined much as other natural historical events, such as: Did three hundred Spartans under King Leonidas attempt to hold off a vast Persian army at the gate of Thermopolae in 480 B.C.? Were the Roman emperors descended from the Gods? Did Constantine see a divine omen, or was this explicable in astronomical terms?

If a person claiming to be a prophet came forth today delivering divinely inspired revelations, we could, of course, submit him or her to careful scrutiny, asking for corroboration. We would submit such extraordinary historical claims to the best available tools of circumstantial evidence. Of course, it is often difficult to ascertain the reliability of historical claims, since the factual data may be lost, and, at best, only fragmentary evidence may have survived. The field of Biblical, Koranic, and Mormonic criticism is putatively amenable to skeptical scientific inquiry. Investigators can use the established methods of science: linguistic analysis, archaeological corroboration, carbon-14 dating, the examination of other documents of alleged eyewitnesses that are available, etc. This means that the historical reconstruction of past claims, whether natural or paranatural, are open to careful checking; that is, if some extant evidence could be recovered; if none, then the only response is that of the agnostic, though many would shy away from this posture.

There has been widespread reluctance historically to engage in such inquiries, since they were considered dangerous to the Faith. But after two centuries or more of meticulous scientific and scholarly criticism, there is a substantial literature that questions the received doctrines. Proponents of the Faith do not wish it questioned by agnostics or apostates. It is still considered in bad taste to be skeptical about these claims in America today; and indeed dangerous to one's health in other parts of the world where scientific inquiry is often considered blasphemous. "Yours is to believe or die," is the old adage, and thus to question revered beliefs is an egregious crime, liable to provoke an Inquisition or a *fatwa*.

There is of course an historic theological-philosophical debate of the case, pro and con. While this is important and intriguing, we are dealing here primarily with *arguments*, not evidence for or against the existence of the God of revelation. The God of the philosophers or theologians is not the same as the God of revelation; for the latter is a question of historical fact. Clearly, I believe that scientific-historical inquiry by skeptics is important; believers are apt to be biased *a priori* in favor, and they allow their faith commitments to intrude. We need independent, reliable skeptical inquiry into these basic questions, especially since such historical claims have a powerful effect on the contemporary world. We are not here raising idle abstract questions, but those which have a profound influence on human behavior. I submit that no matter what the danger, skeptical inquiry can and should be applied to such religious claims.

The key point about this form of skepticism that has developed, I reiterate, is that it cannot be equated simply with *a priori* doubt, but rather with *inquiry* and the quest for reliable knowledge.

Science itself incorporates the methodology of skeptical inquiry into the very process of discovery. Namely, scientists must be prepared to doubt hypotheses or theories unless or until they are verified or tested by predictions; and/or are consistent with other well-tested theories. Objective peer review is an essential ingredient in the process of questioning any aspect of the prevailing paradigm and seeking to overturn it by more parsimonious and/or elegant-tested theories. Science is thus *fallible*; and doubting is intrinsic to its inquiries. However, the goal is not to debunk, but to achieve *reliable knowledge*. This is constructive and positive, not negative or destructive; and it has moral significance. The quest for truth is ongoing and should apply to every area of human interest.

But in religion many worry this may have negative consequences for cherished beliefs and values. The hidden premise of those who object to scientific inquiry into the paranatural claims of religious beliefs often is their fear that such inquiries may be destructive of traditional social institutions. Yet is there not some moral imperative that human beings apply skeptical inquiry to religious claims, in order to ascertain which are true or false? For religious claims are often competing and contradictory, and they can be a source of intense conflict. To shake at the foundations of belief, insists the believer, may leave people in a hopeless quandary. But need it? If a person finds that the historical evidence for the truth of X in whom he has an abiding faith is unreliable, what would this do to the entire framework of ethical and social beliefs that he values, and what effect will this have on the institutional forms that have been developed to sustain them? Would skeptical inquiry into the foundations or religious belief thus undermine the entire deck of cards that we have piled high?

Should skeptical scientific inquiries be concerned with the ethical implications of their considered doubts reached after a process of inquiry? The dilemma posed today is: If skeptical inquiry shakes at the foundations of traditional religious belief, might it not undermine the entire fabric of beliefs and values? When this happens, can science and reason be applied to ethics and values to help us find rational alternatives?

I submit that many ethical questions may indeed be resolved by scientific inquiry. Ethical principles do not in all cases depend upon religion, nor do they require a supernatural and/or occult foundation. For example, the applied sciences frame value judgments all the time, in engineering, architecture, the practice of medicine, psychiatry, economics, politics, and education. Thus scientific or skeptical inquiry into religious beliefs need not lead to moral collapse or nihilism, for there are alternative systems of ethics that we may find both reasonable and viable, independent of appeals to faith or authority. How and to what extent this is possible is a topic, I submit, that the skeptical community needs to address.

Note

1.   This article first appeared in *Skeptical Inquirer* 28, no. 2 (March/April 2004), pp. 32–33.

XII

Why I Am a Skeptic about Religious Claims[1]

Unbelievers have debated the proper way to describe their position. Some scientists and philosophers—notably Richard Dawkins and Daniel C. Dennett—have recently been sympathetic to the use of the term *bright*. Proponents thought it a clever idea, hoping that *bright* would overcome the negative connotations that other terms such as *atheist* have aroused in the past. Many find this to be an attractive advantage. Critics of the use of *bright* have commented that it is presumptuous for us to suggest that we are "bright," i.e., intelligent, implying that those with whom we disagree are dull-witted or dumb. Clearly, many people have been turned off by the term *atheism*, which they perceive as too negative or dogmatic. Others may seek refuge in some form of popular "agnosticism," which suggests that they are simply uncertain about the god question—though this may simply enable them to resort to "faith" or "fideism" as an artful dodge.

I would like to introduce another term into the equation, a description of the religious "unbeliever" that is more appropriate. One may simply say, "I am a *skeptic*." This is a classical philosophical position, yet I submit that it is still relevant today, for many people are deeply *skeptical* about religious claims.

Skepticism is widely employed in the sciences. Skeptics doubt theories or hypotheses unless they are able to verify them on adequate evidential grounds. The same is true among skeptical inquirers into religion. The skeptic in religion is not dogmatic, nor does he or she reject religious claims a priori; here or she is simply unable to accept the case for God unless it is supported by adequate evidence.

The burden of proof lies upon theists to provide cogent reasons and evidence for their belief that God exists. Faith by itself is hardly sufficient, for faiths collide—in any case, the appeal to faith to support one's creed is irrational in its pretentious claim based on the "will to believe." If it were acceptable to argue in this way, then anyone would be entitled to believe whatever he or she fancied.

The skeptic thus requires evidence and reasons for a hypothesis or belief before it is accepted. Always open to *inquiry*, skeptical inquirers are prepared to change their beliefs in the light of new evidence or arguments. They will not accept appeals to authority or faith, custom or tradition, intuition or mysticism, reports of miracles or uncorroborated revelations. Skeptical inquirers are willing to suspend judgment about questions for which there is insufficient evidence. Skeptics are in that sense genuinely *agnostic*, in that they view the question as still open, though they remain *unbelievers* in proposals for which they think theists offer insufficient evidence and invalid arguments. Hence, they regard the existence of any god as *highly improbable*.

In this sense, a skeptic is a nontheist or an atheist. The better way to describe this stance, I submit, is to say that such a person is a *skeptic* about religious claims.

"Skepticism," as a coherent philosophical and scientific posture, has always dealt with religious questions, and it professed to find little scientific or philosophical justification for belief in God. Philosophers in the ancient world such as Pyrrho, Cratylus, Sextus Empiricus, and Carneades questioned metaphysical and theological claims. Modern philosophers, including Descartes, Bacon, Locke, Berkeley, Hume, and Kant, have drawn heavily on classical skepticism in developing their scientific outlook. Many found the "God question" unintelligible; modern science could proceed only by rejecting occult claims as vacuous, as was done by Galileo and other working scientists—and also by latter-day authors such as Freud and Marx, Russell and Dewey, Sartre and Heidegger, Popper and Hook, Crick and Watson, Bunge, and Wilson.

The expression "a skeptic about religious claims" is more appropriate in my opinion than the term *atheist*, for it emphasizes *inquiry*. The concept of inquiry contains an important constructive component, for inquiry leads to scientific wisdom—human understanding of our place in the cosmos and the ever-increasing fund of human knowledge.

In what follows, I will outline some of the evidence and reasons many scientists and philosophers are skeptical of theistic religious claims. I will focus primarily on supernatural theism and especially on monotheistic religions that emphasize command ethics, immortality of the soul, and an eschatology of heaven and hell. Given space limitations, what follows is only a thumbnail sketch of the case against God.

Succinctly, I maintain that the skeptical inquirer is dubious of the claims

1. that God exists;
2. that he is a person;
3. that our ultimate moral principles are derived from God;
4. that faith in God will provide eternal salvation; and
5. that one cannot be good without belief in God.

I reiterate that the burden of proof rests upon those who believe in God. If they are unable to make the case for belief in God, then I have every right to remain a skeptic.

Why do skeptics doubt the existence of God?

- First, because the skeptical inquirer does not find the traditional concept of God as "transcendent," "omnipotent," "omnipresent," or "omnibeneficent" to be coherent, intelligible, or meaningful. To postulate a transcendent being who is incomprehensible to the human mind (as theologians maintain) does not explain the world that we encounter. How can we say that such an indefinable being exists, if we do not know *in what sense* that being is said to exist? How are we to understand a God that exists outside space and time and that transcends our capacity to comprehend his essence? Theists have postulated an unknowable "X." But if his content is unfathomable, then he is little more than an empty, speculative abstraction. Thus, the skeptic in religion presents semantic objections to God language, charging that it is *unintelligible* and lacks any clear referent.
- A popular argument adduced for the existence of this unknowable entity is that he is the first cause, but we can ask of anyone who postulates this, "What is the cause of this first cause?" To say that he is uncaused only pushes our ignorance back one step. To step outside the physical universe is to assume an answer by a leap of faith.
- Nor does the claim that the universe manifests Intelligent Design (ID) explain the facts of conflict, the struggle for survival, and the inescapable tragedy, evil, pain, and suffering that is encountered in the world of sentient beings. Regularities and chaos do not necessarily indicate design. The argument from design is reminiscent of Aristotle's teleological argument that there are purposes or ends in nature. But we can find no evidence for purpose in nature. Even if we were to find what appears to be design in the universe, this does not imply a designer for whose existence there is insufficient evidence.
- The evolutionary hypothesis provides a more parsimonious explanation of the origins of species. The changes in species through time are better accounted for by chance mutations, differential reproduction, natural selection, and adaptation, rather than by design. Moreover,

vestigial features such as the human appendix, tailbone, and male breasts and nipples hardly suggest adequate design; the same is true for vestigial organs in other species. Thus, the doctrine of creation is hardly supported in empirical terms.

- Another version of the Intelligent Design argument is the so-called fine-tuning argument. Its proponents maintain that there is a unique combination of "physical constants" in the universe that possess the only values capable of sustaining life, especially sentient organic systems. This they attribute to a designer God. But this, too, is inadequate. First because millions of species are extinct; the alleged "fine-tuning" did nothing to ensure their survival. Second, great numbers of human beings have been extinguished by natural causes such as diseases and disasters. The Indian Ocean tsunami of 2004 that suddenly killed over 200,000 innocent men, women, and children was due to a shift in tectonic plates. This hardly indicates fine tuning—after all, this tragedy could have been avoided had a supposed fine tuner troubled to correct defects in the surface strata of the planet. A close variant of the fine-tuning argument is the so-called anthropic principle, which is simply a form of anthropomorphism; that is, it reads into nature the fondest hopes and wishes of believers, which are then imposed upon the universe. But if we are to do this, should we not also attribute the errors and mistakes encountered in nature to the designer?

- Related to this, of course, is the classical problem of evil. If an omnipotent, omnipresent, and omnibeneficent God is responsible for the world as we know it, then how to explain evil? Surely, humans cannot be held responsible for a massive flood or plague, for example; we can explain such calamities only by inferring that God is malevolent, because he knew of, yet permitted, terrible destructive events to occur—or by suggesting that God is impotent to prevent evil. This would also suggest an unintelligent, deficient, or faulty designer.

- The historic religions maintain that God has revealed himself in history and that he has manifested his presence to selected humans. These revelations are not corroborated by independent, objective observers. They are disclosed, rather, to privileged prophets or mystics, whose claims have not been adequately verified: there is insufficient circumstantial evidence to confirm their authenticity.

- To attribute inexplicable events to miracles performed by God, as declared in the so-called sacred literature, is often a substitute for finding their true causes scientifically. Scientific inquiry is generally able to explain alleged "miracles" by discovering natural causes.

- The Bible, Koran, and other classical documents are full of contradictions and factual errors. They were written by human beings in ancient civilizations, expressing the scientific and moral speculations of their day. They do not convey the eternal word of God, but rather the yearnings of ancient tribes based on oral legends and received doctrines; as such, they are hardly relevant to all cultures and times. The Old and New Testaments are not accurate accounts of historical events. The reliability of the Old Testament is highly questionable in the events and personages it depicts; Moses, Abraham, Joseph, etc. are largely uncorroborated by historical evidence. As for the New Testament, scholarship has shown that none of its authors knew Jesus directly. The four Gospels were not written by eyewitnesses but are products of oral tradition and hearsay. There is but flimsy and contradictory evidence for the virgin birth, the healings of Jesus, and the Resurrection. Similarly, contrary to Muslim claims that that religion's scriptures passed virtually unmediated from Allah, there have in fact been several versions of the Koran; it is no less a product of oral traditions than the Bible. Likewise, the provenance of the *Hadith*, allegedly passed down by Muhammad's companions, has not been independently confirmed by reliable historical research.

- Some claim to believe in God because they say that God has entered into their personal lives and has imbued them with new meaning. This is a psychological or phenomenological account of a person's inner experience. It is hardly adequate evidence for the existence of a divine being independent of human beings' internal soliloquies. Appeals to mystical experiences or private subjective states hardly suffice as evidential support that some external being or force caused such altered states of consciousness; skeptical inquirers have a legitimate basis for doubt, unless or until such claims of interior experience can somehow be independently corroborated. Experiences of God or gods, or angels or demons, talking to one may disturb or entrance those persons who undergo such experiences, but the question is whether these internal subjective states have external veracity. This especially applies to those individuals who claim some sort of special revelation from on high, such as the hearing of commandments.

Second, is God a person? Does he take on human form? Has he communicated in discernible form, say, as the Holy Spirit, to Moses, Abraham, Jesus, Muhammad, or other prophets?

- These claims again are uncorroborated by objective eyewitnesses. They are rather promulgated by propagandists of the various faith traditions that have been inflicted on societies and enforced by entrenched ecclesiastical authorities and political powers. They are supported by customs and traditions buried for millennia by the sands of time and institutional inertia. They are simply assumed to be true without question.
- The ancient documents alleging God's existence are preliterate, prephilosophical, and, in any case, unconfirmed by scientific inquiry. They are often eloquent literary expressions of existential moral poetry, but they are unverified by archeological evidence or careful historical investigation. Moreover, they contradict each other in their claims for authenticity and legitimacy.

- The ancient faith that God is a person has not been corroborated by the historical record. Such conceptions of God are anthropomorphic and anthropocentric, reading into the universe human predilections and feelings. "If lions had gods they would be lionlike in character," said Xenophon. Thus, human Gods are an extrapolation of human hopes and aspirations, fanciful tales of imaginative fiction.

Third, the claim that our ultimate moral values are derived from God is likewise highly suspect. The so-called sacred moral codes reflect the socio-historical cultures out of which they emerged. For example, the Old Testament commands that adulterers, blasphemers, disobedient sons, bastards, witches, and homosexuals be stoned to death. It threatens collective guilt: punishment is inflicted by Jehovah on the children's children of unbelievers. It defends patriarchy and the dominion of men over women. It condones slavery and genocide in the name of God.

- The New Testament consigns "unto Caesar the things that are Caesar's"; it demands that women be obedient to their husbands; it accepts faith healing, exorcisms, and miracles; it exalts obedience over independence, fear and trembling over courage, and piety over self-determination.
- The Koran does not tolerate dissent, freedom of conscience, or the right to unbelief. It denies the rights of women. It exhorts *jihad,* holy war against infidels. It demands utter submission to the Word of God as revealed by Muhammad. It rejects the separation of mosque and state, thus installing the law of *sharia* and the theocracy of imams and mullahs.
- From the fatherhood of God, contradictory moral commandments have been derived; theists have often lined up on opposite sides of moral issues. Believers have stood for and against war; for and against slavery; for and against capital punishment, some embracing retribution, others mercy and rehabilitation; for and against the divine right of kings, slavery, and patriarchy; for and against the emancipation of women; for and against the absolute prohibition of contraception, euthanasia, and abortion; for and against sexual and gender equality; for and against freedom of scientific research; for and against the libertarian ideals of a free society.
- True believers have in the past often found little room for human autonomy, individual freedom, or self-reliance. They have emphasized submission to the word of God instead of self-determination, faith over reason, credulity over doubt. All too often they have had little confidence in the ability of humans to solve problems and create a better future by drawing on their own resources. In the face of tragedy, they supplicate to God through prayer instead of summoning the courage to overcome adversity and build a better future. The skeptic

concludes, "No deity will save us; if we are to be saved it must be by our own efforts."

- The traditional religions have too often waged wars of intolerance not only against other religions or ideologies that dispute the legitimacy of their divine revelations but even against sects that are mere variants of the same religion (e.g., Catholic versus Protestant, Shiite versus Sunni). Religions claim to speak in the name of God, yet bloodshed, tyranny, and untold horrors have often been justified on behalf of holy creeds. True believers have all too often opposed human progress: the abolition of slavery, the liberation of women, the extension of equal rights to transgendered people and gays, the expansion of democracy and human rights.

I realize that liberal religionists generally have rejected the absolutist creeds of fundamentalism. Fortunately, they have been influenced by modern democratic and humanistic values, which mitigate fundamentalism's inherent intolerance. Nevertheless, even many liberal believers embrace a key article of faith in the three major Abrahamic religions, Christianity, Islam, and Judaism: the promise of eternal salvation.

Fourth, we are driven to ask: will those who believe in God actually achieve immortality of the soul and eternal salvation as promised?

- The first objection of the skeptic to this claim is that the forms of salvation being offered are highly sectarian. The Hebrew Bible promises salvation for the chosen people; the New Testament, the Rapture to those who have faith in Jesus Christ; the Koran, heaven to those who accept the will of Allah as transmitted by Muhammad.

In general, these promises are not universal but apply only to those who acquiesce to a specific creed, as interpreted by priests, ministers, rabbis, or mullahs. Bloody wars have been waged to establish the legitimacy of the papacy (between Protestantism, Roman Catholicism, and Eastern Orthodoxy), the priority of Muhammad and the Koran, or the authenticity of the Old Testament.

- A second objection is that there is insufficient scientific evidence for the claim that the "soul" can exist separate from the body and that it can survive death as a "discarnate" being, and much less for the claim that it can persist throughout eternity. Science points to the fact that the "mind" or "consciousness" is a function of the brain and nervous system and that with the physical death of the body, the "self" or "person" disappears. Thus, the claim that a person's soul *can* endure forever is supported by no evidence whatever, only by pious hope.

Along the same line, believers have never succeeded in demonstrating the existence of the disembodied souls of any of the billions who went before us. All efforts to communicate with such discarnate entities have been fruitless. Sightings of alleged ghosts have not been corroborated by reliable eyewitness testimony.

- The appeal to near-death experiences simply reports the phenomeno-logical experiences of persons who undergo part of the dying process but ultimately do not die. Of course, we never hear from anyone who has truly died by any clinical standard, gone to "the other side" and returned. In any case, these subjective experiences can be explained in terms of natural, psychological, and physiological causes.

Fifth, theists maintain that one cannot be good unless one believes in God.

- Skepticism about God's existence and divine plan does not imply pessimism, nihilism, the collapse of all values, or the implication that "anything goes." It has been demonstrated time and again, by count-less human beings, that it is possible to be morally concerned with the needs of others, to be a good citizen, and to lead a life of nobility and excellence—all without religion. Thus, anyone can be righteous and altruistic, compassionate and benevolent, without belief in a deity. A person can develop the common moral virtues and express a good will toward others without devotion to God. It is possible to be empathetic toward others and at the same time be concerned with one's own well-being. Secular ethical principles and values thus can be supported by evidence and reason, the cultivation of moral growth and development, the finding of common ground that brings people together. Our principles and values can be vindicated as we examine the consequences of our choices and modify them in light of experience. Skeptics who are humanists focus on the good life here and now. They exhort us to live creatively, seeking a life full of happiness, even joyful exuberance. They urge us to face life's tragedies with equanimity, to marshal the courage and stoic forbearance to live meaningfully in spite of adversity, and to take satisfaction in our achievements. Life can be relished and is intrinsically worthwhile for its own sake, without any need for external support.
- Though ethical values and principles are relative to human interests and needs, that does not suggest that they are necessarily subjec-tive. Instead, they are amenable to objective, critical evaluation and modification in the light of reason. A new paradigm has emerged that integrates skepticism with secular humanism, a paradigm based on scientific wisdom, eupraxsophy, and a naturalistic conception of nature. Thus, the skeptic in religion, who is also a humanist in ethics,

can be affirmative and positive about the potentialities for achieving the good life. Such a person can not only live fully but can also be morally concerned about the needs of others.

In summary, the skeptical inquirer finds inconclusive evidence—and thus, insufficient reason to believe—that God exists, that God is a person, that all ethical principles must be derived from God, that faith in divinity will enable the soul to achieve eternal salvation, and that ethical conduct is impossible without belief in God.

On the contrary, skepticism based on scientific inquiry leaves room for a naturalistic account of the universe. It can also recommend alternative secular and humanist forms of moral conduct. Accordingly, one can simply affirm, when asked if he or she believes in God, "No, I do not; I am a skeptic," and one may add, "I believe in doing good!"

Note

1.   This article first appeared in *Free Inquiry* 26, no. 4 (June/July 2006), pp. 30–33.

XIII

Religion in Conflict: Are "Evangelical Atheists" Too Outspoken?[1]

The recent publication of four books—*The God Delusion*, by Richard Dawkins; *The End of Faith* and *Letter to a Christian Nation*, both by Sam Harris; and *Breaking the Spell: Religion as a Natural Phenomenon* by Daniel Dennett—has provoked great controversy and consternation.[2] The fact that books by Dawkins and Harris have made it to *The New York Times* best-seller list has apparently sent chills down the spines of many commentators; not only conservative religionists but also some otherwise liberal secularists are worried about this unexpected development. What disturbs me is the preposterous outcry that atheists are "evangelical" and that they have gone too far in their criticism of religion.

Really? The public has been bombarded by pro-religious propaganda from time immemorial—today it comes from pulpits across the land, TV ministries, political hucksters, and best-selling books. Indeed, at the present moment, the apocalyptic Left Behind series, coauthored by evangelist Tim LaHaye, is an all-time blockbuster. Other best-sellers include *The Purpose-Driven Life* by Rick Warren and a slew of books attacking liberal secularists and humanists by pro-religion conservatives such as Ann Coulter and Bill O'Reilly.

Let's be fair: Until now, it has been virtually impossible to get a fair hearing for critical comment upon uncontested religious claims. It was considered impolite, in bad taste, and it threatened to raise doubts about God's existence or hegemony. I have often said that it is as if an "iron curtain" had descended within America, for skeptics have discovered that the critical examination of religion has been virtually *verboten*. We have experienced firsthand how journalists and producers have killed stories about secular humanism for fear of offending the little old ladies and gentlemen in the suburbs, conservative advertisers, the Catholic hierarchy, or right-wing fundamentalists. It is difficult to find any politicians who are not intimidated and will admit that they are disbelievers or agnostics, let alone atheists. Today, there are very few, if any, clearly identified atheist personalities in the media—Bill Maher is a notable exception. The war against secularism by the Religious Right is unremitting.

Even *New York Times* columnists are running scared. We note the column by Nicolas Kristof (December 3, 2006) calling for a "truce on religion." He deplores the "often obnoxious atheist offensive" of "secular fundamentalism."

Science columnist William J. Broad, in a piece published earlier this year in the *Times* (February 28, 2006), criticized both Daniel C. Dennett and Edward O. Wilson (another Center for Inquiry stalwart). Dennett, complains Broad, "likens spiritual belief to a disease" and looks to science "to explain its grip on humanity." Broad faults E.O. Wilson for writing in an earlier book (*Consilience* [Knopf, 1998]) that "the insights of neuroscience and evolution … increasingly can illuminate even morality and ethics, with the scientific findings potentially leading 'more directly and safely to stable moral codes' than do the dictates of God's will or the findings of transcendentalism." Broad remonstrates against such views, maintaining that they exhibit "a kind of arrogance," and he likewise recommends that scientists declare a truce in their critiques of religion. To which I reply that it is important that we apply scientific inquiry as best we can to all areas of human behavior, including religion and ethics. I fail to see why it is "arrogant" to attempt to do so.

Another *Times* op-ed piece by Bernard A. Shweder of the University of Chicago ("Atheists Agonistes," [November 27, 2006]), denigrates the Enlightenment and reminds us that John Locke, author of "Letter Concerning Toleration," defended tolerance in democratic societies for everyone *but* atheists.

We note that the *National Review* and the Jewish *Forward* are also worried by "militant secularists" who question established religions—they were objecting to an advertisement the Center for Inquiry/Transnational ran on the op-ed page of *The New York Times* (November 15, 2006), headlined "In Defense of Science and Secularism." We think it appropriate to defend the integrity of science and the importance of secularism at a time when both are under heavy attack.

We should point out that, over the years, Prometheus Books, a company I founded, has consistently published books examining the claims of religion. Now, the fact that mainline publishers, largely owned as they are by conglomerates, have published books by scientists critical of belief in God—because they see that they can make a buck by doing it—has shocked the guardians of the entrenched faiths.

But why should the nonreligious, nonaffiliated, secular minority in the country remain silent? We dissenters now comprise some 14 to 16 percent of the population. Why should religion be held immune from criticism, and why should the admission that one is a disbeliever be considered so disturbing? The Bush administration has supported faith-based charities—though their efficacy has not been adequately tested; it has prohibited federal funding for stem cell research; it has denied global warming; and it has imposed abstinence programs instead of promoting condom use to prevent the spread of AIDS. Much of this mischief is religiously inspired. How can we remain mute while Islam and the West are poised for a possible protracted world conflagration in the name of God?

Given all these facts, why should the criticism of religion provoke such an outcry?

Theological versus Humanist Ethics

One charge often hurled at disbelievers is that we have nothing positive to offer. On the contrary, I maintain that it is possible for an individual to lead a good life and be morally concerned about others without belief in God. I have pointed out that the traditional creeds often condoned heinous crimes: censorship, repression, slavery, war, torture, genocide, the domination of women, the denial of human freedom, and opposition to new frontiers of scientific research. We surely cannot condemn all religions, and I recognize that some religions have performed good works: providing charity to the poor and consoling the sick and weak at times of suffering or tragedy. Religions are among the oldest human institutions on the planet. They developed in agricultural and nomadic societies. "The Lord is my shepherd, I shall not want" expresses the metaphors of premodern and prescientific cultures. Many of them would later oppose modern secular trends and fight against democratic reforms. Indeed, the achievements of human progress in the past have often been in spite of opposition from devout religious believers. Today is another day, and religious liberals now support many of the ideals and values of modern secularism and humanism; they may support science and even not be unsympathetic to biblical criticism. Yet in spite of this, they often cling to earlier mythological creeds spun out in the infancy of the race.

What is often overlooked by the critics of "evangelical atheism" is that skepticism about the existence of God does not by itself define who and what we are. For there is a commitment to the realization of human freedom and happiness in this life here and now and to a life of excellence, creativity, and fulfillment. Life is meaningful without the illusion of immortality. There is also the recognition that the cultivation of the common moral decencies—caring, empathy, and altruism—is an essential part of our relating to other human beings in our communities of interaction. Humanists have always been concerned with achieving justice in society. Many of the heroes and heroines in human history were freethinkers who contributed significantly to democratic progress and a defense of human rights. Indeed, the agenda of secular humanism is two-fold: first is the quest for truth, a critical examination of the assumptions of supernatural religion in the light of science; second is the development of *affirmative* ethical alternatives for the individual, the society in which he or she lives, and also the planetary community at large. To label us "evangelical atheists" without recognizing our affirmative commitment to secular humanist morality is an egregious error.

Sunni versus Shiite Muslims

Of special horror today is the carnage inflicted by the Sunnis and Shi-ites, the two major branches of Islam, upon each other in Iraq. We're told that the conflict is "sectarian," as though we should leave it at that. We beg to differ. This is a *religious* conflict, driven by clashes over theology and history. That fact, which the blander word *sectarian* underemphasizes, should not be overlooked.

The horrendous slaughter between two factions of Islam, claiming thousands not only killed but tortured each month in Iraq, proceeds from doctrinal differences about the origins of Islam and the proper successors of Muhammad. The Shiites (concentrated mostly in Iran, Iraq, Azerbaijan, Lebanon, Afghanistan, and Pakistan) comprise about 15 percent of the world's Muslims; the Sunni most of the remainder.

The Shia Muslims believe that the rightful successor of Muhammad after his death should have been Ali, the second person to accept Islam (after Muhammad's wife Khadija). Ali was the male head of "the people of the prophet's house" (Ahlul Bayt). Shiites believe that Ali was appointed by direct order of Muhammad himself. The branch supporting Ali is also known as the "Party of Ali." Upon the death of Muhammad, however, the majority of Muslims favored Abu Bakr as the first caliph. He was succeeded by the second and third caliphs, Umar and Uthman; the fourth was Ali. The Sunnis recognize the heirs of the four Caliphs (including Ali) as the only legitimate Islamic leaders, the Shia recognize *only* those of Ali. There are also important doctrinal differences in the interpretation of the Hadith, allegedly based on the testimony of the Prophet's original companions.

One can only imagine why, thirteen centuries later, men and women are so concerned about these differences that they will destroy each others' mosques and slaughter one another over them. This, of course, is reminiscent of the battles between Roman Catholics and Protestants in Europe, such as the Hundred Years War in the early modern period, when there were disputes about the hegemony and authority of the Bishop of Rome. The alleged statement of Jesus to Peter in the New Testament, "you are Peter, and on this rock I will build my church," has led to vast bloodshed and violence when Protestants and the Eastern Orthodox rejected the authority of the pope. But this happened centuries ago, and Christians by and large have learned to tame their animosities and have abandoned the Inquisition and Holy Crusades. Apparently, the disputes in the Muslim world are as great as ever, and the world watches in horror as violent jihad is unleashed. The key lesson to learn is that it's not so much the existence of God (or Allah) that is in dispute, for both factions claim to believe in the deity, but the authenticity and legitimacy of divine Revelation, delivered, in this case, to Muhammad, who transmitted it to humanity. The key issue is whether these ancient revelations (those of Muhammad, Jesus, Paul, Moses, Abraham, etc.) have been corroborated by reliable eyewitnesses or rather have been corrupted by an oral tradition and insufficient eyewitnesses. But that is another matter.

"Enough already," we say in disgust. Surely, there must be other sources of morality besides religion. From the fatherhood of God, one can deduce all sorts of contrary moral prescriptions, as one can justify bloodshed, torture, punishment, and death in the name of Allah. This is an old story in human history that has been repeated time and time again. When religion becomes dogmatic, when it becomes thoroughly entrenched in human civilization and institutions, the only way to overcome differences of creed seems to be violence. The best antidote for such devastating nonsense, in my judgment, is the cultivation of critical thinking and the administration of a dose of scientific skepticism to unmask the claims of faith.

The Iraqi Bloodbath

The war in Iraq has degenerated into a bloody religious war between two factions of Islam on the one hand, yet, on the other, it is also a brutal confrontation with Western interests and values.

I opposed the U.S. invasion of Iraq in 2003. I argued that a preemptive strike against Iraq without the support of the United Nations had no legal or moral justification, unlike Afghanistan. The fear that Saddam Hussein had amassed weapons of mass destruction was mistaken. Weapons of mass destruction could not be found. There did not seem to be any direct connection between Al Qaeda supported terrorism and the Iraqi government. While we were well aware of the dangerous ideological views of radical Islamists across the region, we were concerned that the invasion of Iraq could make matters worse by exacerbating the situation (as it has).

I submit that the plausible motive for the preemptive strike against Iraq was to secure a base in order to protect the future export of oil and gas deposits in the region. The claim that we wished to establish democracy and human rights in Iraq (a noble, if perhaps impractical, goal) might be viewed as a rationalization after the fact.

One aspect of the Iraq war that has been unfortunately minimized by the media is the vast numbers of casualties among the Iraqi people. The lands surrounding the Tigris and Euphrates rivers—the "cradle of civilization"—have undergone absolute devastation, an enormous human tragedy for the Iraqi people. The destruction of cultural artifacts and treasures in Iraq's museums illustrates the insensitivity to priceless historic values. The number of Iraqi refuges who have fled the country is enormous. The malnutrition suffered by Iraqi children during the years of sanctions as well as during the war is another concern. We are especially disturbed, however, by the excessive loss of life in the civilian population—let alone the dead and wounded American soldiers.

Representative Dennis Kucinich (D–Ohio) convened a special House hearing on December 12, 2006, devoted to an examination of the extent of "collateral damage," as it is euphemistically called. This was broadcast over C-SPAN. The key participants were Les Roberts (Columbia and Johns Hopkins) and Gilbert Burnham (Johns Hopkins), who had conducted a survey to ascertain the number of civilian deaths caused by violence over and beyond normal death rates. Their work was published in the British medical journal *The Lancet*, one of the leading publications of its kind in the world. Roberts and Burnham used the "cluster method" of tabulation, in which a randomized selection process in certain areas throughout Iraq was used as the basis for the survey. The *Lancet* article estimated that 650,000 to 900,000 Iraqi civilians had died since the American and British invasion in 2003. The mass media have basically ignored or underreported the number of casualties. The Bush administration insisted that the number was much lower, but Roberts and Burnham maintain that there were actually *at least* 650,000 deaths among people who are in essence noncombatants. Some defenders of the administration question the cluster methodology for estimating deaths, but Roberts and Burnham insist it is reliable. (It was reliable enough to be used by the American military in Bosnia, the Congo, and elsewhere.)

The basic issue concerns *innocent* civilians, not Iraqi soldiers nor the combatants of the various tribes that wander the streets and kill people. On the basis of these tragic casualties, a good case can be made that the "gang of four" (Bush, Rumsfeld, Cheney, and Rice) have made enormous blunders and that President Bush may have committed impeachable offenses.

Notes

1. This article first appeared in *Free Inquiry* 27, no. 2 (February/March 2007), pp. 4–7.
2. *The God Delusion*, by Richard Dawkins (Houghton Mifflin, 2006); *The End of Faith* and *Letter to a Christian Nation*, both by Sam Harris (W.W. Norton and Company, 2004, and Knopf, 2006, respectively); and *Breaking the Spell: Religion as a Natural Phenomenon* by Daniel Dennett (Viking Adult, 2006).

XIV

The Passion as a Political Weapon: Anti-Semitism and the Gospels[1]

The Passion of the Christ is not simply a movie but a political club; at least it is being so used against secularists by leading conservative Christians. TV pundit Bill O'Reilly clearly understands that Mel Gibson's film is a weapon in the cultural war now being waged in America between traditional religionists and secular protagonists—such as the *New York Times*, Frank Rich, Andy Rooney, and the predominant "cultural elite." Newt Gingrich chortled that the movie may be "the most important cultural event" of the century. James Dobson of *Focus on the Family* and a bevy of preachers herald it as "the greatest film ever made."

Busloads of devoted churchgoers were brought daily to view the film, which portrays the arrest, trial, crucifixion, and death of Jesus with graphic brutality. It is used to stir sympathy for Jesus, who, half naked, suffers violent sadomasochistic whippings at the hands of his persecutors; and it has engendered hostility to Jews, secularists, and separationists who have dared to question Gibson's allegedly scripturally accurate account.

The Passion of the Christ reinforces a reality secularists dare not overlook: more than ever before, the Bible has become a powerful political force in America. The Religious Right is pulling no punches in order to defeat secularism and, it hopes, transform the United States into a God-fearing country that salutes "one nation under God" and opposes gay marriages and the "liberal agenda." The interjection of religion into the public square (which in fact was never empty) by powerful religious and political forces has ominous implications. James Madison, framer of the Constitution, rightfully worried about factions disrupting civil society, and religious factions can be the most fractious.

Movies are a powerful medium. Film series including *Star Wars, The Lord of the Rings, Harry Potter, Star Trek, The Terminator,* and *The Matrix* all draw upon fantasy; and these have proved to be highly entertaining, captivating, and huge box office hits. *The Passion of the Christ*, however, is more than that, for it lays down a gauntlet challenging basic democratic secular values. It also presents fantasy as fact, and for the unaware and the credulous, this is more than an exercise in poetic license; it is artistic and historical dishonesty.

A Distorted Version of the Bible

According to Mel Gibson, *The Passion of the Christ* is "a true and faithful rendition of the Gospels." This is hardly the case. For there are numerous occasions when it presents material not found in the New Testament, and when it does, it distorts the biblical account. Gibson uses poetic license with abandon. Commentators have pointed out that Gibson distorts the character of Pontius Pilate, making him seem to be a tolerant, benevolent, and fair-minded judge—when independent non-Christian historical texts indicate that he was a mean-spirited political opportunist. The film also portrays Pilate's wife Claudia as a kind of heroine. She is sympathetic to Jesus and thinks his punishment is unjust; there is some basis for that in the Bible. But Gibson goes beyond this in his portrayal, for Claudia acts kindly to Mary, the mother of Jesus, and Mary Magdalene at one point in the film, approaching them with a gift of linen cloths. Gibson has Mary use them to wipe pools of blood from the spot where Jesus was flogged by the Romans. Nowhere are these scenes found in any of the four Gospels. Church historian Elaine Pagels has said that it is "unthinkable" that Jewish women would have sought or received any sympathy or succor from the Romans.

Nor do the Gospels provide any support for the severe beatings inflicted on Jesus by the Jewish soldiers and guards who arrest him in the Garden of Gethsemane prior to those inflicted by the Romans. In one gruesome scene, as Jewish troops bring Jesus back to Jerusalem heavily bound, they constantly beat him and at one point, even throw him off a bridge. There is no account of this in the Gospels. It is tossed in to underscore the brutality of the captors.

All the Gospels say is that a large crowd sent by the priests came to the garden to arrest Jesus. There was a scuffle and Jesus told his disciples to lay down their swords. (Here as elsewhere, Jesus does not seem to be a part of his own cultural and religious Jewish milieu; both he and his followers are consistently characterized as renegades and "other" than their social environment.) Matthew 26:57 states: "Jesus was led off under arrest to the house of Caiaphas the High Priest." Mark 14:53

reads: "Then they led Jesus away to the High Priest's house." Luke 22:54: "Then they arrested Him and led Him away." John's version in 18:12: "The troops with their commander and the Jewish police now arrested Him and secured Him. They took Him first to Annas... the father-in-law of Caiaphas."

If Jesus' abuse by the Jewish guards did not come from the Scriptures, from where did Gibson borrow it? From the supposed revelations of a Catholic nun and mystic, Anne Catherine Emmerich (1774-1824). Indeed, much of *The Passion* is taken from Emmerich's book first published in 1833, known in English as *The Dolorous Passion of Our Lord Jesus Christ*. A current edition proudly asserts on its jacket that it is "the classic account of Divine Revelation that inspired" the Mel Gibson motion picture.

Emmerich, a passionate devotee of the practice of meditating on the "sacred wounds of Jesus," described how after Jesus was arrested, he was tightly bound, constantly struck, dragged, and made to walk with bare feet on jagged rocks. Let us focus on a bridge, which they soon reached, and which Gibson depicts in the film. Emmerich states, "I saw our Lord fall twice before He reached the bridge, and these falls were caused entirely by the barbarous manner in which the soldiers dragged Him; but when they were half over the bridge they gave full vent to their brutal inclinations, and struck Jesus with such violence that they threw Him off the bridge into the water.... If God had not preserved Him, He must have been killed by this fall" (Emmerich 2003, p. 71).

I refer here to this scene only to show that Gibson went far beyond the texts of the Gospels and inserted non-Scriptural events mostly drawn from Emmerich. Remember that these are the subjective visions of a psychic-mystic rendered over 1800 years after the events they concern. I went to see the movie a second time to see if any credit line is given to the Emmerich book at the end of the film. I could find none, a glaring omission.

A good deal of the focus of *The Passion of the Christ* is on the flogging (scourging) of Jesus. Two Gospels state simply that Pilate "had Jesus flogged and handed over to be crucified" (Matthew 27:26, Mark 15:15). John's description agrees (19:1-2): "Pilate now took Jesus and had Him flogged." Luke's account (23:16) has Pilate saying: "I therefore propose to let Him off with a flogging."

What the Gospels state as a matter-of-fact and without narrative elaboration is luridly expanded by Emmerich: First they used "a species of thorny stick covered with knots and splinters. The blows from these sticks tore His flesh to pieces; his blood spouted out..." (Emmerich 2003, p. 135). Then she describes the use of scourges "composed of small chains, or straps covered with iron hooks, which penetrated to the bone and tore off large pieces of flesh at every blow" (p. 135). Moreover, nowhere do the Gospels describe who watched the flogging. Emmerich states that "a Jewish mob gathered at a distance." Gibson has the high priests watching the brutal flogging (with a feminine incarnation of Satan looking on with them). Nowhere is this described in the Bible. Gibson thus goes far beyond the New Testament account, implying that the Jews and their leaders were accomplices in the brutal beatings of Jesus.

The New Testament account next states that the high priests and crowd in the square before Pilate called for the crucifixion of Jesus, and when given the choice, selected Barabbas to be freed rather than Jesus. This is fully depicted in Gibson's *Passion*.

The film, however, is silent about the fact that Jesus, his mother Mary, Peter, James, and the other disciples and supporters in the crowds were themselves Jews. In the depiction of Emmerich and Gibson, the Jews come off as the main enemies of Jesus, provoking the Romans not only to crucify him, but to torture him and inflict maximum suffering. I think the point in the film is even more anti-Jewish: it's that Pilate tries to placate the Jews with the beatings, but they won't be satisfied—some real blood-thirstiness here!

Is *The Passion of the Christ* anti-Semitic? Yes, flagrantly so, in my judgment. *The Passion* repeats the description of the Jews portrayed in medieval art and Passion Plays, which provoked in no small measure anti-Semitic pogroms and persecutions suffered by the "Christ killers" for centuries. Much has been said about the fact that Mel Gibson's 85-year-old father Hutton Gibson is a Holocaust denier. He has been quoted as saying that Vatican II was "a Mason plot backed by the Jews." Mel Gibson removed from the subtitles of the original version of his film the statement from Matthew (27:25-26): "The blood be on us, and on our children," though apparently it remains in the spoken Aramaic text.

To his credit, Pope John Paul II in 2000 made an historic apology, declaring that the Jews of today cannot be held responsible for the death of Christ. Still, *The Passion* debuts at a time when anti-Semitism is growing worldwide, especially in Europe and throughout the Islamic world.

According to Scripture (especially the Gospel of John), Christ died on the cross because God sent His only begotten Son to die for our sins; thus, all sinners are responsible, not simply the Jews of ancient Israel. Mel Gibson has himself blamed all sinners for the crucifixion. If this is the case, the crucifixion of Christ had to happen, and was for that matter foretold by Him.

Why God was willing to allow His only beloved Son to suffer a horrible death is difficult to fathom, but according to Christian apologetics it was preordained so that those who believed in Christ could be saved. Thus it was God—not the Jews alone or the Romans—who was responsible for the crucifixion of Jesus. One might even say that if this was part of a divine plan, the Jews should get the credit for carrying it out.

Is the Biblical Account Reliable?

Is the account of Jesus as described in the New Testament—in this case of his trial, crucifixion, and death (let alone his birth, ministry, and resurrection)—an accurate account of historical events? I doubt it. This negative appraisal is drawn from careful, scholarly, and scientific examination of the New Testament account.

The key point is the fact that the authors of the Gospels were not themselves eyewitnesses to the events described in these documents. If Jesus died about the year 30 CE (this is conjectural, since some even question whether he ever lived), the Gospel according to Mark was probably written in the 70s of the first century; Matthew and Luke in the 80s; and John anywhere from 90 to 100 CE. They were thus written some forty to seventy years after the death of Jesus.

The Gospels are based on an oral tradition, derived at best from second- and third-hand testimony assembled by the early band of Jewish Christians and including anecdotal accounts, ill-attributed sayings, stories, and parables. The Gospels' claims are not independently corroborated by impartial observers—all the more reason why some skepticism about their factual truth is required. They were not written as history or biography per se—and the authors did not use the methods of careful, historical scholarship. Rather, they were, according to biblical scholar Randel Helms, written by missionary propagandists for the faith, interested in proclaiming the "good news" and in endeavoring to attract and convert others to Christianity. Hence, the Gospels should not be taken as literally true, but rather as a form of special pleading for a new ideological-moral-theological faith.

In writing the Gospels the authors evidently looked back to the Old Testament and found passages that were suggestive of a Messiah who would appear, who was born of a young woman (or a virgin), and could trace his lineage back to David—which is why Matthew and Luke made such a fuss about having Jesus born in Bethlehem. Accordingly, the

Gospels should be read as works of literary art, spun out of the creative imagination, in order to fulfill passionate yearnings for salvation. They are the most influential fictional works to dominate Western culture throughout its history. Whether there is any core of truth to them is questionable; for it is difficult to verify the actual facts, particularly since there is no mention of Jesus or of his miraculous healings in any extant non-Christian literature.

Tradition has it that Mark heard about Jesus from Peter. Eusebius (260-339 CE) is one source for this claim, but Eusebius wrote some three centuries after the death of Jesus. In any case, Matthew and Luke most likely base their accounts on Mark. The three synoptic Gospels are similar, though they contradict each other on a number of significant events. Scholars believe that Mark was possibly derived from still another literary source (Q or quelle in German, or "source") that has been lost.

Another historical fact to bear in mind is that the Gospels were written after a protracted war between the Romans and the Jews (66-74 CE), which saw the destruction of Jerusalem and of the Temple (70 CE). Hundreds of thousands of Jews were killed in these wars and were dispersed throughout the Mediterranean world. Jerusalem was eventually leveled in 135 CE. The synoptic Gospels were influenced by the political conditions at the times of the various authors who wrote the Gospels, not during the years of Jesus. John's Gospel, written somewhat later, reflected the continuing growth of Christianity in his day. The other book attributed to John, Revelations, which is so influential today, predicts the apocalyptic end of the world, the Rapture, and the Second Coming of Jesus. This book in the view of many scholars reflects the ruminations of a disturbed personality. We have no reliable evidence that these events will occur in the future, yet hundreds of millions of people today are convinced that they will—on the basis of sheer faith.

Let us consider another part of the historical context in the latter part of the first century, when most of the New Testament was composed. Two Jewish sects contended for dominance. First was Rabbinic Judaism, which followed the Torah with all its commandments and rituals (including circumcision and dietary laws). Drawing on the Old Testament, Rabbinic Judaism held that the Jews were the "chosen people." Once slaves in Egypt, they had escaped to the Promised Land of Palestine. Someday, after the Diaspora, the Jews would be returned to Israel, and the Temple would be rebuilt. The second sect was early Jewish Christianity, which attempted to appeal not only to Jews but to pagans in the Roman Empire.

It could do so effectively only by breaking with Rabbinic Judaism. This is the reason for increasing negative references in the Gospels to "the Jews" (especially in John), blaming them for the crucifixion of Jesus. Christianity was able to make great strides in recruiting converts and competing with other sects, such as the Mithraic religion. But it could only do so by disassociating itself from Rabbinic Judaism. It developed a more universal message, which, incidentally, was already implicit in The Letters of Paul (written some fifteen to twenty years after the crucifixion of Jesus): The new Christians did not need to be circumcised nor to practice the dietary laws.

Thus, the biblical texts drawn on in *The Passion of the Christ* should not be read literally as diatribes against the Jews per se, but rather as the record of a dispute among two Jewish sects competing for ascendancy–between traditional and Christianized Judaism.

If one reads the four Gospels side-by-side, as I have done numerous times, one finds many omissions. Evidently their writers never knew Jesus in his own lifetime. Each Gospel was crafted post hoc to satisfy the immediate practical needs of the new Christian churches then developing. They were contrived by human beings who were motivated by the transcendental temptation to believe in Christ as the Son of God and the Savior of mankind. The Gospels thus are historically unreliable, and insofar as *The Passion of the Christ* used them the film is also historically unreliable. But Gibson goes even beyond the Gospels, as I have indicated.

The Establishment of Christianity

I submit that there are two important inferences to draw from this analysis: First, the union of a religious creed with political power can be extremely destructive, especially when that creed is supported by the power of the state or the Empire. It was the conversion of the Emperor Constantine (around 312 CE) that led to the establishment of Christianity as the official religion of the Roman Empire, some three centuries after the crucifixion of Jesus.

The "Nicene Creed," which was the product of the counsel of Nicaea (convened in 325 CE), said that Jesus was crucified under Pontius Pilate. It also declared Jesus the divine son of God "in one substance" with the Father. The decision which books should be included in the New Testament was political, determined by the vote of the bishops attending the council of Nicaea. At this and other church councils, various apocryphal books revered by particular Christian communities were omitted from the canonical Scriptures. So much for historic objectivity.

The Emperor Julian (331-363 CE), a nephew of Constantine and a student of philosophy, became skeptical of Christianity and was prepared to disestablish the Christian church, which he probably would have done had he not been murdered, most likely by a Christian soldier in his army. In any case, Christianity prevailed and the great Hellenic-Roman civilization of the ancient world eventually went into decline. But this occurred in no small measure because of political factors: the grafting of the Bible with the sword, and the establishment of an absolutist Christian creed, intolerant of all other faiths that disagreed, and willing to use any methods to stamp out heresy.

By the fifth century more and more of the inhabitants of the Roman Empire became members of Christian churches, which replaced pagan religions. Christianity reigned supreme across Europe, North Africa, and the Middle East. The latter two were overrun by the Muslims in the seventh and eighth centuries, but feudal Europe remained stolidly Christian as it entered into the so-called Dark Ages. Only with the Renaissance, the Reformation, and the development of science and the democratic revolutions of our time was the hegemony of Christianity weakened. The secularization of modern society brought in its wake naturalistic ideas and humanist values.

The union of religion and political power has generated terrible religious conflicts historically, pitting Catholics against Protestants, opposing Jihadists versus Crusaders, and triggering constant wars among Christians, Jews, Muslims, Hindus, and others. God save us from God-intoxicated legions that have the power to enforce their convictions on those who disagree! This is all the more reason to laud the wisdom of the authors of the American Constitution who enacted the Bill of Rights, including the First Amendment, prohibiting the establishment of a religion.

Freedom of Inquiry

The second inference to be drawn is that the origins of the Christian legend have for too long lain unexamined, buried by the sands of time. The New Testament was taken by believers as given, and no one was permitted to question its sacred doctrines allegedly based on revelations from On High. But skepticism is called for—the same skepticism that should also be applied to the alleged revelations by Moses on Mount Sinai and other prophets of the Old Testament. Orthodox Jews who accept the legend of a "chosen people" and the promise that God gave Israel to the Jews likewise base this conviction on uncorroborated testimony.

Today, thanks to the tools of historical scholarship, biblical criticism, and science developed in the past two centuries, we can undertake sophisticated scholarly and scientific inquiries. These tools enable us to use circumstantial evidence, archaeology, linguistic analysis, and textual criticism to authenticate or disconfirm the veracity of ancient literary documents. Regrettably, the general public is almost totally unaware of this important research. Similarly for the revelations of Muhammad and the origins of Islam in the Koran. Since they are similarly uncorroborated by independent eyewitnesses, they rest on similarly questionable foundations. There is again a rich literature of skeptical scrutiny. But most scholars are fearful of expressing their dissenting conclusion.

The so-called books of Abraham—the Old and New Testaments, and the Koran—need to be scrutinized by rational and scientific analyses. And the results of these inquiries need to leave the academy and be read and digested more widely. Unfortunately, freedom of inquiry had rarely been applied to the foundations of the "sacred texts." Indeed, until recently severe punishment of religious dissenters was the norm in many parts of the world.

Given the tremendous box office success of Mel Gibson's film, there are bound to be other Jesus movies produced—for Jesus sells in America! *The Passion of the Christ* unfortunately may add to intolerance of dissenters; and this may severely endanger the fragility of social peace. It may further help to undermine the First Amendment's prohibition of the establishment of religion, which has been the mainstay of American democracy. This indeed is the most worrisome fallout that the Gibson film is likely to produce.

Questions for Further Reflection

1. In what ways can one construe *The Passion of the Christ* as anti-Semitic?
2. How historically reliable are the Gospels?
3. Is Gibson's film historically accurate?
4. How does the use of Emmerich's visionary book affect the understanding of Gibson's film?
5. Is what ways could one argue that Gibson's film is socially dangerous?

Note

1.   This article appeared in *Mel Gibson's Passion and Philosophy: The Cross, the Questions, the Controversy*, edited by Jorge J.E. Gracia, Open Court, Chicago,

Ill. (2004): pp. 90–99. A slightly different version also appeared in *Free Inquiry* 24, no. 4 (June/July 2004), pp. 50–53.

References

John Dominic Crossan, *Who Killed Jesus? Exposing the Roots of Anti-Semitism in the Gospel Story of the Death of Jesus*. San Francisco, CA: Harper, 1995.

Anne Catherine Emmerich, *The Dolorous Passion of Our Lord Jesus Christ,* trans. Klemens Maria Brentano. El Sobrante, CA: North Bay Books, 2003.

Randel Helms, *Gospel Fictions*. Amherst, NY: Prometheus Books, 1988.

R. Joseph Hoffmann, *Jesus Outside the Gospels*. Amherst, NY: Prometheus Books, 1984.

Paul Kurtz, *Transcendental Temptation: A Critique of Religion and the Paranormal*. Amherst, NY: Prometheus Books, 1991.

George Wells, *Did Jesus Exist?* Amherst, NY: Prometheus Books, 1980.

XV

Creating Secular and Humanist Alternatives to Religion[1]

The question that has intrigued me for the lion's share of my life is whether it is possible to develop secular and humanistic alternatives to theistic religion. I have been puzzled by the persistence of ancient narratives of revelations from God and promises of salvation. They are "news from nowhere," for they are uncorroborated by reliable empirical evidence. Supernatural tales about Moses, Abraham, Jesus, Muhammad, and other prophets endure, despite the advances of modern science, the increase of literacy, and the availability of higher criticisms of biblical and Koranic claims. Fictionalized parables of miraculous wonderment still captivate countless human beings, virtually everywhere—astonishingly, even in the United States with its highly educated public.

Still, not everyone on the planet is fixated on a transcendental realm or tempted by its false lures. Religion has declined dramatically in secular Europe, Japan, China, and other countries of the world. Why is it still so prominent in other areas, and why does it affect some credulous individuals and not others?

Two questions are often posed. The first is, *why does religion persist?* The second is, can we create secular and humanist alternatives?

There are several explanations that have been suggested in answer to the question: Why does religion persist? One reason is that vast numbers of human beings have been exposed to pro-religious propaganda through the ages by the proponents of the Bible, Koran, and other so-called sacred books. Too often, they have lacked access to skeptical critiques of the highly questionable claims of revelation from On High. It is now abundantly clear that the ancient documents on which the great historic religions are founded contain gross exaggerations and untruths, were written by evangelical propagandists for specific faiths, and are products of an unsophisticated, prescientific age. Monotheistic religions are among the oldest institutions in human history. Rational critiques of revealed religions were usually forbidden in most societies. It was generally a crime to question the Word of God or blaspheme his name, however much the orthodox religions of the day might have disputed among themselves over which religion was authoritative. Just in recent times, Catholics and Protestants, Christians and Jews, Hindus and Muslims have vehemently disagreed and persecuted one another. Today, Shiites and Sunnis slaughter each other with abandon. Past and present, all this violence is carried out "in the name of God."

Nonbelief is still punishable by death in many Islamic countries. Although Western countries no longer torture or burn heretics, all sorts of sanctions are applied to nonbelievers; at the very least, it is still considered in bad taste to doubt the sacred icons of society, no matter how bizarre or preposterous they may seem. U.S. polls consistently identify atheists as the nation's most unwelcome minority. In most cultural milieus today, it is very difficult for iconoclasts of any type to make themselves heard, given the fact that the young are indoctrinated into the creeds of their parents from the very earliest, and powerful institutions have been erected to propagate and defend the faith.

Richard Dawkins has introduced the concept of the "meme" to account for, among other things, religion's persistence (*The Selfish Gene*, 1976; see also Susan Blackmore, *The Meme Makers*, 1998). *Memetics* refers to the imitative process whereby humans transmit ideas, values, beliefs, and practices to each other. The memes that catch on are conditioned by repetition and imbibed by subsequent generations. Memes are the conveyors of customs and traditions. The concept of the meme is highly suggestive; it would apply to all kinds of cultural information that can be passed down through repetition and imitation. Critics maintain that memetics lacks a precise scientific definition. Nevertheless, I find the arguments rather persuasive that memes function in ways analogous to genes, which, as we know, are transmitted biologically by natural selection. Memes supported by religious or ideological sanctions may function as "viruses of the mind." Some invasive biological viruses can be cured by antibiotics, and some cannot; invasive memes are often very difficult to root out. There are vaccines that can inoculate us against infectious diseases. Is there something analogous to a vaccine that can protect us from noxious memes? Yes, I think that there is: the use of critical thinking and skeptical inquiry are the best therapies for nonsense!

Daniel C. Dennett has also drawn upon the meme concept to explain the "spell" that supernatural religion often casts on people infected by it and the difficulty they experience in breaking its grip (*Consciousness Explained*, 1991; *Breaking the Spell*, 2006). He argues that we need to pursue the scientific investigation of the causes of religious beliefs in order to weaken their hold on human culture. If humans better understood the origins of religious myths, perhaps they could be released from their noxious influence.

The origin of any given meme is usually forgotten, especially if it was implanted in the deep historical past. I was graphically reminded of this recently when my three-year-old grandson, Cameron, began to sing the English nursery rhyme, "Ring around a Rosy." I chimed in and we both laughed and fell down when we were supposed to:

Ring around a rosy
A pocket full of posies
Ashes, ashes
We all fall down!

I had sung the nursery rhyme to my children and had been taught it by my parents. Yet the original source of the story was largely unknown to us. The rhyme is believed to refer to the bubonic plague (or Black Death) that struck Europe in the fourteenth century. "Ring around a rosy" refers to the pink circles that would appear on a sick person's body; later the circles would turn black and the person would die. *Posies* refers to flowers that people thought would purify the air if breathed through. *Ashes* apparently refers to the fact that they burned the dead and the houses they lived in. And "all fall down" means falling dead. How ghastly this innocent rhyme, its real source buried by the sands of time; yet it has been repeated for centuries. If parents really understood the true meaning of the rhyme, no doubt they would be hesitant to pass it on.

Apply this memes principle to religious beliefs and rituals that are deeply ingrained in the young: witness the *madrassas*, schools in Islamic countries where young boys are taught to memorize Koranic verses by rote; or the five prayers a day required of Muslims in which phrases are intoned by repetition. No wonder these ancient memes continue to possess devout believers, who are willing to die for Allah. This process of indoctrination is similar among Orthodox Jews, who put on *tefillin* and prayer shawls daily and repeat phrases from the Torah; devout Catholics, who rub their rosary beads and recite Hail Marys; or Protestants, who avow the Nicene Creed at Sunday services. Religious memes whose origins are largely unknown have driven their roots so deep into the psyches of devout believers that they are difficult to erase. Of course, there are fairy tales—such as Santa Claus—that everyone knows are pure fiction. But when Gospels are taken as absolute truth and never questioned, this may become destructive of other genuine human values. For example, ardent faith may incline believers against accepting the findings of the sciences, as in the case of those true believers today who refuse to accept evolution.

There is still another possible explanation for the persistence of religious memes and the difficulty believers encounter in shedding them. In my book *The Transcendental Temptation: A Critique of Religion and the Paranormal*,[2] I postulate a "transcendental temptation," that is, a quest for an unseen spiritual reality behind this world. That temptation explains in part the recurrent persistence of religiosity. It has deep roots in cultural history and genetic disposition. The transcendental temptation is expressed by human beings overcome by the fragility of life and yearning for a deeper purpose to the universe. A common fear of death and nonbeing gnaws at the innards, goading humans to seek balm for the aching heart and to find solace in the promise of deliverance. The "quest for certainty," as John Dewey called it, seems to offer a secure anchor in a contingent universe for those seeking such security. Thus the belief in God and immortality expresses our imaginative flight toward an ultimate sanctuary beyond death. If this is the case, then perhaps another reason religious memes continue to be propagated and to flourish is that they satisfy some need (real or apparent) for their holders. These spiritual responses are no doubt spurious, exacerbated by false prophets selling their wares and services. Nevertheless, the transcendental message still resonates with individuals who hunger for existential comfort.

This deep-seated temptation is not present in all human beings, nor in all cultures, to the same extent; at the least, it takes on different forms, particularly in secular societies that encourage a naturalistic worldview. Thus, magical tales of a transcendental realm do not entrap all human beings in an ancient "fixology."

This leads to the second question, which is especially intriguing: *Is it possible to create naturalistic-existential-moral poetries, narratives of sufficient power and intensity to attract and supplant the ancient memetic systems of religion?* The question of truth is an enduring problem for human civilization, and it is especially central to secular humanists. It is apparent that inerrant fundamentalist religions are not only false, but also dysfunctional, insofar as they have blocked scientific research, denigrated individual autonomy, repressed sexual freedom, and denied the possibility of human beings solving their own problems without reliance on God. Still, religious creeds have provided important support systems, and they have cultivated charitable efforts and the bonds of moral cohesion. I readily grant that, where mainline religious denominations have built what were in fact secular communities of friends, they have satisfied important psychological-sociological needs, often without imposing authoritarian overlays. Secular humanists can learn much from the denominations about the need to build communities. But secular humanists differ from the religious in that they are unable to make the leap of faith required to believe in the messianic message of the ancient prophets, even if reinterpreted in metaphorical or symbolic language. These original rituals for salvation were contrived by our nomadic-agricultural forbears, and, however liberalized, they are difficult for highly educated and sophisticated moderns to swallow. Secular humanists, skeptics, and rationalists affirm that they believe in the unvarnished truth, not mythological poetry. They prefer new truths and values, based on conceptions of reality drawn from scientific understanding, not from the ancient religious classics. Modern humans need new, secular prophets of liberation.

The secular humanist outlook relies heavily on cognition and reason. It is committed to the following principles:

- The consistent use of objective methods of inquiry for testing truth claims, based on science and critical thinking;
- Conceptions of "reality" derived largely from empirical research; its cosmic view is naturalistic and evolutionary, and the human species is viewed as part of nature, not separate from it;
- Sharp skepticism of a theistic God or immortality of the soul, for it finds insufficient evidence for these claims;
- The belief that human values are relative to human experience, interests, and needs, and that objective principles can be developed for realizing human happiness and improving the human condition; this includes the belief in maximizing individual freedom and in expressing altruistic concerns for the needs of others;
- Commitment to the democratic society, predicated on freedom and equality, tolerance, the right of dissent, respect for the open society and the rule of law, majority rule and minority rights, and the separation of church and state;
- Recognition of our global interdependence; it believes that we need to develop new planetary ethics that are devoted to the preservation of the planet Earth, biodiversity, and the creation of a genuine planetary civilization in which all members of the human species are considered

equal in dignity and value. This new Planetary Humanism seeks to transcend the ancient racial, religious, ethnic, national, and gender differences of the past in order to develop a peaceful and prosperous world community.

If secular humanists are to be effective in creating institutions that provide alternatives to traditional, theistic religions, then, I submit, we need to satisfy the following conditions:

- First, we need to confront directly the root existential questions about the "meaning of life" and respond cogently to the quandaries that trouble so many human beings. We need to help people withstand the blows of outrageous fortune: illness, grief, suffering, conflict, failure, and death—*weltschmertz*, as the Germans call it. It is vital that we bolster the courage to go on in spite of the sometimes tragic dimensions of human existence. We need to marshal a stoic attitude, which resolves us to persevere in spite of adversity while it recognizes the bountiful satisfactions still available in human life.
- Second, we need to develop an appreciation for ethical values and principles that are firmly grounded in human experience and reason, rigorously tested by their consequences in practice, yet sufficiently attractive to inspire dedication, a sense that life is really worth living, and a respect for the obligations that we owe to others. This includes a moral recognition that we *ought* to help build a better world for ourselves and our fellow human beings.
- Third, we need to appeal to the heart as well as the mind, the passionate and emotional dimensions of life as well as the cognitive and intellectual. For secular humanists, life is discovered to be intrinsically satisfying, rich with various potentialities for joyful exuberance: sexual fulfillment, creative expression, and genuine humanitarian concerns. The arts illustrate the power of aesthetic experiences. Literature, novels, poetry, and drama open us to new forms of the flowering creative imagination. The visual arts, such as painting, sculpture, and architecture, expose us to objects of beauty. Photography and cinematography offer vivid insights, while music, singing, and dance carry the promise of enthralling rapture (in a secular sense, of course).
- Fourth, we need to use the arts to create new narratives that celebrate life (not deny or denigrate it) and that also dramatize the rites of passage: birth, graduation, love and friendship, marriage or civic unions, career-building, retirement, and death. Humanist ceremonies are necessary ingredients to a life well lived, intrinsically good for their own sake. The message of the humanist is emphasis on the potential goodness of life, the power of reason, and the determination to resolve human problems. In short, we need to arouse emotional commitment to inspiring humanistic values, the beauty of life and shared experiences, the joys of discovery, the satisfaction in reaching accords.

We also need to arouse a sense of the splendor and majesty of the natural world by viewing the expanding galaxies in full color and light as seen through the telescopes of astronomy or in studying the rich diversity of life as we discover it in the biosphere.

We especially need to celebrate the power of science and reason to unlock the secrets of the universe and invent new technologies for the betterment of life. It is not blind faith but the objective methods of inquiry that best help us to solve the problems that beset us and offer us the means to ameliorate life on our planet. The march of reason through history, in spite of setbacks and defeats: the sheer joy of achieving progress in conquering disease, improving health and nutrition, reducing pain and suffering, overcoming ignorance and poverty, and expanding the opportunities for education and cooperation—these are the great discoveries and breakthroughs that the human species should herald, rather than supplicating in fear and trembling before the unknown forces of the universe. It is the Promethean person who is able to enter into the world and change it for the better, not the masochistic mystic who petitions unknown forces, unable to summon the resources to overcome challenges by creating new tomorrows.

- Fifth, in building naturalistic alternatives to religion, we need to focus on exemplary role models in history: humanist heroes and heroines, scientists and thinkers, poets and artists, authors and composers, explorers and adventurers, statesmen and stateswomen, humanitarian and progressive battlers for beloved causes and an improved world, people who have made life better. Among these are Solon and Pericles, Socrates and Hypatia, Galileo and Darwin, Shakespeare and Beethoven, Einstein and Salk, Sartre and de Beauvoir, Dewey and Russell, Margaret Sanger and Carl Sagan, E.O. Wilson and Richard Dawkins. These are the great free thinkers, independent persons, and iconoclasts who have exemplified excellence and nobility in their lives, for themselves and others, and who have illustrated the fullness of humanity that is both creative and caring.
- Sixth, we need especially to develop communities of sympathetic persons, committed to science, reason, and free inquiry in every area of human interest, yet able to cultivate goodwill and a moral regard for others. I cannot overestimate the importance of the need to establish alternative secular communities for humanists and naturalists. These institutions must demonstrate by example that it is possible to be a creative individual, a loving person and friend, a loyal member of the society in which he or she lives, rational and affectionate, intelligent and empathetic to those within one's communities of interaction.

The great challenge that humankind faces in the twenty-first century is the need for a New Renaissance. This is the special challenge that the Center for Inquiry movement has taken upon itself (however modestly) as it focuses on building Centers and Communities dedicated to both inquiry *and* human enrichment. Our efforts are directed at developing *new* communities as moral-aesthetic-intellectual substitutes for the ancient religious dogmas and rituals spawned in the infancy of the race and encrusted by memes and customs that are no longer fully functional.

We should respond with optimism and dedication to the proposition that *it is possible to transcend the transcendental temptation* and to infuse any such temptation with humanistic rational, poetic, and existential alternatives. This would focus on both the individual and his or her quest for creative exuberance and the communities in which we live—and preeminently to the Planetary Civilization of which we are all a part.

Melting Glaciers and Global Warming

I recently returned from a glorious educational cruise to Alaska aboard the Holland American liner, the *Westerdam*. We sailed from Seattle, Washington, and Victoria, British Columbia, to Juneau and Sitka, Alaska; and we visited Glacier Bay. Perhaps I should qualify the term *glorious* by saying that the spectacle that we viewed was tinged with sadness, for though we had a splendid opportunity to behold the wondrous snow-covered mountain peaks and pristine temperate rainforests, we also witnessed the great glaciers of Alaska rapidly disappearing. We visited the impressive Mendenhall Glacier, which receded 250 feet the year before last (when it was very warm) and 170 feet just last year, and which continues to melt year in and year out. We observed with great remorse the rapid calving of icebergs, the falling of large chunks into Glacier Bay and floating out to the Pacific Ocean. We learned from Mark Bowen (author of *Thin Ice: Unlocking the Secrets of Climate in the World's Highest Mountains*, John Mac-Rae Books, 2005) that the glaciers are melting all over the world and that, in time, they may very well disappear; this is also true of the snowcapped mountain peaks in Peru, the snows of Kilimanjaro in Africa, and of the great Mount Everest in Nepal. If this process of global warming continues, then water levels will rise everywhere. This would be a worldwide disaster, not only for human populations in low-lying coastal areas such as Florida and Bangladesh, but also for the biosphere in general. In his new book, *The Creation* (Norton, 2006), E.O. Wilson warns that we face an unimaginable crisis in the ecosystem of the planet with the accelerating pace of the death of species.

It is difficult to deny the reality of global warming, though some scientists and politicians, financed by powerful oil companies, have attempted to do just that. How much of global warming may be attributed to the pollution caused by human civilization or to natural forces is open to debate. The preponderance of scientific judgment is that the release of carbon dioxide into the atmosphere—known as the "greenhouse effect"—is a major contributing cause. Al Gore is perhaps the leading American politician to shout this warning, especially in his new film, *An Inconvenient Truth*. These facts have been denied by religious conservatives, who believe that the Earth is made for humans, to be used as they wish for their own purposes. Those who love our blue-green dot, as it appears when seen from afar, need to work together with all members of the planetary community in order to take whatever measures we can to prevent this, if there is still time. This is incumbent not only on the United States, the major user of fossil fuels, but also on the underdeveloped world as it rapidly industrializes.

While aboard ship, we read aloud the following pledge of allegiance, which sets forth our ethical obligations to our planetary abode:

Planetary Allegiance

We pledge allegiance to the planetary community of which we're all a part: one planet, indivisible, with liberty and justice for all. We recognize that all persons are equal in dignity and value. We defend human rights and cherish human freedom. We vow to honor and protect the global ecology and biodiversity, not only for ourselves but for generations yet unborn.

One lesson to be learned from this discussion of global warming is that it is a mistake to think that secular humanism begins and ends with skeptical critiques of religion (the false "idols of the tribe," according to Francis Bacon). The question that is often raised is, if you reject the discredited beliefs of the religious systems of the past, what do you offer in their place? To which I respond: clearly, there are humanist values and principles, which are tested by human experience that are relevant. Implicit in the question of global warming is the basic human imperative to strive today to preserve the natural ecology of the planet. This is so apparent that only a foolhardy person would deny its moral authority.

Notes

1. This article first appeared in *Free Inquiry* 26, no. 5 (August/September 2006), pp. 4–9.
2. Paul Kurtz, *The Transcendental Temptation: A Critique of Religion and the Paranormal* (Prometheus Books, Amherst, N.Y.: 1986).

Section 4

Humanism and Politics

XVI

Is America a Post-Democratic Society?[1]

At the conclusion of the Constitutional Convention in Philadelphia in September 1787, a citizen approached Benjamin Franklin and asked what sort of government the assembled statesmen had given them. "A republic, if you can keep it," Franklin is reputed to have replied.

Can we keep it? That is an urgent question that needs to be asked anew today, more than two centuries after the American Republic began. The Roman Republic lasted but two centuries, and then it was supplanted by the Roman Empire. Has the American democratic republic, too, become so fragile that its survival is in doubt?

This gnawing question is being raised again, as we face ominous terrorist threats and as demands for security preempt concerns for civil liberties, at least in the minds of many. America has faced awesome challenges in its past. Slavery engulfed the young republic in discord, for it contradicted the very premise of the new democracy—that each person was equal in dignity and value. Only the Civil War could resolve that conflict. The Great Depression of the 1930s and the Cold War that followed World War II also posed awesome challenges. Similarly, the exclusion of women, blacks, gays, and other minorities from full participation in American democracy aroused bitter controversy.

There were ominous threats to our democratic republic during the Bush administration, and I wish to examine some of these trends. Many democrats are disturbed by the implications of the "War on Terror," the enactment of the PATRIOT Act, the tightening of our borders, xenophobic fear of the "enemy," and the severe reduction of civil liberties. But there are still other threats to democracy. Most of these have been building for decades—well before the confrontation with the new Islamic *jihad*. As a result, American democracy has eroded so seriously that perhaps we have already become a *post-democratic* society. The United States has just undergone a drawn-out and acrimonious, even bitter, national election. As we go to press, Mr. Bush has been declared the winner of the presidency; and the Republicans have maintained control of the Congress.

Now, I do not wish to be a Cassandra of doom. Many people said that the candidates squared off vigorously during the campaign, indicating that democracy is still alive. In my view, much of this campaigning was pure façade; for neither of the two major candidates addressed some of the basic issues that confront American society. There are, of course, differences in degree, if not in kind, between the two parties—and no doubt Mr. Bush's victory means that our democratic institutions will continue to erode more rapidly than if Mr. Kerry had gained the presidency. These trends will most likely continue in the future—and they can only be turned back if there is massive public recognition of the grave dangers to democracy that we now face. But as we shall see, given corporate control of the media, this is difficult to achieve.

The erosion of democracy is especially disheartening to the humanist outlook, which has been intimately tied to the democratic philosophy. Indeed, humanist and liberal philosophers have contributed to the intellectual underpinnings and theoretical justification of democracy.

Beginning in the seventeenth and eighteenth centuries, John Locke, the French *philosophes* of the Enlightenment, and the founders of the American Republic (especially Paine, Jefferson, and Madison) paved the way, establishing the Right of Revolution, declaring the Rights of Man, and designing the American constitutional system (influenced of course by Montesquieu). Democracy was not based upon divine fiat but upon the rights of the people to secure life, liberty, and the pursuit of happiness, and to limit the power of monarchs. John Stuart Mill in the nineteenth century eloquently defended liberty, the free market of ideas, and the rights of minorities against any tyranny of the majority.

Twentieth-century thinkers, including John Dewey, Sidney Hook, and Karl Popper, continued democratic philosophy's development. John Dewey presented a new defense of liberal democracy. He argued that the "method of pooled intelligence" was the best way of solving social problems and achieving necessary reforms. This presupposed the primary importance of education, as the best guarantee of democratic freedom and an informed citizenry capable of making wise judgments. Humanist philosopher Sidney Hook argued that the democratic philosophy presupposed certain ethical principles: the centrality of human freedom, which a democratic society should enlarge and enhance; and the principle of equality—each person in society was guaranteed equality before the law and entitled to an equality of concern, the poor person no less than the rich. Hook's defense of democracy is unique. It did not draw upon a metaphysical doctrine of inherent human rights (though it demanded that the rights of citizens be recognized and defended); rather, democracy was to be justified *empirically* by its pragmatic consequences. Democratic societies tended to engender less cruelty, duplicity, and fear than undemocratic ones, and they tended to contribute to more peaceful, freer, and prosperous societies with greater opportunities for cultural enrichment than did nondemocratic authoritarian or totalitarian societies. Hook was indefatigable in his battle against fascism in the 1930s and 1940s and against communist totalitarianism from the 1930s through the 1980s. Karl Popper, in his influential book *The Open Society,* argued that the open pluralistic society was essential for a functioning democracy, in contradistinction to closed totalitarian societies.

Political democracy is a precondition for a just democratic society. In a political democracy, the basic policies of a nation and the actions by key officials of its government to carry them out depend upon the freely given consent of a majority of the population of adult citizens voting in free elections. Representative democracy presupposes (a) the legal right of opposition; (b) civil liberties; (c) the right to petition the government for redress of grievances; (d) widespread participation of citizens at all levels of decision making; (e) the rule of law (a just legal system with open trials); and (f) a strong civil society.

For democracy to function fully, *not* merely formally but in actuality, it is essential that at least four other basic preconditions be fulfilled:

First, *economic democracy*: (a) a large middle-class with rising expectations of improved living standards; (b) some measure of equality of opportunity for the sons and daughters of the disadvantaged—their ability to rise to the top, creating a meritocracy, not a plutocracy based on wealth or conditions of birth; (c) some fairness in the distribution of income for the fruits of one's labor; and (d) the ability of ordinary people to accumulate savings and own property.

Second, *social democracy*: (a) nondiscrimination based on class, race, religion, ethnic origin, gender, sexual orientation, or age; (b) the nonexclusion of anyone from public facilities and amenities; (c) educational opportunity for all children and adults and broad access to cultural enrichment in the arts and sciences; (d) the right to leisure, rest, and relaxation; and (e) a peaceful and harmonious society without excessive fear, intimidation, or coercion.

The American experiment in democracy was unique in adding two further preconditions: third, that there would be *no establishment of religion*, entailing the free exercise of religion and the separation of church and state. Freedom of conscience was thus guaranteed by the First Amendment. Fourth, especially in recent decades, has been the recognition of the *right of privacy* of each person to follow his or her own moral values and fulfill goals, as long as these do not prevent others from fulfilling theirs.

These theoretical principles are no doubt familiar to advocates of the democratic philosophy, and the American system has functioned remarkably well as the land of liberty, equality, and opportunity. Wave after wave of new immigrants has "made it in America." Virtually every racial, religious, and ethnic group is represented here, and individuals have been able to pursue their diverse careers and lives in relative freedom. Formerly repressed groups are being gradually emancipated—blacks, women, gays, handicapped people, and other groups—and they are taking their rightful places in American society.

There are many serious threats to this democratic framework that now confront us. Because of a lack of space, I will touch on only four of what I consider to be the especially dangerous trends.

Plutocracy

The first danger is *the growth of plutocracy*, which I define as "government of, for, and by the wealthy class in society." Ours is hardly the first time in American history in which the moneyed classes have held great power: the Founding Fathers were well-established men of wealth and influence; the plantation owners of the South controlled much of its wealth and held inordinate power (they would be defeated only by the Civil War); during the Gilded Age of the late nineteenth century, "robber barons" amassed great wealth and power, unburdened by income or estate taxes; then consider the Roaring 1920s stock-market boom (followed by the 1929 crash) and the Reagan-Clinton go-go years of the 1980s and 1990s. It is this latter phenomenon that should bother us. Between the booms of the 1920s and the 1980s came the New Deal and the Great Society, a time of great strides toward equality. Average workers after World War II improved their economic standing dramatically. These gains now seem to have been curtailed, even reversed, especially since the Reagan years. For more than two decades, we have been deluged by the *libertarian mantra*: that government is evil, that regulations and taxation have stifled the free market, that welfare is abused and needs to be drastically reduced, and that the amassing of wealth is the basic American virtue. A form of *plutomania* has overcome us, as, for example, during the speculative stock-market bubble of the 1990s. Many Americans considered this period of exponential growth to be sanctified by God. I have called the reigning sacred cow "Evangelical Capitalism." Marxism has been virtually defeated, and all too few critics have risen in its place to decry the excesses of capitalist greed or to defend social justice and the principles of fairness.

Our entire political system has been polluted by corruption. Lobbyists run amuck at all levels of government—from the Congress and the White House to state legislatures and county and municipal governments. Pork-barrel perks are doled out to favorites with abandon. A key element of this corruption is the disproportionate influence of campaign contributions upon elections; both major political parties are guilty on this charge, as Ralph Nader and Noam Chomsky have pointed out. The Democrats no less than the Republicans drink deeply at the well of corporate largesse, and both have wealthy men and women in positions of leadership. The Bush dynasty is very wealthy. Senator Kerry (though undoubtedly sympathetic to the poor and disadvantaged) is also wealthy, due to the inherited wealth of his wife. Why are members of the Congress and the state legislatures predominantly businessmen or lawyers? Why do so few teachers, professors, nurses, computer specialists, housewives, scientists, philosophers, artists, and labor union people represent us in our nation's highest legislative bodies? It costs money to run for office, and this prevents ordinary persons from serving.

Undoubtedly, Democrats are more amenable to social-welfare policies than are Republicans. Yet both parties bear responsibility for the present crisis, in which 45 million Americans lack health insurance; retirement coverage has been cut; an adequate minimum wage has not been enacted; American workers work an estimated 350 more hours per year than their European counterparts (this is being amended somewhat by German and French firms that are attempting to increase the workweek), and they enjoy less vacation time; and the United States has the highest ratio of two-income households including women with children who need to work (64 percent). All too few *radical reforms* are enacted by our legislative system, because the plutocrats control it and they assiduously protect their interests—with all too few notable exceptions. In one sense, the heated debates between candidates serve as a cover, for the basic interests of those who control the country are very rarely in contention.

Kevin Phillips, in his remarkable book *Wealth and Democracy*,[2] points out that the United States now has the highest degree of inequality of income and wealth of any of the major affluent democracies. An entrenched plutocratic class has emerged, and its power is growing. Phillips presents statistics showing that "between 1979 and 1989 the portion of wealth held by the top 1% nearly doubled, skyrocketing from 22% to 39%" (p. 92). At the same time, average Americans were falling behind, even during the Clinton years. He shows that in 1999 "the average real aftertax income of the middle 60% of the population was lower than in 1977" (p. 111). Even during the Clinton years, these disparities continued. The stock-market boom of the 1990s perhaps inflated these figures. But, ever since the presidency of George W. Bush began, these trends have accelerated, and the gap in wealth continues to widen.

One can scan the *Forbes* 400 every year to see who the billionaires are; new billionaires enter the list each year as emerging industries shoulder aside the real estate, oil, and heavy-industry fortunes of the past. Phillips shows that the plutocratic classes pass on their wealth to their families in the form of trusts (such as the Rockefellers and DuPonts), which provide income for future generations; these fortunes often continue to grow, even into the fourth and fifth generations. He estimates that at least 100,000 families (1/10 of 1 percent of the population) doubled or quadrupled their wealth between 1982 and 1999. But there are also multimillionaires who are part of the top 1 percent. The top 1 percent share of household wealth had grown from 19.9 percent in 1972 to 40.1 percent in 1997. This inequality is greater than in France, England, and other class-ridden societies.

Indeed, we are today in danger of developing a *hereditary aristocracy* of absentee landlords and shareholders. This trend will dramatically solidify if the taxation-reduction policies of the George W. Bush administration are not repealed. I am referring here to (a) estate taxes ("death taxes," as falsely labeled by the Republicans), which are being reduced annually and will disappear entirely in a few years (if this is allowed to stand, huge fortunes will compound untouched), and (b) the rollback of higher tax brackets for the wealthy, including the reduction of capital gains and dividend tax rates (the current rate is 15 percent).

Bush's latter tax-reduction plan, supported by a significant number of Democrats and virtually all Republicans, was enacted in order to bolster the faltering stock market and to increase the "wealth factor." Three caveats are in order. First, the bulk of these tax perks went to the wealthy. Second, why is unearned income taxed at a lower rate than income earned by labor or services? The entire socialist critique of capitalism—now largely discredited—was based on the "labor theory of value." It held that laboring workers (industrial, technological, or service) are unable to buy the goods and services they produce with their wages. Social-democratic critics today maintain that is unfair to tax profits, dividends, and capital gains (often based on purely speculative growth) at a lower rate than money earned by labor, particularly for those who inherit their wealth, by paying reduced taxes on dividends and capital gains even into the second, third, or fourth generations. Third, the gradual undermining of the principle of progressive taxation is thus deplored on *moral* grounds.

A functioning democracy presupposes a strong middle class. Unfortunately, we are today dismayed by the exportation of jobs overseas (outsourcing) and the increased "Wal-Marting" of the workforce in America, with lower-paying jobs and benefits doled out at home.

Mega-Corporations

This brings to the fore a second danger to the democratic state: the emergence of corporations as dominant players in the marketplace. This economic reality has been well over a century and a half in the making. Two implications flow from it. First, it degrades the classical Adam Smith model of a free market, which presupposed small firms and independent entrepreneurs, consumers, and working people. Smith's focus on supply and demand presumed a free market undistorted by powerful and entrenched interests. Yet, in many industries today, just two or three major corporations (oligopolies) dominate production and distribution. And these companies are almost always incestuously intertwined with politicians, legislatures, and the courts. In response to corporations' vast scope, industrial unions attempted to counter their power in the earlier part of the twentieth century by bargaining collectively. The labor movement has since declined in the percentage of the labor force it represents, and many of its members today work in government rather than the private sector. In earlier days, the role of government was to act as a countervailing force between labor and management; today, government is more like a handmaiden of business interests.

Thus, the regulative role for government has been drastically curtailed. In part, its power has been blunted because powerful corporations eager to reduce costs can simply threaten to move out of a community or country if government fails to do its bidding. The same bargaining chip is used by management against labor to reduce workers' benefits and hold the line on wage increases. The key new factor is that corporations have become global; the largest of them are larger in financial power and political clout than most national governments. These are transnational *mega-corporations*, such as General Electric, General Motors, Daimler-Benz, Sony, Exxon-Mobil, Lever Bros., and Citicorp. In the United States, municipalities and states compete with each other in order to have companies stay in their area or to relocate from another region or state. All sorts of incentives are offered—lower real estate, utility, or tax rates, investment in the infrastructure for the company by local and state governments, and other inducements. Corporations, not governments, hold the upper hand.

For many conservative thinkers, as Calvin Coolidge said, the business of government is *business*, and business takes precedence over all other considerations, such as preserving the environment, reducing global warming, strengthening the healthcare system, building viable transit systems, or providing affordable housing in the inner cities. Democratic legislatures can enact whatever they want, but not if it means that corporate employers will depart for lower-tax havens. In the last analysis, all too often, economic forces trump political considerations.

To see one result of this trend, consider what has happened to U.S. corporate tax rates in the past two decades. From 1996 to 2000, 63 percent of U.S. corporations paid no taxes at all, while 94 percent paid taxes equal to less than 5 percent of their net income. Moreover, the CEOs of corporations paid themselves huge salaries plus bonuses and stock options, even if their corporations had no increase in profits; this at a time when millions of jobs were lost through outsourcing and wages increased slowly if at all.

What is the upshot of my argument? Neither classical democratic theory nor the economic theory of the marketplace are able to accommodate huge transnational mega-corporations and conglomerates that have amassed inordinate power and are able to compete with the power of the state; these make decisions that governments, executives, or legislatures are unable to control or circumvent. Is America already in a post-democratic stage of development, in the sense that political leaders and the public at large are impotent in controlling corporate power?

Theodore Roosevelt introduced legislation to break up huge trusts and monopolies at the beginning of the twentieth century; later presidents, including Woodrow Wilson and Franklin Delano Roosevelt, struggled to restrain corporate power. Today, it is difficult to regulate the activities of mega-corporations, though the European Community attempts to do so, as do, fitfully, the castrated Federal Communications Commission and the Federal Trade Commission within the United States. Transnational in scope, many of today's mega-corporations have no single national homeland; they are beyond the power of any one country to restrain. The mega-corporate sector is in significant ways beyond the power of states to control, and this constitutes a major problem for national democratic governments.

I wish to conclude this section with one further observation, and that is the warning of President Dwight Eisenhower that Americans should be cautious of the growth of the military-industrial complex and its great influence on public policy. I wish to reiterate this warning and add *technology* to the description of the complex. America's overwhelming power in the world is made possible because of its military-industrial-technological capacities: American foreign policy is intimately related to its economic power and its global military capability. This enormous power has led to American triumphalism and the trappings of empire. We are afforded great opportunities to spread our democratic ideals world-wide, but there are also great dangers inherent in the military adventures that we embark upon—not the least is the fact that we are now extended worldwide beyond our means.

Media-ocracy

This brings us to a third threat, which some consider to be virtually a "clear and present danger" today. The *central* principle upon which liberal democratic society rests is arguably its dependence on a *free market of ideas*. John Stuart Mill argued that a democratic society encourages the free exchange of ideas. John Dewey held that the method of pooled intelligence enables the public to make reflective judgments. Popper extolled the open society.

This concept had some meaning at a time when individual citizens could speak out on a soapbox at Hyde Park or Union Square or distribute pamphlets and leaflets on street corners, when many voices could be heard in the town hall, and every major city published several newspapers.

Today, the public square has been inundated by mass communications media, which all too often drown out dissenting viewpoints. Secularists and humanists opposed totalitarian societies, because the ministries of propaganda spewed forth the official party line and squelched opposing viewpoints. We are surely not at that point yet, but a kind of iron curtain is closing American society; a quasi-official propaganda line is too often the only one heard. For example: it is widely held that capital punishment is the only way to deal with murderers; that violence is the most effective response to evil; that long prison sentences are necessary for drug dealers and heavy users; that government is wasteful; that the free market is the only way to get anything done; that we need to privatize everything and judge all services by the bottom line; that we should consider those who possess great wealth to be role models (e.g., Donald Trump); and that self-righteous chauvinistic nationalistic patriotism, which venerates God, country, and the flag, is the only posture to assume, *ad nauseam*!

In the media, too, we see again the influence of mega-corporate domination. Today, there are fewer and fewer large players: General Electric (NBC, CNBC, MSNBC); Time Warner (CNN); News Corp (Rupert Murdoch's Fox network); Disney (ABC); and Viacom (CBS). Mega-corporations dominate television and radio, and they own most of the cable networks and movie production studios.

But mega-corporations also gobble up the print media and book and magazine publishers. I am familiar with book publishing, where I have seen independent publishers, in the thirty-five years since I founded Prometheus Books, undergo acquisition by mega-corporations. Similarly for book chains, distributors, and wholesalers. Five companies now control 75 percent of the U.S. book market. Two of these companies are transnational: Bertelsmann, a German mega-corporation, publishes 30 percent of the trade books in the United States; Pearson, a British company, dominates 30 percent of the American textbook market. In the United States, increasingly, chains own newspapers and magazines. In France, only two corporations, Groupe Industriel Marcel Dassaut and Lagardère, own 70 percent of the French press.

This phenomenon is true in other capitalist countries: for example, in Italy, Silvio Berlusconi, head of state and megacorporate tycoon, dominates the television mass media. Media moguls in Germany, France, the United Kingdom, and other countries do the same, though in these countries the consolidation of corporate broadcasting is somewhat mitigated by the presence of alternative public television and radio networks—the United States still lacks a truly effective public broadcast system, despite the efforts of PBS and NPR.

The principal danger in this is a worrisome shift in the focus of programming. Media mega-corporations are interested first and foremost in profits; hence, they produce media programs in terms of their marketability. The criterion is what will sell, not what is true. Entertainment outmatches information and education. Inevitably, diversity in ideas and values dries up, and the parameters of the open, free, and democratic society are constrained. I am not overlooking the role of the Internet, which we all use. Once the Net was hailed as an anarchic domain of free expression; I suspect that a limited number of main players will come to dominate this medium as well. Granted that there is a modest split between the owners of Fox and NBC on the one side and ABC, CBS, and Time Warner on the other. But even here all such media conglomerates very rarely criticize their own power.

In my view, we need to apply the Sherman antitrust laws to media conglomerates, bring back the Fairness Doctrine (killed off during the Reagan years), and establish at least one other independent public radio and television network to stand alongside PBS and NPR and ensure a broadcast outlet for genuine dissent.

Theocracy

The fourth major danger to our democratic republic is the frightening possibility that the United States is becoming a theocracy, or at the very least a quasi-theocracy. Major assaults are being made on the First Amendment; and the fairly widespread public support that the principle of the separation of church and state enjoyed only two decades ago is now being rapidly eroded.

Major assaults have been advanced by the Religious Right. Should this powerful force further consolidate its alliance with religious conservatives, we are in for a fundamental challenge to our view that the United States is a secular democracy, that it should be neutral about religion, and that it should not favor religion over nonreligion. The First Amendment states that "Congress shall make no law respecting an establishment of religion, or prohibiting the free exercise thereof." This is being reinterpreted by Supreme Court Justices William Rehnquist, Antonin Scalia, and Clarence Thomas to mean that Congress shall not favor—or establish—any one sect or denomination of religion over any other; but this does not mean, they say, that the government cannot favor religion over nonreligion. There seems to be strong public support for civic monotheism (even among many liberals)—that is, for those religions that emanate from the Book of Abraham (Christianity, Judaism, and Islam)—at the very least, some form of ceremonial deism is being established. Inasmuch as there are millions of Hindus, Buddhists, Sikhs, atheists, agnostics, and secular humanists in the United States, it is difficult to see what legal argument any future conservative Court may introduce to deny them equal protection under the First Amendment. But there are determined forces that make no bones about their desire to do so. The effort by the Bush administration to support faith-based charities, vouchers, and provide public monies for religious organizations is an ongoing battle. This of course draws on the free-exercise clause of the First Amendment. The continued effort to appoint religious conservatives to the courts in the future will solidify these trends. Positively, Democrats in the Congress have opposed these efforts, though regrettably most Democratic politicians have expressed their piety in public (including Mr. Kerry) and almost none has been willing to admit any nonreligious identity.

The assault on the First Amendment by the right wing has not been taken sufficiently seriously in my judgment by the humanist movement in the United States. When the label "secular humanism" entered popular parlance in the late 1970s and early 1980s, the Religious Right maintained that "secular humanism is a religion," and as such, they maintained it must be extirpated from the public schools and universities, the courts, and all other governmentally supported institutions. The legal argument for this is rather convoluted. If secular humanism is a religion, they say, it violates the establishment clause of the First Amendment. The Council for Secular Humanism has denied that secular humanism is a religion, though other humanist organizations maintain that humanism, as they practice it, is religious in character.

This challenge took two forms in the early 1980s. First, in Mobile, Alabama, Federal District Court Judge Brevard Hand banned forty-five books from the public schools (by authors ranging from John Dewey and Abraham H. Maslow to Richard Hofstader), claiming that they espoused "the religion of secular humanism." I was asked by the American Civil Liberties Union and People for the American Way to represent the view that secular humanism was not a religion. I maintained that Judge Hand's ruling smacked of a New Inquisition. Fortunately, it was overturned in the Appeals Court. It was never taken to the Supreme Court. If this challenge were re-introduced today, it is doubtful that it could be turned back again.

A second series of legal challenges sought to have "creation science" taught in the public schools alongside evolutionary theory, which the Religious Right again represented as a tenet of "the religion of secular humanism." None of these challenges was successful; and by the 1990s most liberals and humanists thought that these legal arguments had been defeated—at least until the year 2000.

For concurrent with the election of George W. Bush, similar outcries were again being heard. These challenges were ignited by Tim LaHaye (author of the *Left Behind* series of novels, the most popular ever published) and David Noebel, head of Summit Ministries. The gauntlet was laid down in their book *Mind Siege* (World Publishing, 2000). This book even hit the *New York Times* best-seller list. In it, the same litany of charges is recycled; namely, that secular humanism is a religion and that millions of evangelical foot soldiers need to root it out from all walks of life, including the public schools, but especially the colleges and universities. A campaign is now underway in tens of thousands of churches. Hundreds of thousands of books have been distributed free on college and university campuses to help to rout secular humanism.

Should this challenge be taken seriously, or should it be dismissed as nonsense? Regrettably, Tim LaHaye and his cohorts have had strong influence on the Bush administration; *New York Times* columnists Paul Krugman and Nicholas Kristof, CBS's *60 Minutes*, and others have pointed out their powerful influence in the corridors of power. Will the Religious Right continue to intimidate those in power and force everyone to invoke the deity, no matter which political party they represent?

The ferocious creationist challenge has resurfaced again, but this time clad in sheep's clothing, repackaged as "intelligent design," with new allies. Evolution is being challenged in state after state to provide equal time for "intelligent design." Since Bush will no doubt appoint more conservative judges, these challenges most likely will be waged in the courts anew. Given the shift in the public square in favor of pious religiosity, we have no guarantee that the Religious Right will not prevail. Even if Mr. Bush fails in his bid for a second term, I am afraid that this battle will not go away and that the challenge to defend secularism—even the integrity of freedom of inquiry and science—will be ongoing. Remember, Michael Newdow's challenge to "under God" in the pledge of allegiance could find no friends in the United States Congress. The public square is no longer "naked," but seethes with religiosity and piety—what a shift in the attitudes of public officials, none of whom dare to defend the right of dissent.

It is time to draw some conclusions from my analysis. I submit that American democracy is endangered because of (1) the growth of an entrenched *plutocracy* with enormous wealth and power; (2) the emergence of global *mega-corporations* allied with the military-industrial-technological complex; (3) the virtual domination of the media of communication by media mega-corporations (a *media-ocracy*); and (4) the danger that we are becoming a *quasi-theocracy*: one nation *under God* while unbelief is considered un-American.

We need to ask: are we already in a *post-democratic* stage? Is it still possible to stem this tide and restore American democracy? In my *opti-*

mistic mood, my response in the short and mid-run is "Yes, we can," but we face enormous political battles. In the long run, we need to embark upon a New Enlightenment, defending reason, science, free inquiry, and nonreligious ethical alternatives—if there is still time to do so.

In my *pessimistic* mood, I recognize yet another source of danger to democratic institutions. It is virtually impossible for any one nation-state (democratic or nondemocratic) to solve its economic, cultural, social, and environmental problems alone. Neither France nor Germany, China nor Brazil, Britain nor the United States is capable of dealing with these problems in isolation from their impact on others in the world. For the problems we face are planetary in scope. The Europeans have discovered this truth, and they are working hard to strengthen new European institutions—a European Parliament and a new Constitution—and of course the World Court.

Only the present leadership of America stands in haughty isolation, refusing to acknowledge the legitimacy of the World Court or to abide by treaties; only the United States has abandoned the principle of collective security and the United Nations; only the United States assumes for itself the role of policeman to the world. Possessing a preponderance of weapons of mass destruction, it seeks to impose its will on others. Incredibly, among the major powers only the United States is fixated on a premodern theological worldview. Whether a future Democratic administration could change this trend is at this point questionable—unless there is a genuine realignment of the centers of power in the United States.

These developments provide a great challenge for liberal humanists to lead the way—in recognizing and working for a *global democratic world*. American foreign policy had been a beacon in the past—Presidents Wilson, Roosevelt, Eisenhower, Kennedy, Johnson, Nixon, Carter, and others worked for democracy and human rights on a planetary scale. And this battle seems to augur a great opening for planetary humanism. We need to intensify our efforts in favor of new, transnational democratic institutions: a democratic World Parliament, the World Court, collective security, an environmental monitoring agency, a world income tax to stimulate development in the underdeveloped portions of the globe. In particular, we must establish some global institutions with the capacity to regulate the activities of mega-corporations.

The key ethical principle enunciated in *Humanist Manifesto 2000* is that *every person on the planet should be considered to have equal dignity and value*. Thus we should do what we can to defend and extend democracy to every country and region of the world, on a decentralized basis. But we also need uniquely to build new, viable democratic institutions on the planetary level. In my view, this is the daring new frontier for democracy in the twenty-first century.

Thus, the battleground is not simply to restore democracy in the United States, but more importantly to expand democratic institutions on the global scale. If this noble goal is to be achieved, we need to overcome intolerant xenophobic, racist, ethnic, nationalistic, and religious prejudices. We need to vigorously criticize religious fundamentalism on all sides with courage and determination. We need to define and defend planetary ethics, to strive to build a new democratic humanistic civilization based on shared human rights and values. This battle both at home and on the planetary scale is awesome, but we have no viable option but to strive to bring it about.

Notes

1. This article first appeared in *Free Inquiry* 25, no. 1 (December 2004/January 2005), pp. 19–25.

2. Kevin Phillips, *Wealth and Democracy: A Political History of the American Rich*, Broadway Books (an imprint of Random House), New York, N.Y.: 2002.

XVII

The New American Plutocracy[1]

I am deeply troubled by the fact that during the presidential and congressional elections there is little or no debate on what I consider to be a *central* issue for the American future: the emergence of a new and powerful plutocracy wedded to corporate power. Regrettably, none of the major candidates will deign to even discuss this vital question. Only Ralph Nader has identified it. But he has largely been ignored or parodied by the mass media. Typically, Paul Krugman, op-ed columnist for the *New York Times*, has ridiculed Nader precisely for his attacks on "corporate power." Senator John McCain did raise the issue of the special interests and soft money corrupting the political process. But he has been rebuffed and has climbed into the same bed with Bush. Many do not consider Nader to be a viable candidate, for the Green Party does not represent an effective political coalition. Neither *Free Inquiry* nor the Council for Secular Humanism can endorse political candidates, but this should not preclude me from presenting my own *personal views* about the deeper humanist issues at stake.

A plutocracy is defined as "government by the wealthy." The critical question that should concern us is whether the United States is already a plutocracy, and what can be done to limit its power. This question, unfortunately, will not be taken seriously by most voters—but it damned well ought to be.

Ancient Greek democracy lasted only a century; the Roman republic survived for four, though it was increasingly weakened as time went on. As America enters its third century we may well ask whether our democratic institutions will survive and if so in what form.

As readers of these pages know, I have been concerned by the virtually unchallenged growth of corporate power. Mergers and acquisitions continue at a dizzying pace, as small and mid-sized businesses and farms

155

disappear; independent doctors, lawyers, and accountants are gobbled up by larger firms; and working men and women are at the mercy of huge global conglomerates, which downsize as they export jobs overseas.

I have also deplored the emergence of the global *media-ocracy*, whereby a handful of powerful media conglomerates virtually dominate the means of communication. A functioning democratic society depends upon a free exchange of ideas; today fewer dissenting views are heard in the public square, as diversity is narrowed or muffled.

The Tribune Company, publisher of the *Chicago Tribune* and other newspapers and radio and television companies, bought the Times-Mirror, publisher of the *Los Angeles Times*, etc.; the Gannett chain purchased Central Newspapers, publishers of the *Indianapolis Star*, the *Arizona Republic*, and other newspapers. News Corporation (Rupert Murdoch) has announced its intention to take over Chris-Craft's extensive television holdings. And Viacom has offered to buy out the remaining stock it doesn't own in the giant radio network, Infinity Broadcasting. Although Clinton's Justice Department has been attempting to stem the merger juggernaut by questioning a limited number of acquisitions, this may be viewed as mere window dressing, as too little and too late.

This trend toward the concentration of ownership should be of special concern to secular humanists and rationalists. The regnant corporate outlook increasingly espouses a spiritual/religious/supernatural mystique, and it seeks to marginalize iconoclastic viewpoints. Unfortunately for secular humanists, *pro ecclesia et commercia* (for church and commerce) has become the ideology not only of the Religious Right, but is being marketed daily to consumers in the mainstream.

Corporate Control

Corporate domination of the democratic process by means of campaign contributions blocks the emergence of independent voices willing to defend the public interest. Lobbyists subvert the integrity of the Congress and of state legislatures throughout the land by buying influences and votes. Big oil, media, pharmaceutical, tobacco, gambling, insurance, and financial companies thus dominate the legislative process. For example, the banks and credit card companies charge usurious rates and use deceptive marketing practices, fleecing millions of unwary consumers and forcing them into bankruptcy, yet effective legislation to protect consumers was blocked in Congress by the banking industry. Surreptitiously, large companies are now reducing retirement benefits with nary any political opposition. Corporations today—such as General Electric and Exxon-Mobil—are earning huge profits.

Some may say that my appraisal is too pessimistic, for stock ownership is widely distributed, and that corporate efficiency contributes to the current American prosperity. Granted, we do not wish to undermine our economic prosperity, but much of this is also due to new scientific and technological discoveries and to an educated labor force, not simply corporate oligopolies.

We need to ask the questions: should corporations be the primary arbiters of the public will, and should "market forces" alone determine the conditions of social justice? Unfortunately, a relatively small number of corporate managers and stockholders of the new plutocracy control the corporate state, and it is the incestuous relationship between corporate economic power and politics that is most disturbing. For example, Dick Cheney departed from Halliburton, the large oil exploratory company, according to the *New York Times*, with a $20 million package of stock options and other benefits. Today a corporate-military plutocracy rules virtually unchallenged, manipulating and manufacturing the news and safeguarding its position of power.

The War on Estate Taxes

The attempt by the outgoing Congress to get rid of estate taxes is only the latest brazen effort to advance the interests of the plutocracy. Unfortunately, there is now a strong majority of the Congress for repeal, and this includes many Democrats—although President Clinton has threatened to veto the measure. Those who rail against estate taxes mislabel them "death taxes." But one can make a persuasive ethical case for estate taxes as fair—and I am arguing only the *ethical*, not political issue—for they would provide a more level playing field for the disadvantaged and equalize, however modestly, the widening gap between rich and poor. One can argue that it is in the public interest to reduce estate taxes on small businesses and farms in order to protect them from extinction at the hands of larger corporations, but to exempt the huge fortunes of multimillionaires and billionaires is morally unconscionable. Repealing the estate tax would expand the financial wealth of the plutocracy that now rules this country. It would ensure the perpetuation of the existing financial elite with very few limits on its economic and political power. In 1998, the top 1 percent of the population, according to an article in the *Wall Street Journal*, owns 38.1 percent of the wealth of the country; the top 20 percent—87.4 percent; the rest of the population—80 percent—own only 12.6 percent of the wealth! These disparities are growing. In the past twenty years, the after-tax income of the wealthiest 1 percent of the population increased by 119.7 percent, whereas the bottom 60 percent by only 12 percent.

Hypocritically, the Religious Right supports the elimination of estate taxes. Incredibly, it has sought to enshrine Greed by Divine Sanction: "God rewards the thrifty and virtuous," ideologues assert; "those with wealth deserve to keep it"—even if they made their money in specula-tion or by inheritance. The Religious Right opposes gun control, is for capital punishment, and is against legislation to extend medical care to the millions who cannot afford it, or prescriptions for the elderly, yet it supports aid to the affluent.

A century ago Teddy Roosevelt helped enact and enforce the Sherman Anti-Trust Law, and later Woodrow Wilson introduced the progressive income tax. Where are the political leaders today, willing to restrain corporate trusts and the new plutocracy? Who will speak out for the ordinary citizen? Who will defend the humanistic principles of equity and fairness?

Piety in the Public Square

Secular humanists are independent-minded persons who will most likely support a variety of candidates in the upcoming elections. They will in their evaluations of platforms no doubt appeal to humanist values. A vital test will be how well candidates support the separation of church and state and the First Amendment.

The recent political conventions—heavily supported by corporate money—at times looked like religious revival meetings; for most of the major candidates praised the Lord and religious faith repeatedly.

There is a fine line that ought to be drawn between private conscience and public professions of religious belief. Candidates have every right to hold their religious convictions or practice the rituals of their tradi-tions; but is it too much to ask that they restrain proclamations of their personal piety in the public square? Our president and vice president should represent *all* the people, not simply the Judaic-Christian tradition; and this includes Unitarians, Mormons, Buddhists, Hindus, Muslims, Sikhs, Scientologists, minifidians, nullifidians, and just plain backslid-ers. Rationalists, skeptics, atheists, agnostics, and secular humanists are American citizens too!

There is widespread moral diversity in America. To simply assume that faith in the Old or New Testament is the only basis of "morality" is ill-informed. Had the candidates taken an introductory philosophy course at their universities, they would have seen that there is within Western civilization an historic nonreligious and rational humanist basis for morality. Moreover, humanist values are central to American civic virtues—a commitment to human rights, including in the Old or New Testament is the only basis of "morality" is ill informed. Had the candidates taken an introductory philosophy course at their universities, they would have seen that there is within Western civilization an historic nonreligious and rational humanist basis for morality. Moreover, humanist values are central to American civic virtues—a commitment to human rights, including freedom of conscience, autonomy of choice, the right to dissent—none of which is easily found in the ancient religious documents. Indeed, these documents have been used in the past to justify the divine right of kings, aristocracy, and oligarchy.

Our political leaders should be cautious before they seek to judge public policies by their own religious biases. A cherished aspect of American democracy is respect for diversity. We need to resist any attempts by the reigning plutocrats to impose religious conformity as the test of American patriotism.

Note

1.   This article first appeared in *Free Inquiry* 20, no. 4 (fall 2000), pp. 5, 60–61.

XVIII

Can We Bridge the Great Cultural Divide?[1]

Most secular humanists I know were dismayed by the election of George W. Bush to a second term, and doubly so because of the wide margin of his victory (if we assume the official figures are correct), and by the fact that conservative Republicans solidified their control of the Senate and House. Mr. Bush said he had a mandate to fulfill his agenda. Perhaps it is too much to ask, but we would be heartened if the President adopted the role of statesman and moved his administration more toward the center of the political spectrum. The United States is beset by horrendous problems, not least including a growing deficit and the misbegotten, tragic war in Iraq. The president and Congress need all the help they can muster from all Americans. It would be a worthy goal to try and bridge the great divide that separates us.

James Madison, the father of the Constitution, worried that factions might engender conflicts within the new American Republic. One reason why he introduced the Establishment Clause of the First Amendment, which forbade lawmaking respecting an establishment of religion, was to avoid religious factionalism. Surely, we are on the brink of religious factionalism today; yet there is still time to appeal to the good sense of the American people and to turn back the prospect of religious warfare in the public square.

This magazine has never endorsed political candidates nor supported political parties *per se*. We are deeply concerned, however, with defending the core moral principles of American democracy. We are especially apprehensive that the Bush Administration will continue to cater to its base, the evangelical Right. If it does so, then a radical transformation of democratic values and principles is likely to occur, and factional conflicts engendered by religious hostilities may engulf the public square.

The first reaction of many secular humanists to the Bush victory was to want to flee the country. That is surely not a realistic option; instead, we ought to stay and attempt to persuade our fellow citizens of the importance of defending traditional American ideals as we interpret them. We have hardly reached the eve of the last days, as had the Weimar Republic facing Nazism in pre-World War II Germany. Hopefully, there is still time to modify the agenda of the Bush Administration. In any case, we ought not to give up trying to do so.

Which issues divide Americans? There are many, but I will focus on five of the most urgent:

First is the failure of the evangelical Right to recognize that there exist alternative moral conceptions of virtue and value and differing principles of fairness. We deny that all morality must be faith-based; surely throughout history, men and women have sought to ground moral values on rational considerations. This has been recognized in both secular and religious traditions. An appeal to reason enables human beings to modify their value judgments in the light of their consequences and also to more peacefully negotiate differences with others. No one party has a monopoly on righteousness; those who insist that their principles are absolute are apt to feel entitled thereby to tyrannize others.

Second, in the present context of American society, we are concerned about continued assaults on the First Amendment and especially its principle of the separation of church and state. The fact that America has until now withstood efforts to establish a specific religion, whether Christianity or Judeo-Christianity in general, is a credit to the American experiment in democracy. We are also disturbed about the dangers to our civil liberties implicit in the PATRIOT Act and Homeland Security. In our view, the "War on Terrorism" has been used to frighten the public. We do not deny that there are terrorists, but we question excessive paranoia about them. The departure of John Ashcroft is welcome news. Whether his replacement, Judge Alberto Gonzales, will be an improvement remains to be seen.

Third, we are disturbed that the Bush Administration will most likely insist on appointing reactionary, strict-constructionist judges to the federal courts. Such judges may drastically re-interpret the Constitution and trample on the rights of dissenting and nonreligious Americans. Need I reiterate that Hindus and Buddhists, Jews and Sikhs, Muslims and secular humanists, atheists and agnostics are still citizens? Similarly, we fear that the expansion of federal funding for so-called "faith-based charities" will only exacerbate the trend toward establishing monotheism as the generic religion of the country.

Fourth, we deplore the demeaning of the scientific, naturalistic, and secular contributions to American culture with which our nation's history is so rich. These developments are virtually synonymous with modernism. They are responsible in no small way for the democratic movements of our time and for the extension of equal rights, liberties, and educational opportunities to all citizens. Science and technology have played a central role in improving the conditions of life, in enhancing health care and longevity, in decreasing drudgery and pain, and in making possible the bountiful abundance of consumer goods, economic well-being, and leisure for all sectors of society. To seek to restrict scientific research on allegedly moral grounds (as in the ban on stem-cell research) is short-sighted and destructive of what could be enormous benefits for humankind.

Fifth, we are troubled by the unilateral pre-emptive foreign policy of the Bush Administration, though we support the effort to build democracy in the Middle East, as difficult as that may now seem. This means a defense of human rights, civil liberties, and secular, nontheocratic states. It is sheer hypocrisy to support the separation of mosque and state in the Islamic world at the same time that the separation of church and state is being weakened at home. We grieve for the mounting numbers of American men and women killed or wounded in Iraq, but also for the massive loss of innocent civilian lives there. We believe that the United States should participate in helping to build a world community and that it should be a cooperating partner in the United Nations in matters of collective security. The departure of Colin Powell and the reappointments of Condoleezza Rice and Donald Rumsfeld in Bush's second term are not good signs that the needed changes are likely to occur. With the ending of the Cold War, many hoped that a peaceful and prosperous world would result. Instead, a new and awesome arms race seems to be developing.

A Pivotal Battle over Moral Values

According to exit polls, a significant portion of the voters indicated that their support of President Bush was based on "moral values." When you ask *which* values, there is clearly room for disagreement among Americans, but there is also some common ground—especially our shared belief that America is the land of opportunity and that to realize this entails freedom and equality for all. In talking about morality, the Religious Right has focused primarily on sexual issues, such as abortion and same-sex marriage. The morality of their position is surely arguable. A majority of Americans still believe in reproductive freedom, the right of a woman to control her own body without being forced to carry a pregnancy to its full term. This is justified by an appeal to "freedom of choice," a basic American value. Similarly, same-sex marriages were banned in eleven states, no doubt because they offended moral sensibilities; but this also raises the moral question of the denial of equal rights to some citizens. At one time, interracial marriages too offended the sensibilities of many Americans and were banned in numerous states. Hopefully, a compromise can be reached by recognizing civil unions for same-sex partners (even President Bush at some point said he believed in this), thus guaranteeing them equal rights under the law in matters such as visitation, property, insurance, and the like. The basic principle at stake here is, of course, "the right of privacy," which is a basic American right, and which I submit that the Religious Right, which claims also to believe in individual liberty, ought to respect.

On the scale of moral values, secular humanists emphasize "life, liberty, *and the pursuit of happiness*" as basic to the scheme of American values. Indeed, most Americans strive for personal happiness in their own lives. One might think that high-profile preachers who emphasize obedience to God's commandments and eternal salvation would therefore renounce the search for happiness. Yet I do not see Pat Robertson, Tim LaHaye, or Jerry Falwell abandoning pleasures, even luxuries, in their lives. On the contrary, they willingly enjoy the goods of modern life that our consumer economy affords them. I do not see them giving up their fine cars, good homes, jets, fine clothing and jewelry, and the other accoutrements of good living. Nor do most believers in the pews renounce the finer things of life when they can afford them. The tastes for such things seem to me to be thoroughly secular values, which might shock Jesus if he were to return from ancient Palestine, a land of deprivation and sorrow.

Contemporary American culture extols the virtues of the self-made person, the indomitable spirit of the individual entrepreneur, of the adventurer or explorer, of trailblazers like Henry Ford, Andrew Carnegie, Thomas Edison and others. Most Americans seek good jobs and hope to succeed in their careers. This highlights the value of *individual freedom and autonomy and the achievement motive,* all of which express thoroughly secular, humanistic, and libertarian values.

Still other humanistic values are widely cherished, including the encouragement of *creativity* and the attainment of *excellence.* Indeed, our universities and colleges strive to provide opportunities for students to realize their creative potentials. *Self-actualization* is thus a noble goal. Surely, it is not immoral.

May I point out again that there is an historic philosophical and cultural heritage implicit in Western civilization, which encourages morality based on principles of *reflective intelligence, prudence, and reason*, not simply faith. This approach has been appealed to by Aristotle, Aquinas, Spinoza, Kant, Mill, and even Confucius in ancient China. The need for moral inquiry is not sufficiently appreciated by many evangelicals, who likewise face moral dilemmas in life. We often are confronted with difficult choices, not necessarily between good and bad or right and wrong, but between two goods or two rights, both of which we cannot have, or between the lesser of two evils. In such situations, whatever a person's moral grounding, some reflective wisdom is essential in helping us to make wise choices. I wonder if President Bush took an introductory philosophy or ethics course at Yale, and if so, whether he learned something from it? If he had, we all would be better off.

There are any number of complex moral issues about whose solutions morally earnest people can honestly disagree. These concern questions of war and peace, capital punishment, euthanasia, assisted suicide, infanticide, animal rights, the distribution of goods and services in society, and more. On these issues, religious as well as secular persons may end up on either side of any question. For example, Mr. Bush, fundamentalist Baptists, and Muslims favor capital punishment, while the Catholic Bishops of America, liberal Protestants, Jews, individual Catholics, and many secularists are opposed. We see a similar diversity regarding questions about "the moral justification of euthanasia or assisted suicide." Roman Catholics and evangelical Protestants are usually opposed, while many liberal religionists and secularists may support "death with dignity" or the principle of informed consent as stated in a living will.

Economic and political policies engender heated controversies in society, but they also express profound differences in moral values. There are those who support laissez-faire policies, believing that the government should play little or no role in the private sector, while others believe that the government has an obligation to be concerned with social welfare. Those committed to "Evangelical Capitalism" believe that tax policies favoring the wealthy reward those who deserve it, a status that is in some sense divinely decreed. This often simply masks hypocrisy, greed, and corruption. Laissez-faire policies, evangelical capitalists believe, are powerful incentives for economic growth. Others appealing to "principles of fairness" support progressive taxation, a rising minimum wage, and universal health care. They oppose the elimination of estate taxes and preferential treatment for dividends and capital gains.

Many people, religionists and secularists alike, believe in extending moral caring beyond our own society to all members of the global community; others are adamant that our primary concern should be our own country. Secular humanists in particular have advocated the development of a new planetary ethics, in which each and every person on the planet is considered to have *equal dignity and value.*

The Principles of Fairness versus "Gott Mit Uns!"[2]

The cultural divide in America cuts deep, separating two contending conceptions of morality. Those who believe that there is a need for a moral reformation based on the principles of fairness confront "evangelical foot soldiers" convinced that God is on their side (*"Gott mit uns!"*) in an all-out battle between good and evil.

The first form of morality is humanistic and secular. Its chief aim is to realize human happiness in "the city of humankind." It wishes to rely on reflective intelligence in resolving moral dilemmas. It emphasizes tolerance and the negotiation of differences. It holds that men and women are responsible for their own destinies and that they can, with some measure of goodwill, achieve meaningful and enriched lives for themselves and their communities. It advocates the civic virtues of democracy and the extension of universal human rights to all persons on the planet.

The second form of morality is traditional religious morality, which has taken on an extremist evangelical and fundamentalist twist in recent years. It is focused on the "City of God" and the coming, apocalyptic end of civilization as we know it. Rooted in religious faith, allegedly revealed to our forebears who lived in a nomadic and agricultural culture of the past, it declares that humans are "sinful" and that their ultimate duty is to obey the moral Commandments, divinely delivered. Since we are dependent upon God for salvation, human beings in themselves are incapable of achieving moral virtue. There are absolute commandments that a person must believe in and follow. Evangelical doomsday prophets today declare that the end times are approaching. They view the wars in the Middle East as signs of divine deliverance. Those who believe in Jesus as their savior will be saved by the divine Rapture, those who do not will be, as in Tim LaHaye and Jerry Jenkins's best-selling novels, "Left Behind" to suffer terrible punishment. Secular humanists are skeptical of this apocalyptic interpretation of human history and cosmic destiny.

It would be difficult to take this dramatic tale seriously, if not for the fact that it is taken so seriously by tens of millions of well-meaning Americans who hold considerable political and economic power.

Secular humanists turn instead to modern science for their interpretation of the cosmos and the place of the human species within it. Science explains the emergence of the human species as a product of evolution; it seeks to explain the universe in natural, causal terms. Secular humanists' moral outlook is not weighed down by anthropocentric concepts of sin, guilt, redemption, and salvation. It is optimistic about the potentialities for improving the human condition.

Fortunately, many liberal religionists are equally disturbed by fundamentalist doomsday prophecies, and they are sympathetic to the principles and values of humanist morality. Although they are surely influenced by the Old and New Testaments, they tend to interpret Scripture in nonliteral terms. They realize the complexities of decision making and are less doctrinaire in their approach to the moral life. Humanists hold that there are widely shared moral virtues (the common moral decencies and also basic values (the ethical excellences) that both religious and nonreligious people respect. Humanists and liberal believers share a commitment to tolerance and the civic virtues of democracy. They agree that there are universal human rights, though these are not to be found in the Bible. And they are dubious of intransigent religious absolutes. They agree that religious piety by itself is no substitute for using human intelligence, fallible as it may be, to solve moral problems. Both humanists and liberal believers wish to apply modern science for the betterment of the human condition. Unfortunately, their views are often drowned out by loud evangelical-fundamentalist voices.

The dispute between extremist religious moralists (orthodox and fundamentalist) on the one side and secular humanists and liberal religionists on the other takes many forms today. Extremist religious moralists consider America to be "one nation under God" (they equate patriotism with religious faith). Both secular and religious liberals fear theocracies; they cherish the First Amendment and the separation of church and state.

Extremist religious moralists oppose abortion, euthanasia, contraception, and women's rights. They consider homosexuality sinful. They are all too often xenophobic about the rest of the world. They object to any questioning of their absolute certainties, whether from science, reason, humanism, democracy, the United Nations, or the World Court. Secular humanists believe in individual freedom, the right of privacy, and the building of a world community—convictions that, fortunately, most religious liberals share.

Homogamy, Anyone?

One issue caught in today's cultural divide is same-sex marriage. Some conservative religious moralists seek to enact a constitutional amendment that would prohibit it. They insist that marriage must be between one man and one woman, as is divinely sanctified by the Bible; further, they believe that heterosexual marriage is threatened by gay marriage.

This dispute over marriage is rather puzzling, since religious denominations often disagree vehemently about the institution. Conservative Roman Catholics oppose divorce under any circumstances (although not annulments), and they defend the unnatural state of celibacy; liberal Protestants, Jews, and religious humanists will allow divorce under certain conditions and are more receptive to sexual expression generally. Muslims also approve of divorce; in addition, they have sanctioned polygamy. Women are considered inferior to men and devoid of basic human rights in most parts of the Islamic world. Judaic-Christian religions have defended monogamy and are opposed to polygamy or bigamy. Yet the Old Testament condones patriarchy, concubinage, and polygamy: Abraham had many concubines and wives. Rachel bore Jacob no children, so she gave him her slave-girl Bilhah, who bore him sons. Jesus apparently never married and bade his disciples to leave their wives. Paul admonished wives to obey their husbands. So much for traditional biblical morality and its anti-family and anti-woman attitudes!

Secular humanists today would recognize marriages between two individuals, no matter what their gender. Mature adults should be permitted to work out their own living arrangements, and if they choose to join together should enjoy the same rights—economic, political, and social—as persons in religiously sanctified marriages. Liberal Episcopalians, Methodists, Jews, and Catholics empathize with this viewpoint. There is considerable evidence that homosexuality is genetic (for example, homosexual behavior is found in other species). Given this, civil society ought not to discriminate against same-sex preferences. The right of privacy between consenting adults is at stake. Nor should society fear the creation of new or extended marital forms. The reality of modern society is already that the nuclear family represents only a minority of households, and *de facto* there is pluralistic diversity in relationships. Romantic affairs and a high divorce rate are omnipresent among heterosexuals. Partly in response to the AIDS epidemic, large numbers of gays have abandoned promiscuity and have sought stable relationships—in defense of marital bonds, as it were.

Incidentally, I prefer the term *civil union* rather than *marriage* (though I would accept either), for what is at issue is equal protection under the laws for all adult couples: equal rights in property, taxation, inheritance, insurance, retirement, health care, visitation rights, etc. *Homogamy* (same-sex unions) seems to me to best describe the relationship of two individuals of the same sex, similar to *heterogamy* for heterosexuals. I think that a constitutional amendment banning same-sex marriage or civil unions would be an unfair violation of human rights.

Present state laws specifying who may marry are grossly unfair to the nonreligious: secular humanists, atheists, and agnostics. States issue marriage licenses. However, the only officiants allowed to conduct a marriage ceremony are those authorized by religious institutions or governmental officials (a justice of the peace, judge, mayor, etc.). Regulations differ state by state, but in the United States, approximately forty-five states of the union offer no provision for couples to have a binding public marriage ceremony officiated by a private secular organization of their choice, such as a university, fraternal organization, or humanist organization. I have conducted humanist wedding ceremonies for many couples, but these are not legally recognized in New York State. To solemnize their vows in the eyes of the law, the couple must have another wedding with a priest, minister, rabbi, or public official in attendance. This constitutes egregious discrimination. European countries recognize civil ceremonies; why not the United States? Public ceremonies performed by the Council for Secular Humanism (which is an educational organization) are not recognized in most states. The Church of Scientology, Baptists, Jehovah's Witnesses, Mormons, Hindus, and Muslims are recognized, but not secular institutions. Talk about unfairness!

Religious Censorship of Science

A second area of contention today is the dispute regarding biogenetic research. Traditional religious moralists once opposed artificial insemination; yet millions of happy children and parents have benefited from these procedures. Today, they seek to ban cloning research of any kind, therapeutic or reproductive. This is not only shortsighted, but hypocritical. The same conservatives who oppose governmental regulation in the economy now clamor for it in science.

Leon Kass, chairman of the President's Council on Bioethics and a professed devotee of the Old Testament, vigorously opposes embryonic stem-cell research. That there should even be a presidential council in the first place is highly questionable, especially since this body, which is biased, has become the chief exponent of censorship. (Indeed, a dissident liberal member of this body was recently fired.) In an op-ed piece in the *Wall Street Journal* ("Reproduction and Responsibility," April 2004), Kass called for a series of "legislative moratoria" to prohibit various "new reproductive techniques." In particular, Kass wishes to ban any research on embryos older than ten to fourteen days. Presumably, he is reflecting the Roman Catholic doctrine of "ensoulment" that has recently been adopted by fundamentalist Protestants. If and when this legislation is brought to the Congress, it would exacerbate the cultural war; for traditional religious moralists believe this research on embryos is sinful; whereas secular humanists and their liberal religious allies wish to use science to improve the human condition. Such repressive policies could block efforts by biogenetic scientists to eliminate disease, reduce suffering, and extend life. Shades of the censorship of Galileo and Darwin!

Traditional religious moralists have often sought to block scientific progress on the basis of little more than fear of the unknown. In my view, any limits placed on research should come from within the scientific community, not from the protests of extreme religious moralists who are willing to use governmental power to bludgeon scientific inquiry.

The Principles of Fairness

The double standard of traditional religious morality is apparent. I need hardly point out that the Vatican, which opposes same-sex marriage and cloning research as immoral, at the same time confronts a celibate priesthood, a significant minority of whose members have practiced pedophilia.

There are numerous actions and policies condoned by extreme religious moralists that secular humanists find abhorrent, especially those that violate the principles of fairness. I will mention some of them:

1. The demands for censorship of sexual displays are today prominent. Traditional religious moralists rail against Janet Jackson for having bared her breast during the Super Bowl, and they object to the use of vulgar expletives by Howard Stern, but where are their criticisms of the excessive violence in television, radio, movies, and throughout the mass media?
2. Nor do traditional religious moralists criticize the resort to violence by state or federal governments. Capital punishment is opposed by many liberal humanists and religionists on moral grounds. Traditional

religious moralists attempt to justify the death penalty by appeals to the Old Testament's principle of retribution. Susan Jacoby, in her new book, *Freethinkers: A History of American Secularism,*[3] cites Antonin Scalia in a 2002 speech: "Death is no big deal," he said, and then advocated the death penalty on constitutional and divine grounds. Virtually all of the European democracies have prohibited the death penalty. The World Court recently criticized the United States for sentencing fifty-one Mexican citizens to death without allowing them to consult their own embassy; capital punishment is illegal in Mexico.

3.   Many religious traditionalists have defended preemptive wars, a policy deplored by many of America's friends and allies. Extremist religious moralists are all too eager to express self-righteous patriotic, nationalistic, and chauvinistic slogans in support of the use of military force.

4.   Traditional religionists who loathe sexual transgressions have largely ignored greed and avarice. All too often, wealth is considered as synonymous with virtue (consider just two examples, Pat Robertson and John Templeton). Traditionalists carefully ignore the saying attributed to Jesus that it is rare for a rich man to enter into heaven. This corruption has spilled over into the political system, where campaign contributors and lobbyists influence the legislative process, undermining environmental protection and other regulations essential for the common good.

5.   Another point of contention—on moral grounds—is traditionalists' failure to show concern for the welfare of the disadvantaged, the poor, or even the middle class at the same time that the elephantine compensation of corporate executives is extolled. A basic principle of fairness in our democracy is at stake. The CEOs of the two hundred largest companies earned on average $9.2 million in salaries, bonuses, and stock options in 2003. (Of course, some received far more.) Although stock options granted were down from the previous year, cash payments to CEOs increased 14.4 percent, whereas the increase in the average worker's pay was only 2 percent. Moreover, in 2003 there was an increase in unemployment.[4] In addition, the amount of taxes paid by corporations has steadily declined. From 1996 to 2000, 63 percent of U.S. corporations paid no corporate income tax at all, while 94 percent paid taxes equal to less than 5 percent of their net income. Traditionalists accept sharp disparities in income and wealth in America today, are willing to provide lower tax rates for capital gains and dividends as distinct from money earned from labor or work, and refuse to enact an increased minimum wage. All this is typical of their uncaring attitude. All of it fulfills, as I've argued before, the sacred principles of "evangelical capitalism." This is further illustrated by the continued decline of progressive income tax rates, the determined effort to repeal the estate tax entirely, and the amassing of large speculative fortunes in the stock market and real estate. In his disturbing book, *Wealth and Democracy* (New York: Broadway, 2002), Kevin Phillips points out

that the United States is well on its way to becoming an entrenched plutocracy.

Get-rich schemes are in abundance. State-sponsored lotteries, *I Want to Be a Millionaire* game shows, and the building of gambling casinos illustrate the skewing of values. Gambling casinos are going up almost everywhere in the United States, no doubt in the hope that they will improve the local economies. Yet they often appear in depressed communities and attract the poorest sectors of society. The social and psychological costs of gambling, such as dependency, debt, domestic violence, family breakdowns, bankruptcy, and suicide and other deaths, is overlooked in the effort to advertise and promote casinos. I, of course, believe in a free market; however, I also believe that consumers should be warned about the pitfalls of slot machines—it is rare that anyone can make a fast buck, unless he or she stops after a big win.

I am surely not defending any form of Puritan repression but merely pointing out the distorted priorities of the traditional religious moralists. Bill Bennett was the czar of conservative morality in America, attempting to defend the old-time religious morality, yet he lost a fortune in gambling and smoked like a fiend. What is the point? That one person's virtue becomes another's vice.

In defending the principles of fairness or social justice, I am not defending socialism, as one critic has characterized my criticism of evangelical capitalism. The term *socialism* referred to the nationalization of the means of production and/or the domination of the entire economy by the government. I believe in the vitality of the free-market capitalist system. What I am talking about is the application of simple moral principles of equity and fairness.

The two moralities that I've outlined above may be contrasted in the light of Lawrence Kohlberg's stages of moral growth and development.[5] Traditional religious moralists are apt to be authoritarian; they set great store in the traditional sacred cows, condone injustice, extol the wielders of power, and applaud the defenders of wealth and the status quo. In contrast, secular humanists have an altruistic concern for the happiness of all human beings within the planetary community. Liberal religious allies have common cause with secular humanists in the criticism of xenophobic, authoritarian nationalists.

Last but not least, America's growing legions of evangelical foot soldiers are now awaiting the Second Coming of Jesus and the Rapture, or so we are told by the best-selling authors of the *Left Behind* novels.

They are convinced that God will save only their brand of evangelical Protestants (and perhaps those conservative Roman Catholics to the right of Attila the Hun). They will "leave behind" all others who do not accept their form of creedal fascism. Like the earlier defenders of the Aryan race, they insist that God agrees with them, and that all other Christian denominations, Jews, Muslims, Buddhists, Hindus, secular humanists, atheists, agnostics, and freethinkers—the bulk of humankind—will be condemned to hell. Unless you are prepared to believe in our way, say these true believers in our midst, you deserve to go to hell! This means that of the six billion people on the planet, only a relatively small number will enter the kingdom of heaven.

This attitude is similar to that of Islamic terrorists who insist that only those who accept the Koran as revealed by Muhammad will go to heaven—true believers who are prepared to detonate themselves and kill as many people as they can in the name of Allah. A new form of moral intolerance has descended on the world. *Gott mit uns* was a frightening paean to patriotism, intolerance, violence, and hatred sung by fascist storm troopers of another era as they marched off to "redeem" the world.

What will happen to love, compassion, and caring grace, extended to all humans in the community of humankind, no matter what their religious beliefs; what will happen to the common moral decencies and the principles of fairness and equity—if they get their way?

Two Competing Moralities[6]

We are told by the critics of secular humanist morality that, without belief in God, immorality would engulf us. This position is held by many conservative, even centrist, political leaders today. They say that society needs a religious framework to maintain the general order. But they are, I submit, profoundly mistaken.

What they overlook is the fact that humanist ethics is so deeply in-grained in human culture that even religious conservatives accept many (if not all) of its ethical premises—though, like Molière's *Bourgeois Gentilhomme,* who was surprised when he was told that he spoke and wrote in prose, many people will be equally surprised to discover this.

May I point out five aspects of humanist morality that are widely accepted today. Humanist ethics is not some recent invention; it has deep roots in world civilization, and it can be found in the great thinkers, from Aristotle and Confucius to Spinoza, Adam Smith, Mill, and Dewey. What are these philosophers saying?

First, that the pursuit of happiness—*eudaimonia,* as the Greeks called it—is a basic goal of ethical life, both for the individual and society, This point of view came into prominence during the Renaissance; it is expressed in the Declaration of Independence, and indeed in virtually every modern democratic system of ethics. People may dispute about the meaning of happiness, but nonetheless most humanists say that the good life involves satisfying and pleasurable experience, creative actualization, and human realization. We wish a full life in which the fruits of our labor contribute to a meaningful existence. We recognize that religious believers want salvation in the next world, but few today would want unhappiness in this life.

A second principle is the recognition that each person has *equal dignity and value,* and that he or she ought to be considered as an end and not a mere means. This doctrine was implicit in the American and French democratic revolutions; it was used to overthrow slavery and hierarchical societies, and it is appealed to in order to eliminate racial, ethnic, religious, and sexual discrimination.

A third value of humanism is the ideal of *moral freedom.* Humanists defend free societies that allow wide latitude for individuals to express their own needs, desires, interests, goals, and their diverse visions of the good life, however idiosyncratic they may be. Nevertheless, humanist ethics emphasizes the higher intellectual, moral, and æsthetic values, and it focuses on moral growth and development as essential to happiness.

Fourth, this implies that we *tolerate* the diversity of values and principles in different individuals and groups in society. We need not necessarily accept different lifestyles; we simply allow them to co-exist. Moral freedom does not necessarily mean license or corruption; it does not mean a libertine style of life; for there is concern not only with freedom, but also with *virtue.* It does not condone the fleshpot, the shallow or egotistical individual; for even while humanist morality maintains that individuals should be allowed to pursue their own ends without repression, it asks that they learn to behave *responsibly,* that they cultivate the common moral decencies, and that their behavior be considerate of the needs of others. That means that they will develop an appreciation for the basic shared moral virtues of a civilized community—truth, sincerity, integrity, fairness, empathy, etc. This presupposes the development of moral character in the young; for self-control and an altruistic regard for others are essential for the full flowering of the individual.

Fifth, humanist ethics focuses on *human reason* as the basis of ethical choice. This is insufficiently understood by dogmatic religionists who fail to appreciate the fact that there are often difficult choices to be made in life; though we may share principles and values, we need to recognize that society is undergoing rapid change and that new moral problems may emerge. Often we must choose between the lesser of two evils or the greater of two goods, not between good and evil. Thus there are the classical moral dilemmas that all individuals in society encounter, in which competing values and principles contend. Humanists maintain that in such situations ethical inquiry ought to be emphasized, and that a reflective moral intelligence—aware of one's own interests and values and also of the needs and interests of others—should seek to negotiate differences and work out compromises. Humanists believe that science and technology, if used wisely, can help us to improve human life and contribute to the common welfare. Thus, in our view, ethical rationality is essential for moral growth and development.

In any case, humanist values and principles underlie three powerful social movements that have emerged in modern society, especially since the Renaissance. Let me enunciate them.

1. *Secularization:* The institutions of modern society have sought to liberate morality from repressive theocratic creeds. This entails a separation of church and state as a precondition of freedom from authoritarian or totalitarian control.

2. *Democracy:* This is a further precondition for humanist morality to flourish; for it is in a free, open, and democratic society that individuals are allowed to make their own decisions and universal human rights are defended, both on the social and the planetary scale. Democracy entails an open market of ideas, rule by majorities, and the right of dissent.

3. *Consumerism:* Modern economic systems are predicated on the assumption that individual consumers should have the freedom to produce, purchase, and consume goods and services of their own choice. This has led to an enormous improvement of the human condition, the extension of the fruits of industry and of happiness to all citizens.

Yet many religionists today decry humanist ethics and they proclaim absolute declarations and creeds. In the past, they often opposed democracy and moral freedom, tolerance, and respect for diversity. Many emphasize still today the virtue of obedience rather than of individual autonomy. Humanists respond that belief in God is no guarantee of moral virtue. Indeed, devoted believers will often kill each other over differences in doctrine or authority, and they oppose each other on issues concerning public morality: some are for and some against capital punishment, war or peace, the rights of women, minorities, euthanasia, sexual freedom, etc. Dogmatic religious doctrines especially set people against each other, leading to hypocrisy, greed, policies of retribution and punishment, chauvinism, and pride, rather than an empathetic moral regard for the needs of others. Thus there is a genuine humanist alternative to such doctrinaire points of view, which needs to be appreciated.

I submit that humanist ethical ideals, which emphasize the pursuit of happiness, moral freedom, tolerance, moral responsibility, and rational moral inquiry, are basic for social peace and ethical improvement, and that both religious and nonreligious people can share these values. To castigate humanist ethics would endanger the hard-won gains to achieve a secular state, a democratic society, and a prosperous economy serving all the citizens of society. Shall we risk the advances of social, political, and economic progress in the name of an authoritarian creed? To reject humanist morality would do precisely that: It would repeal the modern world.

The Free Market with a *Human* Face[7]

It is an astonishing phenomenon: the predominant influence on America today is a militant minority committed to what might be called "Evangelical Capitalism." Evangelical Capitalists say they are devoted to individual liberty first and foremost. By this they mean economic liberty, which they apparently view as divinely inspired—"the hand of God," as it were—at work in human institutions. This is translated concretely into their demands for business deregulation, lower taxes, and free trade come hell or high water.

Evangelical Capitalists are not talking simply about the *laissez-faire* doctrines of Adam Smith, the freedom of individual entrepreneurs to engage in commerce. They seek unfettered freedom for huge corporations that already dominate national and global markets. They oppose any governmental interference with corporate actions, for the business of government is *business*, not welfare, or education, or public health. Evangelical Capitalists' devotion to economic liberty is so extreme that it seemingly precludes any concern for the common good.

Max Weber, founder of modern sociology, observed that the rise of capitalism is related to the emergence of the Protestant ethic, with its emphasis on thrift, saving, and diligent effort; and also with its view that the accumulation of wealth is a dispensation from God rewarded to those most deserving of it. American workers may be the hardest working and most productive in the world, though we are now told by Evangelical Capitalists (contradicting the work ethic and thrift) that they need to "spend and consume" to stimulate the economy! Evangelicals fervently believe that everything should be left to the free market. This will stimulate economic growth; a rising tide will lift all boats.

No doubt there is some truth to this. The free market, released from the dead hand of inefficient governmental (or corporate) bureaucracy, can be a powerful engine of economic growth, as the former proponents of "social planning"—such as China and now Russia—have learned.

But surely the free market is not a panacea for every social ill, nor an infallible instrument for human progress. One cannot test every human need by the profit it generates. Those who wish to *privatize* everything—perhaps even social security—court enormous risk. And they disregard countless unmet social needs: environmental protection; crumbling national rail and metropolitan transit systems; declining inner cities; the demutualization of life insurance companies for the benefit of stockholders but to the detriment of policyholders; the loss of retirement funds by employees working for bankrupt companies; a static minimum wage; and the disgraceful fact that 42 million Americans have no medical health insurance.

The latter item is especially poignant: the United States, the wealthiest nation in the world, does not have a universal system of health coverage. Here a basic humanistic principle is at stake: the conviction that health care is a human right and that each person is entitled to some coverage.

The legislation now enacted and signed by the president to provide prescription aid for the elderly may be long overdue, but it is also another illustration of "too little, too late." Worse, it rewards private health-maintenance organizations, encouraging them to enter this arena, perhaps one day to supplant government-run Medicare. Nor will this bill allow cheaper drugs to be imported from Canada, a sop to the pharmaceutical industry.

Evangelical Capitalists claim that "we cannot afford" universal health insurance or adequate prescription drug coverage for the elderly. Yet government provides massive handouts to corporations, farm subsidies for agricultural conglomerates, and a huge tax cut and the gradual repeal of estate taxes for the wealthy. Lobbyists toil for the special interests: the hogs feed mightily at the pork-barrel trough and keep the feed coming through deal making lubricated by campaign contributions. There is a long line of suitors buying political influence. No wonder corporate profits today in industry after industry are breaking all records.

Interestingly, as the nation's piety increases, its compassionate concern for those most in need tends to decrease. European democracies are much more secular than the United States and equally committed to free-market economics, yet they manage to supplement private enterprise with principles of social justice. America at present cannot and will not pursue social justice—because it is committed to the dogmas of Evangelical Capitalism. We need a free market, *yes*, but with a *human* face—a free market that also recognizes principles of equity and fairness, welfare and justice, and some concern for the common good.

If freedom and the free market are sacrosanct, then why not privatize the armed forces, the Federal Bureau of Investigation, and the Central Intelligence Agency? The heavens forbid. If freedom from government regulation is sacred, then why not truly defend the rights of individual freedom and privacy? Let's start with a woman's right to choose, the right of terminally ill patients to choose euthanasia, the right of any two individuals to cohabit or marry. The Evangelicals wish to regulate the most intimate part of each person's life. Here liberty ends and piety intrudes.

Farewell Fair Play[8]

Something awful seems to be happening to the traditional American sense of fair play and goodwill. The public response in support of the victims of September 11 notwithstanding, in general there seems to be a decline of empathy and altruism. Perhaps I am overreacting, but this deficiency seems to assume many forms.

What immediately comes to mind is our treatment of prisoners. I refer first to the great flap that emerged worldwide over the Bush administration's refusal to place the prisoners of war captured in Afghanistan under the rules of the Geneva Convention. They are "unlawful combatants," we were told; or they are "dangerous and our guards need to be protected"; or, in still another statement, "They do not deserve any better." I've always thought that the Geneva Convention provided commendable rules governing the treatment of prisoners of war, rules that all civilized nations should follow. The prisoners are being treated "humanely," we were told. Surely, we would want our own soldiers, if captured anywhere in the world, to be treated in accord with the Geneva Convention. How can we demand this in the future if we violate these rules today? President Bush relented after much criticism at home and abroad and grudgingly declared that Taliban prisoners would come under the Geneva Convention, but not members of the Al Qaeda. Many critics believe that this concession does not go far enough.

"The Quality of American Mercy Is Not Strained"

This cavalier dismissal of the Geneva Convention has disturbed civil libertarians in the United States and our allies throughout the world. So has the treatment of thousands of Arabs and Muslims in the United States, recently apprehended by the Justice Department and held incommunicado and without bail. They are "terrorists," says the administration; but how do we know unless they are indicted and put on trial and processed through the American system of justice? Will the infamous deed of September 11—which we all abhor—and the fear of future terrorist acts so erode our sense of justice that we will abandon our traditional adherence to democratic due process?

Perhaps there is something deeply amiss, for a similar vindictiveness is often displayed as well in our treatment of American prisoners, incarcerated for a wide range of infractions. The War on Drugs in particular has taken a vast toll on the American sense of balance, and its result seems close to the development of a police-state mentality. Bursting into homes at all hours to jail alleged drug offenders—even for possession or use of marijuana, for example—seems like an extraordinary overreaction. Drug offenders are considered "wicked." Not that I wish to encourage drug use, but shall we abandon our free society to rout out drug use while we permit cigarette smoking and the abuse of alcohol, the two most noxious drugs available? From all reports, brutality in American prisons seems to be intensifying. Has vindictive justice gotten the best of us? I was interested to see William Bennett, the paragon of Christian virtue, railing against sin recently at a convention of American conservatives, defending the harsh tactics of the drug police. Whatever happened to the quality of mercy among those who express the Christian faith?

Another painful sign of the retributive mentality is seen in the fact that we still exact the death penalty; indeed, the United States is the only democracy that does. Our European allies are offended by capital punishment, and many countries now are refusing to honor extradition to the United States if the accused would risk suffering the death penalty. It is highly questionable that capital punishment serves as a deterrent. Surely we need to deal with those who commit heinous crimes. I would myself recommend life imprisonment for such offenders without the right of parole. But should not one of the aims of incarceration be *rehabilitation*, and should not a civilized society exert efforts to educate and reform offenders so that they may be returned to society? Instead we seem to have an exaggerated sense that punishment is good for its own sake and that those who commit crimes deserve retribution.

It seems to me that what is happening in the United States is that we have been overtaken by a religious sense of retributive justice and that this has taken on exaggerated proportions. Surely one of the purposes of punishment and incarceration is to protect society from criminals. Granted, but beyond that do we need to provide cruel and unusual punishment? Whatever happened to compassion?

The Bloated Defense Budget

I am also dismayed that the end of the Cold War has not reduced our military budget. We seem so frightened by enemies, domestic or foreign, that we are willing to spend vast sums on armaments and reduce our expenditure on domestic programs, such as medical insurance for those who lack it. The United States has also reduced foreign aid assistance throughout the world. The ministers of the wealthy Group of Seven nations have recommended that these nations donate 0.7 percent of gross national product for international aid programs for the poorest nations of the world. The United States currently provides the lowest percentage, only 0.1 percent. Secretary of the Treasury Paul H. O'Neill is a strong opponent of this aid, one reason why the United States is now known as "Uncle Scrooge."

President Bush's proposed military build-up would exceed that of the Reagan years. The administration proposes to increase defense spending by $120 billion over the next five years—at a time, incidentally, when it proposes that taxes be reduced and the deficit increased. It is interesting that the United States now spends an estimated 50 percent of all arms expenditures in the world. The Religious Right seems to need demons, real or imaginary, to guard against—formerly they were Bolsheviks, socialists, left-wingers, liberals, secular humanists, child abusers, drug fiends; there are now terrorists in place of the anarchists of earlier epochs. H. L. Mencken wryly observed: "The whole aim of practical politics is to keep the populace alarmed (and hence clamorous to be led to safety) by menacing it with an endless series of hobgoblins, all of them imaginary." How true this is of the American political scene today.

The America that we love has in the past defended democracy and human rights and offered aid to those suffering disasters worldwide. Has this America become a swashbuckling military power, pursuing a unilateral foreign policy insensitive to the views of the world—such as the abrogation of international treaties? Are we no longer the hope of the world, but a nationalistic state pursuing our own self-interests? Today Afghanistan is defeated. Will we follow the president tomorrow by putting out of commission Iran, Iraq, and North Korea? I fear that America will lose its cherished friends and allies throughout the world, and her self-respect, and pursue imperialist policies that may be turned against us in the future by new coalitions of adversaries. Why Not a Palestinian/Jordanian State?

A New Holocaust?

Six million Jews were lost in the Nazi holocaust of World War II. Will the nearly six million Jews now living in Israel suffer a similar fate? This stark reality may very well confront the world one day unless this festering conflict is resolved. Israel has borders that are barely definable and hardly defensible. Apparently the only thing that stands between it and destruction is Israel's strong defense forces, including nuclear weapons and the United States.

In my view, a creative solution of the impasse between Israel and Palestine that should be explored is to have Palestine merge with Jordan and create a greater Palestinian/Jordanian federation, which could provide a viable homeland for the Palestinian people and enable them to achieve the statehood that they so passionately desire. This state would include the 94 percent of the West Bank and the one-third of Jerusalem already offered by former Prime Minister Ehud Barak and rejected by President Yasser Arafat. Since the Gaza Strip is not viable and is filled with a great number of refugees, there could be an exchange of populations and territories. (The Israelis might vacate the settlements on the West Bank, ceding them to the new Palestinian/ Jordanian state, and the Arabs would in turn cede the Gaza Strip to Israel.) The condition would be that Israel's right to exist be recognized by Palestine and other Islamic states.

I should say right off that I am here speaking personally and not on behalf of this magazine, which represents a wide range of differing political viewpoints. May I wax autobiographical: I was in Germany as a GI with the American Army of Liberation during and immediately after World War II and witnessed the freeing of the survivors of Dachau, Buchenwald, and other concentration camps. When many of these displaced persons told me that they intended to go to Israel to establish a Jewish state, I said that I thought that this was a mistake. I was particularly skeptical of the Old Testament story that God had promised Israel to the Jews. How could fewer than one million Jews, I asked, stand against hundreds of millions of Arabs? Thus, I had serious misgivings about Zionism, and I recommended that survivors stay in Europe or immigrate to other countries of the world. These hapless individuals told me that they had nowhere to go and that most countries would not welcome them.

A Jewish state was established by the United Nations in 1948. Arab armies immediately tried to crush it, but without success. Hundreds of thousands of Palestinians who lived in Israel at that time fled, or in some cases were driven out. Hundreds of thousands of other Jews (estimated at up to 850,000) were forced to leave other countries in North Africa and the Middle East, from Morocco to Egypt and Syria, where they had lived in many cases for two millennia or more. Israel managed to survive in spite of repeated invasions by Arab armies. And it was able to reach accords with both Egypt and Jordan, returning large sections of the occupied land. Any effort to sign a peace treaty with Syria or with Arafat and the Palestinians, as we are well aware, has been to no avail.

To my mind the Oslo Peace Process and the Mitchell Plan seem most promising, and the proposals of Prime Minister Barak a reasonable compromise. Israel would return most of the West Bank and part of Jerusalem, which could be the capital of both the State of Israel and a new Palestinian/Jordanian state. But this plan failed because of the Palestinian demand for the right of return to Israel proper. Given the emergence of suicide bombers, this would have made Israel untenable and its destruction inevitable. This is apparently what Hamas and Hezbollah fervently wish. The carved-up and emasculated state that Arafat insisted upon would make Israel unsustainable, always open to attack; nor would it be sufficient for a viable Palestinian state, divided from the Gaza Strip.

The key point is that Israel now exists *de facto*. To give America and Canada back to the Indians or Australia back to the Aborigines would be impracticable. Likewise to insist that Israel allow the right of return of all Palestinians would not be feasible. Israel fears that the Muslims might eventually overwhelm the Israelis and convert the state into an Islamic theocracy.

No doubt there is some basis for justice on all sides of this tragic situation. An end must be put to the bloodshed of senseless attack and retaliation. The Palestinians want statehood. Israelis want a state with defensible borders. In my view the Palestinians deserve a state, but there are underdeveloped lands to the east. Therefore I would suggest that a new Palestinian/Jordanian federation could provide the Palestinians with a viable nation and that forging such an agreement would enable Israel to live peacefully behind secure borders. As part of this solution I would recommend that the United Nations guarantee peace by monitoring the borders during a period of, say, fifty years.

But this would require an end to religious terror and intolerance. Religions, when taken literally, degenerate into fanaticism. When ancient texts—either the Koran or the Bible—are used to justify present political realities, the result is bloodshed and conflict. A necessary condition of peace is almost certainly that both the Palestinian/Jordanian state and Israel be secular and democratic. I would suggest that the world community work with the Israelis, Palestinians, and Jordanians to come up with a new creative proposal—to create a new Palestinian/Jordanian state and an Israeli state that can live in peace with its neighbors.

A brief historical note is perhaps useful: In ancient days "Palestine" referred to the present state of Israel, the West Bank, and large sections of Jordan. The entire region was occupied by the Turks for centuries. After their defeat in the First World War in 1920, Britain was awarded a mandate over the entire region of Palestine and Jordan (then known as Transjordan). In the Balfour Declaration of 1917, Britain declared its intention to establish a Jewish National Home, and it designated the Arab State as Jordan in 1927. Jordan annexed the West Bank in 1950, but this was occupied by Israel after being invaded by Arab armies in the 1967 Six-Day War. Subsequently there were bloody conflicts between the Palestinian refugees and Jordanians. The Palestine Liberation Organization and Arafat were expelled from Jordan, though 60 percent of present Jordanian citizens were originally Palestinian refugees. There have been intermittent efforts to incorporate the West Bank and Jordan. I suggest that this option be explored anew. If this is to be achieved it is important that Chairman Arafat work out a *modus viendi* with King Abdullah of Jordan. To integrate Jordan and the West Bank could make for a genuinely sustainable and durable society coexisting peacefully with Israel.

Should Religion Be a Private or Public Matter?[9]

Several years ago, the then-Reverend Richard John Neuhaus (now a Catholic priest and editor of *First Things*) criticized those who believed that, in a pluralistic society, religious conviction should be a private, not a public, matter. He complained loudly that religion had been excluded from the public square. Well, the good Reverend Neuhaus has had his way; religion is now intruding into public discourse every day and in a big way. Some of this is no doubt due to President George W. Bush's constant references to divine favor and his efforts to bridge the gap separating church from state. The First Amendment to the United States

Constitution was enacted to avoid the kind of religious factionalism that had engulfed other societies in which religion was a matter of public policy. We hope the civic virtues of democracy are now so well ingrained in American values that rational discourse will prevail in questions of law and policy, without the intrusion of extraneous religious considerations. America is a secular democracy, and as such secular considerations should predominate.

We surely believe in freedom of expression; religious believers have as much right as anyone in society to express their views. The problem arises when a person's religious convictions have an impact on public policy—especially when legislators, government officials, or judges allow their private religious beliefs to determine how they set, implement, or interpret law and public policy.

In the recent national debate about the qualifications of John Roberts and Samuel Alito for the U. S. Supreme Court, one might well ask whether their religious convictions should have been open for consideration. Is a justice's faith a public or private matter?

The selection of Justice John Roberts as chief judge proceeded smoothly, even though liberals knew him to be very conservative. The nomination of Samuel Alito—after the vituperative opposition by religious conservatives to Harriet Miers's nomination forced President Bush to withdraw her name—engendered more heated controversy. Democrats were concerned whether Alito's replacing Justice Sandra Day O'Connor would swing the Court too far to the right. In addition, they were concerned whether either nominee or both would oppose abortion and the right of privacy. Roberts and Alito strove to avoid being pinned down concerning issues that they said would likely come before the Court. Justice Roberts suggested, however, that he thought that *stare decisis* (the principle of precedent) applied to *Roe v. Wade*, which he implied was "settled law" and would not be overturned; he seemed to regard the right of privacy in a similar light. We heard few such assurances from Judge Alito. The question for both nominees that perhaps should have been asked—and was not—was whether their Roman Catholic faith might trump their duty to interpret legal issues like these impartially.

John F. Kennedy undoubtedly took the proper position concerning religion during his campaign for the presidency, when he said that his personal religious convictions, if elected, as a Roman Catholic would not be relevant to discharging the duties of his office. Perhaps this was a moot issue for him, in that he did not seem a particularly devout Roman Catholic. Mario Cuomo, the former governor of New York State, reiterated JFK's position by saying that, although he did not himself support abortion, as governor it was incumbent on him to enforce the law, and abortion was legal in his state and in the nation. The question that we need to ask is: If religion is out in the public square, what do you do if you have a *devout* nominee to the Supreme Court? Which is one's higher duty—to interpret the laws and the United States Constitution or to fulfill one's religious obligations to one's church?

A justice of the Supreme Court is pledged to obey and enforce the Constitution of the United States, which derives its powers from "We the People" and has no theological foundation. Every federal justice takes a judicial oath under 28 USC #453 to "faithfully and impartially discharge and perform all of the duties incumbent upon me under the Constitutional laws of the United States," not the dictates of some foreign authority.

When justices are asked to deliberate about laws that come before the Supreme Court but are contrary to their deepest held religious convictions, should they not recuse themselves? There is a statute that governs these cases: 28 USC #455(a) states that "Any justice, judge, or magistrate in the United States shall disqualify himself in any proceedings in which his impartiality might reasonably be questioned."

There are now two Protestants, two Jews, and a majority of five Roman Catholics on the Supreme Court. The Roman Catholics are Justices Scalia, Thomas, Roberts, Alito, and Kennedy—the first four of whom are not only conservative, but by all accounts also devout. Should this be a concern to citizens in the United States?

If religion is a public matter, many have asked this question in the light of the fact that the Vatican is deeply opposed to abortion in any form, for it considers a human being to be a person "from the moment of conception." This view also drives papal opposition to certain methods of contraception, sterilization, the use of pharmaceutical abortifacients, *in vitro* fertilization, sterilization, and stem-cell research. And it is worth noting that, on similar grounds, papal doctrine is very much opposed to euthanasia and assisted suicide.

I raise these issues in the light of Pope John Paul II's *Encyclical Evangelium Vitae* (the Gospel of Life), issued on March 17, 1995, which no doubt poses a number of questions for devout Catholics who hold public office to ponder. The *Evangelium* states, "I confirm that the direct and voluntary killing of an innocent human being is always gravely immoral. … The deliberate decision to deprive an innocent human being of his life is always morally evil and can never be licit.…"

The pope then goes on to state what this means by quoting approvingly from "The Declaration on Euthanasia," issued by the Congregation for the Doctrine of the Faith on May 5, 1980:

> "Nothing and no one can in any way permit the killing of an innocent human being, whether a fetus or embryo, an infant or an adult, an old person or one suffering from incurable disease, or a person who is dying … nor can any authority legitimately recommend or permit such an action." I reiterate that a human being is defined as "a person from the first moment of conception."

Now, this encyclical was issued *ex cathedra*. This means that it is an article of faith that must be taken as obligatory by every Roman Catholic *and,* on the Vatican's view, by every Catholic official of government, and judges are *not* excepted.

According to the *Catholic Encyclopedia, ex cathedra* is "a theological term which signifies authoritative teaching … by the Roman pontiff.… We teach and define that it is a dogma Divinely revealed that the Roman pontiff when he speaks *ex cathedra,* that is … by virtue of his supreme Apostolic authority … is possessed of … infallibility.…" A teaching so proclaimed is "irreformable" and not subject to revision or alteration.

Thus, Church law holds that all Roman Catholics are obligated to obey this divine ruling. It is dogma, binding not only on laypersons but also on Catholic legislators, administrators, authorities, and judges. Speaking of forbidden acts such as abortion and euthanasia, the *Evangelium* clearly declares: "Nor can any authority legitimately recommend or permit such an action."

What will a devout Roman Catholic justice—who is bound by the laws of his church to obey any dictum that a pope has issued *ex cathedra*—do in judging the constitutionality of a law that deals with any subject on which a pope has written infallibly? Will the law in and of itself drive that justice's deliberations, or will it be trumped by the higher authority that the papacy claims to wield over Roman Catholics? No questions like these were raised during the Roberts or Alito confirmation hearings, but I submit that they should have been.

A 2002 Catholic News Service story describes Justice Antonin Scalia's participation in a panel discussion on the death penalty. Asked why he favored capital punishment when the Catholic Church opposes it, Scalia replied, "This doctrine is not one that the Christian church has consistently maintained." Since the pope's teaching against capital punishment in *Evangelium Vitae* was not given *ex cathedra,* Scalia said, he is not obligated as a Catholic to accept it but only to give it serious consideration. "I have given it careful and thoughtful consideration and rejected it," Scalia said. "I do not find the death penalty immoral. I am happy to reach that conclusion because I like my job and I'd rather not resign" (from "Judge Rejects Church View on Death Penalty" by Michele Martin, *National Catholic Reporter*, February 8, 2002). Scalia is correct about capital punishment, since *Evangelium Vitae*'s *ex cathedra* pronouncement concerns the killing of *innocent* human beings, a class from which persons properly found guilty of capital crimes are arguably excluded, but it *does* condemn all abortion *ex cathedra*.

So now the question is, how would Scalia—and other Catholic justices who are equally devout—rule when issues such as abortion and euthanasia, which *are* prohibited *ex cathedra* by the pontiff, come before them? (The Supreme Court has agreed to hear *Gonzales v. Carhart*, a case concerning late-term so-called partial-birth abortions.) Will the Catholic justices obey the law and recuse themselves? Will they resign? Or will they decide based on the law and their reason, even if this means allowing the Constitution of the United States to trump an *ex cathedra* teaching of their church? The reluctance of senators and pundits to pose these questions is understandable. But in today's America, where religious convictions are so openly expressed in the public square, such uncomfortable questions surely need to be asked, and answered.

Violence in America[10]

All too frequently, the daily news brings us accounts of another devastating shooting somewhere in the United States. Last year at Virginia Tech, a disturbed Korean student, Seung-Hui Cho, went berserk, targeting innocent fellow students and faculty seemingly without reason. Similar Ramboesque massacres have occurred at Northern Illinois University, the University of Texas, and shopping malls in several locales. Some will observe that it is all too easy to buy guns; others defend the Second Amendment as a guarantee that citizens can possess firearms. Beyond the issue of access to guns, there is a more upsetting explanation for the violence that surrounds us: such violence may be endemic to American culture. Surely it permeates all aspects of our national life.

Murder and mayhem are constant fare in movies and on television. As a case in point is the film written and directed by the Coen brothers, *No Country for Old Men*, which won the Academy Award for Best Picture of 2007. The award for Best Supporting Actor went to Javier Bardem, who portrays a psychopathic murderer named Anton Chigurh. Now, I must confess that I am a strong fan of movies. I find that cinema as an art form can have a powerful cathartic effect. But I must say that

Pope John Paul II on the Killing of Innocents

Therefore, by the authority which Christ conferred upon Peter and his Successors, and in communion with the Bishops of the Catholic Church, I confirm that the direct and voluntary killing of an innocent human being is always gravely immoral. This doctrine, based upon that unwritten law which man, in the light of reason, finds in his own heart (cf. Rom 2:14–15), is reaffirmed by Sacred Scripture, transmitted by the Tradition of the Church and taught by the ordinary and universal Magisterium.

The deliberate decision to deprive an innocent human being of his life is always morally evil and can never be licit either as an end in itself or as a means to a good end. It is in fact a grave act of disobedience to the moral law, and indeed to God himself, the author and guarantor of that law; it contradicts the fundamental virtues of justice and charity. "Nothing and no one can in any way permit the killing of an innocent human being, whether a fetus or an embryo, an infant or an adult, an old person, or one suffering from an incurable disease, or a person who is dying. Furthermore, no one is permitted to ask for this act of killing, either for himself or herself or for another person entrusted to his or her care, nor can he or she consent to it, either explicitly or implicitly. Nor can any authority legitimately recommend or permit such an action."

—From Evangelium Vitae*, March, 1995*

"Ex Cathedra" **Defined**

Literally "from the chair," a theological term which signifies authoritative teaching and is more particularly applied to the definitions given by the Roman pontiff. Originally the name of the seat occupied by a professor or a bishop, *cathedra* was used later on to denote the magisterium, or teaching authority. The phrase *ex cathedra* occurs in the writings of the medieval theologians, and more frequently in the discussions which arose after the Reformation in regard to the papal prerogatives. But its present meaning was formally determined by the Vatican Council, Sess. IV, Const. de Ecclesiâ Christi, c. iv: "We teach and define that it is a dogma Divinely revealed that the Roman pontiff when he speaks ex cathedra, that is when in discharge of the office of pastor and doctor of all Christians, by virtue of his supreme Apostolic authority, he defines a doctrine regarding faith or morals to be held by the universal Church, by the Divine assistance promised to him in Blessed Peter, is possessed of that infallibility with which the Divine Redeemer willed that his Church should be endowed in defining doctrine regarding faith or morals, and that therefore such definitions of the Roman pontiff are of themselves and not from the consent of the Church irreformable."

—From (the Catholic Encyclopedia*)*

I believe in an America where the separation of church and state is absolute—where no Catholic prelate would tell the President (should he be Catholic) how to act, and no Protestant minister would tell his parishioners for whom to vote—where no church or church school is granted any public funds or political preference…. I believe in an America that is officially neither Catholic, Protestant nor Jewish—where no public official either requests or accepts instructions on public policy from the Pope, the National Council of Churches or any other ecclesiastical source—where no religious body seeks to impose its will directly or indirectly upon the general populace or the public acts of its officials.

—John F. Kennedy (from his speech before the Houston Ministerial Association, September 12, 1960)

I found this film especially appalling in the kind of violence it depicted. Based on a best-selling novel by Cormac McCarthy, the film opens on a grotesque scene of corpses sprawled across the west-Texas desert near the Mexican border, stumbled upon by a passing hunter (Josh Brolin). The dead were apparently killed in a battle for drug money as a $2 million deal turned sour. The film follows Chigurh, a professional hit man in hot pursuit of the hunter, who has found the money. Sheriff Ed Bell (Tommy Lee Jones) tracks both men. Chigurh is especially violent, murdering innocent people whom he encounters throughout his search. There is one scene in which he considers killing an unaware and innocent gas station owner. He tosses a coin to decide what to do and asks the man to make the call. That man lives, but a later victim does not. "You don't have to do this," the fearful victim says, when offered the call on the coin toss. Chigurh laughs and says nonchalantly, "They always say the same thing."

There are dozens and dozens of violent action films. Another that disturbed me, though it was amusing, was *In Bruges*. In this film, two contract killers, Ray (Colin Farrell) and Ken (Brendan Gleeson), are hiding in a rundown hotel in the beautifully preserved medieval Belgian city of Bruges, with its Gothic architecture and canals. Harry (Ralph Fiennes), the gangster boss who hired them then ordered them to lay low, commands Ken to kill Ray. It seems that Ray, in the course of killing a priest in order to rob him, accidentally killed a young boy. A family man in private life, Harry finds *that* killing highly offensive. Many deaths ensue, including those of innocent bystanders. One bizarre, violent incident entails mistaken identity and a suicide over the death of a dwarf. *In Bruges* has enjoyed a generally favorable critical reception.

The question I must raise is, what is the social impact of the violence that permeates our films and comes as daily fare into our bedrooms, kitchens, and living rooms on television? Most such films are produced in expectation of a strong box-office showing; some, such as *No Country for Old Men,* may aspire to the status of true art. Now, I believe in freedom of expression and I am opposed to any form of censorship whatsoever. Further, I think that Hollywood's one hundred years of cinema have enriched the lives of millions of people with great performances and great dramas, comedies, and tragedies. (Incidentally, the Center for Inquiry/Los Angeles is located on Hollywood Boulevard, about a mile and a half from the Kodak Theater, where the Academy Awards are bestowed every year. Many people associated with the film industry visit CFI/Los Angeles frequently.)

And so I appeal to the producers, writers, and directors to exercise their sense of good judgment, as parents and citizens, in producing extremely violent films. What I dissent from is the ready acceptance of the great number of films that depict cold-blooded murder and suicide without remorse and form so large a part of the media stream consumed by all age groups. Violence is no doubt part of the human experience, but I find the resort to capricious, remorseless depictions of such violence close to obscene. And I wonder whether this cultural immersion in violence explains in part the frequency of violent crimes, including mass murder on campuses and elsewhere, in American life.

Still, violence in the media cannot be the whole answer. Others are in order. First, it is a sad commentary on American culture that 2.03 million people are in prisons, a far greater number than in most other countries—both in absolute and proportional terms. Second, the United States has, since World War II, become a belligerent military state, intervening across the globe more or less at will. Consider the current war in the Middle East. The nightly news depicts suicide bombers who target civilians in Iraq, Afghanistan, and Pakistan. Innocent people are killed in great numbers, in broad daylight—at shopping centers, weddings, and funerals, without compunction. But then again, we are also shown questionable actions of U.S. and coalition forces—to say nothing of U.S.-paid mercenaries—in the Middle East. Some of their actions have seemed as inexplicable, as unjustifiable, as those of our "enemies."

Presidential candidate John McCain says we may need to be in Iraq for a hundred years—a credible period when one considers that we have maintained troops in Europe for almost sixty years and in Korea for half a century.

The U.S. Department of Defense's budget is $500 billion; if we add to this the cost of the wars in Afghanistan and Iraq, an estimated $240 billion, this means that *three-quarters of a trillion dollars* a year is being spent on arms and armies—more than the rest of the entire world combined.

How sad that violence and the threat of violence permeate American culture. No wonder that horrendous shootings happen on the campuses and elsewhere, seemingly at random; for in our arts, in our cities, and in our foreign policy, we are surrounded daily by a culture of death.

America the Beautiful, Open to All[11]

The United States is *not* "a Christian nation" nor even "Judeo-Christian"—contrary to what conservatives and fundamentalists proclaim.

The first Americans, who migrated from Asia to this continent over the Bering Strait some 15,000 to 20,000 years ago, were pagans! Millions of Native Americans were already here when European conquerors—from Spanish Conquistadors to English Puritan dissenters—arrived claiming to "discover" America. White settlers drove the Indian tribes off their lands or slaughtered them as they pushed westward.

Granted, at one time there was a Protestant majority among these White settlers. After heavy Roman Catholic immigration in the nineteenth century, one had to speak of a Christian majority. But add to this the Africans who were forcibly brought here on slave ships, stripped of their native religions, and compelled to convert to Christianity. Later, millions of Jewish immigrants came to the United States seeking freedom.

Successive waves of immigration continue transforming America today. It is the most religiously diverse country in the world. According to the latest census, this process *accelerated* during the 1990s; as never before, immigrants from all corners of the globe are reweaving the fabric of American life.

This latter-day transformation is vividly depicted in a new book by Harvard religion professor Diana L. Eck, *A New Religious America: How a "Christian Country" Has Now Become the World's Most Diverse Nation.*[12] Today Islamic mosques and Buddhist and Hindu temples are being built in virtually every major city or suburb in America. Asian immigration is no doubt a result of the 1965 immigration act signed by President Lyndon Johnson, which repealed quotas tied to national origins. From 1990 to 1999, the Asian population increased by 43 percent, to nearly eleven million. Today there are an estimated six million Muslims (rapidly growing not only through immigration but also because of high birth rates and numerous conversions), millions of Buddhists, one million Hindus, hundreds of thousands each of Sikhs, Zoroastrians, Baháí, Jains, Confucians, Pagans, and Shintoists. There are an estimated 1,350 diverse religious denominations in this country!

Similar changes are occurring in our nation's racial and ethnic mix. Hispanics increased by 38.8 percent, now numbering 33.3 million (many of them evangelical Protestants). Given widespread intermarriage across religious, racial, and ethnic lines, there are many Americans who are of mixed parentage and express diverse talents and outlooks—as Tiger Woods so eloquently illustrates. Added to this mix are the millions of Americans who belong to no religious denomination (47 percent) or do not profess a belief in a god or gods (8 to 11 percent). Twenty percent of Americans believe the Bible to be an ancient book of fables recorded by man.

All of the above are now true-blue Americans, entitled to equal protection of the laws; no one is a second-class citizen. In truth, every American is a member of some minority; even "Baptist" and "Roman Catholic" are minority labels. The United States is nothing less than a microcosm of the planetary community, for it represents multicultural diversity, a plurality of ethnic religious and nonreligious beliefs and values. Given the conditions of freedom inherent in an open democratic society, all individuals and groups—no matter what their racial, religious, gender, age, ethnic, or creedal backgrounds—are entitled to pursue their own lifestyles. As I drive to my offices every day, I pass by Episcopal, Unitarian, Methodist, Christian Science, Mormon, and Roman Catholic churches, as well as Sikh, Hindu, and Chasidic temples.

Actually, history gives no warrant for saying what kind of nation, religiously speaking, our country was meant to be. The United States as a political state did not come into being until the Constitution was ratified in 1787. The Articles of Confederation (1777) and the Declaration of Independence (1776), which preceded the Constitution, did not provide the basic legal framework for this country. The Constitution makes no mention of God and explicitly provides that there is no religious test for office; it guarantees political freedom to every citizen no matter what his or her creed. The Civil War and the suffragist movement eventually extended the franchise and other rights to African Americans and women. The fact that the white colonists were predominantly Protestant in the seventeenth and eighteenth century (ignoring blacks and Native Americans) does not stamp America as indelibly Protestant or even Christian.

The United States is not a monotheistic nation either. Its citizens hold a wide range of beliefs, from atheism through monotheism to polytheism and even pantheism. The vigorous doctrinal disputes that have invigorated life throughout the nation's history should provide sufficient evidence of America's religious diversity.

And yet in spite of this, there are still brazen attempts by fundamentalists—including many within the Bush/Ashcroft administration—to reinterpret the Constitution, and to threaten the rights and liberties of millions of Americans who do not share their own religious predilections.

Tim LaHaye and David Noebel in *Mind Siege: The Battle for Truth in the New Millennium* (Nashville, Tenn.: World Publishing, 2000) still insist that the United States is a Christian country. Would they exclude Asian citizens who hold different beliefs? They claim that secular humanism is the "established" religion of the United States and wish to extirpate its influence from public life. We reply that secular humanism is *not* a religion; it is a philosophical, scientific, and ethical eupraxsophy (good wisdom in conduct). In any case, there is no common religious creed that represents all of the people of the United States. The same battle *against religious tyranny* that Jefferson waged against the fundamentalists of his day apparently needs to be fought again today. James Madison observed in *The Federalist Papers* that, if the Republic is to survive, then it needs to avoid factions, and religious factions are among the most dangerous. Many of the Founding Fathers were deists, not Christians; they recognized that liberty of conscience is precious and that any effort to establish an official American religious creed needs to be opposed.

"For Spacious Skies"[13]

One of the core controversies that has engulfed the United States in the last decade concerns the very *definition* of America itself; in particular, the role of religion in public life has engendered intense definition-mongering.

Religious conservatives insist that America is "one nation under God," which is often interpreted to mean "a Christian nation." They hold that religion and patriotism go hand in hand and that America has a divine destiny. The Republican Party has virtually been captured by this Evangelical Protestant minority, which seeks to redefine America in terms of its own religious outlook.

Surprisingly, this position is supported by Samuel Huntington, the oracle of Harvard, in a new book, *Who Are We?: The Challenge to America's National Identity*.[14] Huntington agrees that America is a Christian country, i.e., an Anglo-Protestant one, and that its religiosity distinguishes it from European democracies that have become highly secularized. He believes that America's core culture is the culture of the seventeenth- and eighteenth-century Protestant settlers who, he claims, "founded America." Huntington is especially concerned that Hispanic immigration, rising demands for bilingualism, and some Hispanics' reluctance to assimilate pose a threat to the dominant Anglo-Protestant culture. He is too pessimistic, in my view, for, like other minorities, Hispanics can in time become fully integrated into American society and seize their opportunity to realize the American dream.

Like most religious conservatives, Huntington is flexible—to a point—when he defines the "real America" as Anglo-Protestant. In fact, his definition of America has been extended to include Roman Catholics and the Eastern Orthodox. Other neo-conservatives have further expanded it to include Jews. Thus, they portray America as a "Judaic-Christian" nation *necessarily* rooted in the Old and New Testaments.

I submit that such a viewpoint is "un-American." It is biased, narrow, and chauvinistic. Let me explain what I mean. The first humans on the American continent were not the English settlers of the seventeenth and eighteenth centuries but the native population of Indians. They had been living on this vast land for thousands of years before the conquering settlers arrived from Europe. The nations and tribes of North and South America numbered millions of people in well-developed societies. These were the real "first Americans," and they were pagans, not Christians! As for the first Europeans who came to America, they were not exclusively Anglo or Protestant. The Spanish, Roman Catholic *conquistadores* occupied sections of the West and South before English Protestants came to New England and Virginia, or the Dutch to New York. Today's Hispanics are not "foreign" intruders; rather, they carry on the historic Spanish influence in the West and Southwest. America was also built by Africans, who were not Anglos. Enslaved against their will, they were brought to the American colonies by biblically drenched Southern Protestants.

In my view, America is best understood as a *universal* culture. What it means to be American is constantly redefined by successive waves of immigrants, who intermarry and blend into the culture to whose content they themselves add spice and vigor. To claim that America can be defined *only* or *primarily* by the seventeenth- and eighteenth-century Anglo colonists and not by any people here before *nor* by immigrants who came later is prejudicial balderdash. I should point out that we *love* Anglo-Protestants; they have contributed massively to modern culture—but let us balance their role with those of so many others.

"For spacious skies," sung in our national anthem, proclaims that America is open to all. The eloquent declaration by Emma Lazarus, inscribed at the base of the Statue of Liberty, perhaps best defines America:

> Give me your tired, your poor,
> Your huddled masses yearning to breathe free,
> The wretched refuse of your teeming shore.
> Send these, the homeless, tempest-tost to me.
> I lift my lamp beside the golden door.

Irish immigrants landed to build the Erie Canal and to work in mines and factories; Scandinavians and Germans (many of them freethinkers), Italians and Poles, Jews and Slavs came to these shores seeking their fortunes, bringing with them non-Protestant values and beliefs, as did the Chinese of the nineteenth century who helped construct the Western railroads. In other words, America encompasses virtually *every* ethnic, racial, religious, and national group in the world. In recent decades, millions of Asian immigrants have arrived—Vietnamese and Koreans, Filipinos and Indians, Buddhists and Hindus, Muslims and Sikhs, Shintoists and Confucians. In what sense can anyone claim that the Anglo-Protestant influence embodies the only *true* definition of America?

In misrepresenting America as "one nation under God," conservatives ignore another important point. The United States Constitution was written by deists and freethinkers as much as by believers. These framers were influenced by the Enlightenment, notably by French writers who were not religious Christians. We see their influence in the absence of any religious test to hold public office under the Constitution. And the First Amendment, authored by Madison and inspired by Jefferson, stipulates that "Congress shall make no law establishing religion or prohibiting the free exercise thereof."

The U.S. Constitution must be understood as a *secular* document, the first of its kind, defending freedom of conscience and the right to believe or *not* believe. What is crucial to the definition of America is *not* that it is Protestant or Roman Catholic or even Christian or Judaic, but that it is and has been a *secular republic*, electing its leadership without a hereditary monarchy and *without* any pretensions of theocracy, whether *de jure* or *de facto*.

The real heart of our national identity is the constant remaking of who and what we are by the countless immigrants who have enriched our culture. Essential to this process have been the *civic virtues of democracy*, which are basically *humanistic*. These grew out of the Renaissance and the Reformation, but also out of the Enlightenment and the democratic and scientific revolutions of the modern world.

What are the core values and principles that have defined us as a nation? I submit that they include at least the following:

- Tolerance for diversity and for the adoption of alternative lifestyles in the pursuit of happiness.
- Respect for individual liberty.
- Equality before the law, for poor as well as rich, commoner as well as aristocrat. The open society, in which civil liberties including freedom of speech and assembly are guaranteed.
- The nonestablishment clause of the First Amendment, vital to our secular republic.

- Americans appreciate individual responsibility, hard work, and dili-
  gence. This is not uniquely an Anglo- Protestant virtue, for Germans
  and Dutch, Irish and Jews, Italians and Asians have shared these
  virtues; the American frontier stimulated heroic efforts from almost
  all who sought to conquer it.
- We share a common language, English—yes! But we also share a
  common set of political principles and values (such as a doctrine of
  human rights), and these are drawn from the French Revolution as well
  as the British parliamentary system (which, in any case, the Founders
  modified by introducing checks and balances).
- We have prized public education for common men and women, in the
  belief that the educated citizen is the most effective way of governing
  a democratic society.
- The history of America is therefore the battle to become more inclusive.
  The Jacksonian presidency, the Civil War, the suffrage movement, the
  New Deal, and the Great Society—all tried to extend democracy to
  more and more persons. Everyone is offered the opportunity to participate in American life: black and white, Protestant and Catholic, Jew
  and Mormon, Muslim and Hindu, Buddhist and freethinker, gay and
  straight, white and brown, red and yellow, believer and unbeliever.
  We are all Americans!

What right does any one portion of our population have to impose
its own exclusive brand of religious dogma on others? The Reverend
Richard John Neuhaus, a Lutheran priest who converted to Catholicism,
in 1985 complained about the "naked public square" because, he said,
it was empty of religion. And it was, for large numbers of Americans
considered religion to be a private matter. Alas, the public square is no
longer naked. Instead, it overflows with public professions of piety; it
is unfortunate if those who wish to redefine America as a Protestant or
Christian or even Judeo-Christian nation would exclude those who cannot accept their religious doctrines. They ignore the fact that America
has always been a land for religious dissenters.

We should welcome the pluralistic diversity (over 1,350 separate
denominations and sects!) that the United States has provided within
the framework of shared democratic values. What unites us is our willingness to negotiate any differences and to reach compromises for the
public good. This is intrinsic to the democratic- humanistic ethic. Each
individual is entitled to his or her own convictions and values, as long as
he or she agrees to abide by the law. The government should, however,
remain neutral about what its individual citizens prefer and it should
not seek to establish Christianity or Judeo-Christian monotheism as the
official creed of the land.

Hurrah for Freedom of Inquiry[15]

There is an ongoing debate among secular humanists as to what our priorities should be. Two subjects have been among the most hotly debated. First is the burning desire of many secular humanists that we engage in political activism. Many secularists, naturalists, and humanists believe that the United States faces so many critical problems that we need to focus far more intensely on the political battles of today, especially the culture wars with the Religious Right. Many insist that we come out strongly against the Bush administration on certain issues, the war in Iraq, recent appointments to the Supreme Court, and other hot-button issues of the day. Some also wish us to enter into the fray between libertarian advocates of the free market and social democrats who worry about the loss of American jobs and wish to restore principles of equity and fairness.

In answer to the political activists, we have indeed dealt with all of these issues but as ethical, not simply political, concerns. I have argued in these pages that we are not a political movement, for we recognize that secular humanists may differ about concrete political and economic issues. However, we have and will continue to deal with political issues, but only when the basic principles and ethical values of secular humanism are directly threatened, as they so often are.

Second, many desire to focus primarily on the critique of religion, to deal with questions such as the existence of God and the human soul, and to defend atheism outright. I have been identified as an "atheist poobah," whatever that means! Although I am nonreligious and skeptical of theistic religious claims, I surely do not wish to be known primarily as an atheist, for our secular humanist agenda is broader than that. I have often said that, although I do not believe in God because I think there is insufficient evidence for the claim, I surely do not define myself by what I am against, but rather by my positive stance. It's what I believe in deeply—what I am *for*—that matters more: we are naturalists, not supernaturalists; secularists, not theocrats; but beyond that, we wish to focus on free inquiry and humanistic ethics, and we have some confidence in a progressive future for humankind.

I surely recognize the importance of the above two issues—political controversies as they emerge on the national and international scene and the need for basic criticisms of theological claims—and this magazine will continue to deal with these questions. But there is another approach in the culture war, which has become increasingly vital today and has emerged in the pages of this magazine. Thus, I submit that we need to focus on the positive and affirmative aspects of the naturalistic, secular, and humanistic outlook, not its negative critiques.

For many of us, it is important today that we define and defend constructive alternatives to the reigning religious moralities. Thus, we have argued:

- that we need to defend free inquiry, critical thinking, reason, and the methods of science;
- that a person can be good without belief in God;
- that the lives of nontheists can overflow with meaning and enrichment;
- that secular humanism and scientific naturalism can contribute immensely to the growth of democracy and the improvement of the human condition on the planet.

Clearly, if God is dead for post-postmodern society, *humans are alive*—and have the responsibility to create a better world for themselves and their fellow human beings. It is not the death of God but the *rebirth of human confidence in the courage to achieve* that we especially need to herald.

We are concerned with educating the public about the ideals of naturalistic and humanistic eupraxsophy. That is why we call for a New Enlightenment, for we believe there is a need for a fundamental reformation of society—indeed, a new cultural renaissance. These goals are far more profound than simply focusing on the political vicissitudes of the day. Focusing on the need for free inquiry in all areas of human endeavor—including religion—seems to us to be a first step in this direction. And this is a goal that has inspired the growth of our Centers and Communities worldwide.

The Best Antidote for Religious Fanaticism

We are confronted today by the continued challenge of religious fundamentalism. The explosive growth of Islamic fundamentalism in the last half of the twentieth century has ignited conflagrations worldwide, as have the fearful responses to it. First and foremost among our concerns, of course, is the brutal war of attrition in Iraq and the continuing toll it exacts both on American soldiers and Iraqi civilians. American forces have suffered some 2,100 dead, 15,500 wounded (many seriously), and tens of thousands more who suffer possible long-range psychological impairment—this according to Representative John Murtha (D–Pa.), who recommends the immediate withdrawal and redeployment of American forces in the Middle East. Recently, all three factions in Iraq—the Shiites, Sunnis, and Kurds—have asked U.S. military forces to leave. The mounting death toll among innocent Iraqi civilians is rarely discussed in the United States. Although President George W. Bush recently admitted to an estimate of 30,000 casualties, we think that the number is probably higher.

Many people hope that the new Iraqi constitution will enable democratic institutions to develop, permit Iraqi forces to police their own nation, and allow American troops to come home. Unfortunately, insurgent attacks, far from abating, have increased, and suicide bombers continue to proliferate. We hope that democracy can be realized in the Middle East one day—and we hope that this is not simply a pious hope.

We at this magazine have opposed the Iraqi war because we thought that it would only exacerbate the conflicts between Islam and the rest of the world. We thought it would likely inflame hatred against the United States and recruit new terrorists—which it has tragically done. It surely has intensified hatred between Sunnis and Shiites and expanded their fratricidal warfare against one another.

Outside of Iraq, too, the conflict goes on as terrorist bombings continue worldwide—in Madrid and London, Tel Aviv and Indonesia, Jordan and Saudi Arabia. Added to this unrest are the recent student riots and car burnings in France by disillusioned young Muslims. The growing Islamic minorities in Europe have aroused xenophobic fears among extreme nationalists such as France's Jean-Marie Le Pen. Liberal majorities in Western Europe are coming to question their earlier multicultural assumption that all cultures are *equal* in value—the code of Sharia, which assigns women a lesser station in society, is surely not morally equivalent to the ethics of contemporary democracy, which defends all human rights, including those of women.

I submit that one reason for this mistaken multiculturalist view is the belief that Islam is a "peaceful religion" or that the followers of Egyptian philosopher Sayyid Qutb and Osama bin Laden are simply misguided radicals who misconstrue the "real" meaning of Islam. Most Muslims take their religion as nominal and perhaps have not understood the implications of violence in the Koran and Hadith. On the contrary, there is considerable contextual support for violence and mayhem within these "sacred texts"; through history, this has frequently motivated passionate hatred against those who resist Islam. This is quite similar to the literal reading of the ancient Hebrew Bible and the New Testament that was used centuries ago to justify the Inquisition and the Crusades. We reiterate what we have said countless times in these pages: there needs to be public discussion of the convictions of fundamentalist religions, including Islam, which teach that they alone possess the absolute truth and the only guaranteed road to salvation and that they can impose their will on all others by violence and slaughter.

What Islam urgently needs today is a critical reading of the Koran and Hadith, both by independent scholars and by educated Muslims. Careful scientific examination carried out under the impetus of Ibn Warraq of the Institute for the Secularization of Islamic Society (ISIS) at the Center for Inquiry indicates that, contrary to the Muslim conviction that the Koran is the most unitary and consistent of all scriptures, there are many versions of the Koran, not just one. Scientific, scholarly, and historical investigations of how the Koran was compiled may weaken Muslim convictions as to its inerrancy; perhaps this will lead to a rise in metaphorical (not literal) interpretations of those scriptures. Current research into the origins of the Koran indicate that what is taken as the revealed word of Allah was influenced by writings from traditions other than those extant in Arab cultures, including extensive borrowings from Christian, Judaic, and Syriac sources.

The Protestant Reformation was able to tame the medieval churches of the West. The Renaissance in the West, as well as the development of biblical criticism and science, further weakened authoritarian forms of Christianity and Judaism. It is clear that there needs to be an Islamic Renaissance and Reformation, a flowering of Koranic criticism, and broad growth in appreciation for science. Only these can help to moderate the Koran and weaken its use by fundamentalists as a club to bludgeon dissent.

A similar fundamentalist mindset, of course, obtains among Christian believers in the Rapture in the United States today, who insist that the Bible is inerrant. We are faced in the United States with fundamentalist extremists who are convinced that only a relatively small number of devout Christian believers will go to heaven while all the rest of humankind will be condemned to hellfire. This is similar to the view held by devout disciples of *jihad*, who abandon any empathy for those they might kill and, in their view, will be cast into hell.

Terrorism of course needs to be rooted out and resisted wherever it appears. But long-range, an important antidote for all such nonsense is the pen, not the sword; the power of ideas, not blind faith; the willingness to engage in free inquiry, not the effort to suppress it by a fatwa or censorship. Most of all, sacred texts should not be held immune to intelligent examination.

Notes

1. This article first appeared in *Free Inquiry* 25, no. 2 (February/March 2005), pp. 5–8.
2. This article first appeared in *Free Inquiry* 24, no. 4 (June/July 2004), pp. 5–8.
3. Susan Jacoby, *Freethinkers: A History of American Secularism*, Metropolitan Books (New York, N.Y.: 2004).
4. "Executive Pay: A Special Report," *New York Times*, April 4, 2004.
5. Lawrence Kohlberg, *The Psychology of Moral Development* (New York: Harper & Rowe, 1983).
6. This article first appeared in *Free Inquiry* 21, no. 3 (summer 2001), pp. 5–6.
7. This article first appeared in *Free Inquiry* 24, no. 2 (February/March 2004), pp. 5–6.
8. This article first appeared in *Free Inquiry* 22, no. 2 (spring 2002), pp. 5–6, 60.
9. This article first appeared in *Free Inquiry* 26, no. 3 (April/May 2006), pp. 4–7.
10. This article first appeared in *Free Inquiry* 28, no. 4 (June/July 2008), pp. 9–10.
11. This article first appeared in *Free Inquiry* 21, no. 4 (fall 2001), pp. 5–6.
12. Diana L. Eck, *A New Religious America: How a "Christian Country" Has Now Become the World's Most Diverse* Nation, HarperCollins (San Francisco, Calif.: 2001).
13. This article first appeared in *Free Inquiry* 25, no. 1 (December 2004/January 2005), pp. 5–6.
14. Samuel Huntington, *Who Are We?: The Challenge to America's National Identity*, Simon & Schuster, (New York, N.Y.: 2004).
15. This article first appeared in *Free Inquiry* 26, no. 2 (February/March 2006), pp. 4–5.

Section 5

The Rise of India and China

XIX

The Industrial-Technological Revolution[1]

The steady economic progress of two mammoth Asian countries—India and China—is a significant achievement. Some have likened this to a Third Industrial Revolution. The First Industrial Revolution occurred in Britain in the late eighteenth and early nineteenth centuries. It replaced manual labor with machinery, as with the mechanization of textile manufacturing in Birmingham and Manchester. It saw the introduction of the steam engine, steamboat, locomotive, telegraph, the iron foundry, and the cotton gin.

The Second Industrial Revolution refers to the rise of industrial countries like Germany and the United States from 1871 to 1914. This ushered in—or set the stage for—the many daring technological inventions that have continued to transform life in the twentieth and twenty-first centuries, such as electricity, new methods of producing steel, skyscrapers, modern sanitary systems, improved medical care with surgery and antibiotics, advances in communications (including the telephone, radio, and television), the introduction of the automobile, the growth of highway systems and suburbs, and air and space travel.

The term "Third Industrial Revolution" has been used to designate the Information Revolution, beginning roughly in 1974, with the introduction of computers and, eventually, the Internet. This has been extended by some today to incorporate other promising technologies, such as nanotechnology and bioengineering. Actually, the Third Industrial Revolution is rather an Industrial-*Technological* Revolution.

Of considerable significance is its impact upon India and China, which have leapfrogged their economies forward. Manufacturing in China is replacing the industrial base of many Western countries. More people in China own cell phones than in the United States, and China is building new cities throughout its territories. Of special importance today is the growth of *outsourcing* to India (as well as other countries). This involves a radical change in the location of the workforce. Alan S. Blinder, the former vice chairman of the Federal Reserve Board and an adviser to former President Clinton, recently emphasized the significance of outsourcing and the risk that it poses to the industrial economies of the United States and Europe. For the first time, workers need not be wedded to an industrial plant, for many types of work can now be transported anywhere by means of computers and satellites. Thus, multinational corporations find it easier to employ the skills of Third World workers at lower cost than those associated with their home-based labor forces. A recent story in *The New York Times* (April 4, 2007) pointed out that many large corporations such as IBM, Citigroup, Accenture, and Aviva are rapidly transporting jobs overseas. Everyone is by now familiar with the fact that airline reservations are now serviced in other countries, and much back-office work is handled offshore by foreign, English-speaking personnel. This trend has spread from financial institutions, banks, and insurance companies to aerospace, pharmaceutical, and other industries, all of which are sending routine communications and manufacturing work overseas. This has led to a surge in the Indian economy, where a newly educated middle class with special skills is developing in cities like Bangalore and Hyderabad.

For many years, India was considered the "basket case" of Asia, with famines threatening continually. From 1991 to 2003, however, India's economy—with Western investment—began to grow at an annual compounded rate of 5.7 percent, a rate far higher than the advanced economies of Europe. Today this is accelerating, due to outsourcing, and is approaching 7–8 percent and even higher. Such growth is absolutely necessary for India's future.

For its part, the Chinese economy keeps growing at breakneck speed, by transporting entire manufacturing operations from affluent countries to China, where labor costs are much lower. Its economy has been growing at rates of 9–10 percent per year, which has transformed Chinese society, though this is projected to level off at 8 percent in future years. China has emerged as a great power, holding vast sums of dollars in reserve due to its enormous trade surplus with the United States. At the same time, America's ballooning trade deficit with China has benefited consumers in the United States, who can buy goods at greatly reduced prices, though it has at the same time decimated industry after industry. Some balance has to be achieved that fulfills the desire to help India and China grow, yet is sensitive to the needs of workers losing their jobs in more affluent countries.

There are increased calls in the United States for erecting tariffs and trade barriers, especially against China, to protect jobs in the home market; and one can sympathize with the reasons for this apprehension. The Bush administration is calling for a crackdown on pirated goods, such as movies, books, and music, as a first step while asking China to import more Western products.

From the standpoint of planetary humanism, we encounter a dilemma. We have argued that as secular humanists "*we have a responsibility to care about each and every person in the planetary community, and ... this obligation should extend beyond our own societies to humanity as a whole*" (see my editorial, "India's Population Time Bomb" *Free Inquiry*, Spring 1999). Thus we wish to see India, China, and other Third World countries prosper and grow. The nation-states that we live in are no longer islands unto themselves: whatever happens anywhere reverberates everywhere. The interdependence of the global economy—especially since the Information Revolution—is apparent when communication is instantaneous and anyone with a computer anywhere can contribute to the production of goods and services. Former Federal Reserve chair Alan Greenspan has said that advanced economies need to retrain workers for new jobs if they are to compete in the global market. Unfortunately, it is overwhelmingly in the low-paying service sector that this process is occurring.

Some critics of this trend mistakenly call it "socialism." It is a far cry from that, for the socialism of an earlier generation called for the nationalization of the means of production; what is happening today is a result of free-market capitalism, pure and simple, on the world scene. Those who rail against competition from abroad are anti-free-market and anti-capitalist. No doubt some balance has to be achieved between free trade and equality of concern for workers at home.

There are many great problems that rapid economic growth has caused in both China and India. I specify only three of them.

First is the need to reduce population growth. In 1950, the population of China was 556 million and that of India 350 million. China's population in 2006 is approximately 1.3 billion; India's is 1.1 billion. It is likely that India's population will outstrip China's in thirty years. By 2050, it is estimated that China will have 1.48 billion people and India, 1.6 billion. World population is projected to grow to 9.3 billion by then. Such continuing growth in absolute terms exerts enormous pressure on resources. Every effort has to be made to lower the rate of growth. China, with its stringent one-child policy, has managed to do that, especially since the year 2000, when the population growth rate was 0.9 percent per year; in

2006, it declined to 0.59 percent per year. In any case there is a significant decline in the birth rate, which is now 1.8 children per couple.

India's population continues to grow at a much higher rate. Last year, it was estimated at 1.38 percent, more than two times China's rate. India had adopted some time ago population measures, including vasectomies for males, sterilization for females, and public support for contraception. Unfortunately, these policies have not kept pace with the country's population growth.

In China, decades of population control have reduced the number of young workers relative to the number of aging elders; is it now a live question whether or not there will be enough working people to support the nonworking population. In India, 35–40 percent of the population is under age fifteen, so its primary challenge is the need to control the rate of population growth. Unless India adopts a rigorous nationwide policy of population control, it will continue to falter, no matter how expansive its economic growth. Interestingly, in India, the Hindu birth rate has declined, but the Muslim birth rate has not. The Muslim population apparently still considers it advantageous to have large families and shows considerable resistance to contraception. The great question for China and India is whether rising levels of affluence will reduce the desire for large families, as it has in other countries. In 1980, India and China had roughly the same income per capita, though China's has nearly doubled since then. India is making great efforts to try to narrow the gap.

The second great challenge that India and China face is the tremendous drain on their natural resources, particularly energy and water. Demand for energy is outstripping the capacity to produce it, with fresh water in increasingly short supply. With this, of course, comes the danger of pollution to the environment, which the Kyoto Protocol is trying to reduce—though, regrettably, Kyoto does not apply to China or India, which are given leeway for their attempts to catch up. Yet China was responsible for an estimated 18 percent of the world's carbon emissions, almost equal to the 21-percent share of the United States (2004 figures), and is likely to outstrip the United States shortly. Fortunately, both India and China have so far been able to feed their populations; as those populations have risen, so the green revolution has contributed to the food supply. Whether this will continue, only the future will tell.

The third great challenge both countries face is the need to overcome poverty in the countryside and to bridge disparities in income. While a large middle class is growing in both societies, large underclasses persist. Concomitant with economic growth, there need to be continued efforts to increase standards of living and provide opportunities for education for the poorest sectors of society. Of considerable significance is the fact that India is a democracy, whereas China still has a long road to travel if it is to become democratic.

From the standpoint of planetary humanism, we need to be concerned about each person on the planet, and we need to try to improve the education, happiness, and well-being of every person. One can only hope that China and India will be able to overcome enormous economic problems and that they will continue to grow, while at the same time limiting population, preserving the environment, reducing poverty, and defending the freedom and rights of their ordinary citizens.

I should point out that, in a modest way, the Center for Inquiry/Transnational is attempting to assist these countries by establishing Centers in India (there are now four—in Hyderabad, Pune, Delhi, and the port city of Kakinada in the state of Andhra Pradesh—and a fifth is planned in Chennai, formerly Madras) and in Beijing, China, which will host a World Congress in October, 2007. The agenda of the Center for Inquiry is to develop the public understanding of science, to reduce levels of superstition, and to develop some public appreciation of humanist values in ameliorating human life. This priority should be high on the agenda of both China and India, if they are to solve their problems and contribute to better lives for their citizens.

Of Human Dignity

In a provocative article in *Commentary*,[2] the neoconservative magazine, Leon Kass raises questions about the relationship between science and biblical religion. Western civilization, he says, draws upon both science and religion, which are necessary to its future. He is concerned that many scientists today reject biblical religion as "irrational." He is especially disturbed that "an aggressive intellectual elite" has converted to "scientism."

He asks whether, given this challenge, biblical religion can respond. This is all the more pertinent today, he says, because of developments within the sciences of genetics, neurobiology, and evolutionary psychology. Kass, professor of social thought at the University of Chicago, served as chairman of the President's Council on Bioethics from 2001–2005. In that capacity, he opposed many proposals brought before the Council on cloning, stem-cell research, and other bioengineering techniques, because he believed they violated "human dignity." He concluded this, apparently, because he believes that these new technologies conflict with biblical religion, and because of his commitment to his own ethnic loyalty to Judaism and the Hebrew Bible.

Astonishingly, Kass refers to the revelation of scripture as the basis of his view that humans possess "dignity." Interestingly, he does not discuss the differences between the Old and New Testaments—which is to say, Judaism and Christianity. Nor does he acknowledge the centuries of hatred and persecution to which these differences have led, or the crimes against humanity often condoned by devout religionists—from the Inquisition, the Crusades, and the protracted wars between Catholics and Protestants to the condoning of slavery, patriarchy, the historic suppression of women and homosexuals, and the opposition to democracy and human rights.

Although Kass grounds his religious view on revelation, he totally excludes any reference to the Koran, a legacy of the Book of Abraham and surely a latter-day claim to knowledge from on high. He disregards centuries of bloody confrontations between different revelatory traditions; this shameful history does little to support his claim that human dignity is rooted in revelation. Given the wars fought in the name of Allah or God, one can ask, "Oh, Dignity, where is thy divine embrace?"

I surely do not deny that religions have some good as sources of meaning, consolation, charity, and hope, but they have also been dysfunctional. The question is whether these religious institutions can be profoundly reformed or replaced by others that are more relevant to the present condition of world (not simply Western) civilization.

Of special interest to secular humanists is Kass's frontal assault on "the luminaries of the International Academy of Humanism—including the biologists Francis Crick, Richard Dawkins, and E.O. Wilson and the humanists Isaiah Berlin, W.V. Quine, and Kurt Vonnegut"—who, in 1997, issued a statement defending cloning research in higher mammals and human beings ("Declaration in Defense of Cloning and the Integrity of Scientific Research," *Free Inquiry*, Summer 1997). That statement deplores the fact that some world religions teach that human beings are fundamentally different from other mammals, for they are "imbued by a deity with immortal souls." The statement goes on to say that, "A view of human nature rooted in humanity's mythical past ought not to be our primary criterion for making moral decisions about cloning."

Kass deplores the fact that leading scientists today are willing to dethrone the traditional idea that humanity is created in God's image and has a special place in the universe. He regrets that these scientists have thrown out not only the "immaterial human soul" but the very idea that we are free and responsible for what we do. He accuses the secular elite of "dehumanizing" humanity from its proper status as "noble, dignified precious, or Godlike." He calls this "soulless scientism." Science, he argues—erroneously, I submit—is totally unable to account for ethical behavior and is "morally neutral." Kass is worried that we stand today on the threshold of an effort by scientists to "perfect" human nature and "enhance" human life. He asks, how do we know that biogenetic engineering (such as embryonic stem-cell research) is worthwhile? Why should we welcome a "post-human" future? This, he insists, is the "moral and religious crisis" we face today. He rails against the use of evolution and neuroscience "as battering rams against the teachings of the Bible and the religions built upon it." Kass brazenly asserts that "[t]he teachings of Genesis 1 are indeed untouched by scientific findings." His case rests on the statement in Genesis 1:31: "And God saw everything that He had made, and, behold, it was very good."

Thus, Kass says, when we ask, "Why should there be something rather than nothing?" we now have it on the highest authority of the Bible that the world, having been created, is *good*. Quoting Joshua Heschel, Kass continues that "the story of creation is not a description of how the world came into being," but an "appreciation" of the glory of the world's having come into being. The point of the creation narrative is to summon us to celebrate with awe and to recognize that the existence of the universe is good and that it calls us to a worthy life, "a life that does honor to the divine likeness."

The first chapter of Genesis, like (Kass declares) no work of science, "invites us to harken to a transcendent voice." It is "a response to the human longing for meaning." This, he says, is more than cognitive, for it answers "the call to righteousness, holiness, and love of neighbor."

Kass concludes "that we should have been given such a life-affirming teaching is, to speak plainly, a miracle."

All of this, it seems to me, is a form of gobbledygook. For Kass assumes that Genesis 1 is in some way divinely given by a "transcendent" voice. In truth, it is only the voices of human beings in an ancient age trying to find existential meaning in the universe and reading into it everything that they longed for.

The Bible is not the word of a distant God, proclaimed by him to humans, but a series of books written by human beings in the distant past, presenting their own visions of reality. To consider the Bible divinely inspired is a pernicious form of the "God delusion," as Richard Dawkins so aptly describes it—the invoking of God to satisfy the human quest for meaning, an anthropocentric God read into the fabric of nature by the hunger for some supernatural purpose. There is something terribly amiss when the former chairman of the President's Council on Bioethics invokes his own religious convictions in an attempt to determine national policy, and when President Bush and his evangelical and Roman Catholic cohorts use the Genesis story to block scientific research. The Vatican's doctrine that human life begins at conception, when an immortal soul is implanted by God, is oblivious to the potential benefits that embryonic stem-cell research may offer in curing diseases and extending life. The same is true concerning other potential discoveries in biogenetic engineering, which Kass fears.

Kass's article does pose a serious challenge to secular humanists and atheists, however: if we reject the religious presumption that dignity has a divine source, then how *do* we justify the ethical principle that *we ought to consider every human person equal in dignity and value?*

Secular humanists respond that human beings are responsible for their own destinies—for themselves and for the wider community of humankind. This does not depend upon an absent deity nor on spurious promises of eternal salvation. Human beings living within communities learn to abide by ethical principles that prescribe how they should treat one another. A basic principle is implicit in the democratic ethic that has developed over the centuries and is now deeply ingrained in human behavior, across cultures and ethnicities: the recognition that we ought to respect the *dignity* of each person as a moral being, not simply within our own nation-state (the dignity of fellow citizens) but within the broader planetary community (the dignity of all humankind). The respect for this dignity is not a divine right inherent in the person himself. It is not a description of an abstract metaphysical property. Rather, it is a general normative prescription that tells us that a civilized community *ought* to recognize the moral equality of each person as such, recognizing the duties and obligations that arise out of his or her relationships to others. These include their rights to life, liberty, and the pursuit of happiness, and also the obligation of society to provide as best it can the means by which each person can satisfy his or her basic needs for survival and growth, including cultural education and enrichment. Implicit is the recognition that society will respect some degree of personal freedom consonant with the preservation of social order.

Also included are prohibitions against physical harm or death without lawful cause. Humans should be treated with kindness and caring (for those deserving of it). The idea of dignity thus has deep roots in human civilization; it is not a contrivance of caprice. It has its expressions in the democratic revolutions of the modern world, in the battles for what Thomas Paine called the Rights of Man, now widely proclaimed through the Universal Declaration of Human Rights and accepted by most of humanity. It entails the concepts of equality before the law, equal opportunity, the right to education, a prohibition of discrimination based on race, creed, ethnicity, national origin, or gender. This ideal has been expressed in the struggles against slavery and the oppression of women and minorities.

These ethical principles are intrinsically humanistic, for they encourage human beings to realize the best life of which they are capable. They respect the right of privacy: the right of individuals to have some latitude in fulfilling their diverse conceptions of the good life, so long as they do not restrict the rights of others. These principles seek to distribute the opportunities for achieving happiness as widely as possible.

How is dignity justified? I would say that, in the last analysis, it is vindicated by its empirical consequences. Those societies that do not respect the dignity of persons and consistently violate the basic rights of humans tend to condone cruelty, duplicity, and repression. Humanistic ethics focuses on the *ends* to be achieved—maximizing the dimensions of freedom and happiness of human beings. But it also entails *an ethic of principles*, holding that some principles are so fundamental that they ought not to be violated by civilized communities. The respect for the dignity of each person is such a principle, justified not only because of its instrumental value but also because it is intrinsically valued for its own sake. As such, it appeals to both our rational understanding and our empathetic and compassionate feeling for others.

Notes

1.   This article first appeared in *Free Inquiry* 27, no. 4 (June/July 2007), pp. 4–9.
2.   Leon Kass, "Science, Religion, and the Human Future," *Commentary*, (April, 2007), pp. 36–48.

XX

The New China and the Old[1]

The Eleventh World Congress of Centers for Inquiry/Transnational convened in Beijing in October 2007, the culmination of almost twenty years of interchange between the Center for Inquiry and Chinese scientists. I will focus on the reasons for the Congress and what we hope will ensue from it. I was fascinated by the remarkable changes that have occurred in China since our first visit in 1988. Lin Zixin, former editor of *Science and Technology Daily*, the largest-circulation scientific newspaper in the world, had invited the Committee for the Scientific Investigation of Claims of the Paranormal (CSICOP) to visit China. Chinese scientists at that time, he said, were concerned about the growth of paranormal and occult beliefs. They wished to critically examine paranormal claims and assess the validity of external Qigong and the reality of Chi, psychokinesis, and alleged psychic diagnoses of medical ailments.

We gladly accepted the invitation and gathered a delegation of six well-known skeptics from North America, including Frazier, James Randi, James Alcock, Barry Karr, Philip Klass, and myself. We did not find any evidence of "extraordinary" paranormal powers and issued a report to that effect (see *Skeptical Inquirer,* Summer and Fall issues, 1988).

We noted the chutzpah displayed by psychics, whether adults or children (much had been made at that time about so-called gifted children), who tried but didn't succeed in hoodwinking us. Intrigued by our methods of testing, our Chinese hosts wanted to remain in contact with us. Actually, the Chinese Association for Science and Technology (CAST), a coalition of over 180 science organizations, sponsored the exchange program. CAST, a nongovernmental organization, is somewhat equivalent to the American Association for the Advancement of Science (AAAS).

The Chinese were especially interested in how they could raise the public's appreciation and understanding of science, combat superstition, and improve scientific illiteracy. In time they created a new organization, the Chinese Research Institute for the Popularization of Science (CRISP), which overlapped with CSICOP in its concern with the prevalence of antiscientific attitudes and the public's captivation with parapsychology, UFO abductions, astrology, alternative healing, and pseudoscience in general.

In the early 1990s, CSICOP became an integral part of the Center for Inquiry/Transnational. It has since changed its name to the Committee for Skeptical Inquiry (CSI) and broadened its agenda to defend science, reason, and free inquiry in every area of human interest. The Council for Secular Humanism (CSH) also became part of the Center for Inquiry. It was especially interested in responding to fundamentalist attacks on evolution and naturalistic methodology. CFI added to its agenda the defense of secularism and advanced humanist values not rooted in religion but secular in nature. The Chinese became interested in questions concerning individual morality and happiness, which were similar to the moral virtues of Confucianism, so they found this aspect of our work useful.

The agenda of CFI continued to interest Chinese scientists, who sent delegations to each of our Skeptics World Congresses (held in Heidelberg, Germany; Sydney, Australia; Padua, Italy; and Burbank and Amherst in the United States). More explicitly, they began to send dozens of students, scholars, and officials every year to the Summer Institute of the Center for Inquiry in Amherst, New York, and they translated many of our articles and books. CFI responded by sending two additional teams to lecture in China, and this eventually led to the establishment of a new Center for Inquiry in Beijing and the co-sponsorship of the Eleventh World Congress by the Centers for Inquiry (co-hosted by CAST, CRISP, CFI/Beijing, the Chinese Academy of Science, and many top universities and scientific institutes). CFI/Transnational was pleased to send a delegation of twenty distinguished scientists and philosophers from several countries to the Eleventh World Congress.

The basic theme of the World Congress was development of the public's understanding of science—its methods of inquiry, its naturalistic worldview, and the relationship of science to ethics. These topics are relevant to many societies, but also to the planetary community. The Chinese are concerned with maintaining internal harmony within China and especially expressed worry about global warming and environmental pollution of the atmosphere and water resources. Although there is a preponderance of evidence about the reality of global warming, Ken Frazier pointed out that a minority of readers of *Skeptical Inquirer* adamantly claim there isn't a problem.

All told, some seventy papers—many provocative—were delivered at the Congress, including those by eminent Chinese scientists, such as Professor Qin Dahe, renowned climatologist and meteorologist and Chinese representative to the world agency concerned with global warming (that had just received a Nobel Prize), Cheng Donghong, executive secretary of CAST, and Ren Fujun, the energetic head of CRISP. Ren and I co-chaired the Congress.

Ren said that they wished to expand the role of the Center for Inquiry in China; the enterprise of science popularization has reached an opportune moment as the country grapples with an incredible development boom. It is important, he said, to continue research cooperation between CRISP, CFI/Beijing, and CFI/Transnational to increase the number of Chinese researchers who will participate in summer training classes at the CFI Institute in Amherst, New York, and to co-sponsor international conferences. Many of our Chinese counterparts expressed a desire to establish CFIs in other cities in China. On our trip to Shanghai we met Wang Xin, director of the Shanghai Association for Science and Technology in their new building, and he affirmed that they would like to establish a CFI/Shanghai.

Thus, the Eleventh World Congress ratified and solidified twenty years of interchange and pledged the continued cooperation in furthering the public's understanding of science.

China's Soaring Economy

The entire world community is vitally interested in the Chinese economy, and many international conglomerates have opened branch offices and invested heavily in China. Friendly governments have supported this. The world is eager to trade with the Chinese, and many countries are importing their goods and services at an increasing rate. This has led to complaints about displaced workers at home, because large companies have discovered that they can manufacture products in China and ship them back cheaper than they can produce them in their own countries, sparking tremendous economic expansion in China. Encouraged by its economic vitality, foreign capital investment in China is increasing. This is similar to what happened historically elsewhere when foreign capital enabled countries to develop.

The opening of China to the free market in the past two decades has led to its explosive economic growth. As Frazier notes, of the leading twenty companies in the world, in terms of stock valuation, eight of them are Chinese (including China Mobile, China Telecom, PetroChina, etc.). The sudden emergence of a new class of billionaires in China is an astounding development. Indeed, there are an estimated 100 billionaires living in mainland China (according to the *Hurun Report* and *Forbes*). Most of the wealth comes from real estate, construction, and manufacturing. The wealthiest person on the list is Yang Huiyan, who received a $17.5 billion gift of stock from her father, a real estate developer. Zhang Yin is worth $10 billion due to a surge in the share prices of his Nine Dragons Paper holdings (he owns 72 percent); Yu Rongman, owner of Shimao Property holdings, has $7.5 billion in wealth. And Huang Guangyu, founder of Gome Electrical Appliances, is worth $6 billion according to estimates. Most of this wealth comes from a real estate boom and soaring prices on the Shanghai and Hong Kong exchanges (similar to Google). The Shanghai and Hong Kong stock markets made more money last year from public offerings than the New York Stock Exchange and NASDAQ combined. China is now the chief engine of economic growth in the world—projections place it second to the U.S. by 2015.

This indicates, perhaps, that China is hardly a Communist country; it has a mixed economy—the private sector continues to grow by leaps and bounds. Official Chinese statistics indicate that privately owned companies comprise one-third of the total economy, but I think that this figure is too low. Chinese capitalism is now the dominant force accelerating the economy. What China is able to do on top of that, which other capitalist countries cannot, is use the power of the State to plan large projects and harness both private and public companies to achieve them—such as the vast effort to reconstruct a large section of Beijing for the Olympic Games.

Environmental, Societal Challenges

I was stunned by the evident progress that China had made in the nineteen years since we were there. Everywhere we went new construction was bustling—factories and stores, highway systems, skyscrapers and apartment houses, and entire new towns and cities. China uses one-third of the cranes in the world, according to estimates. The four cities we visited—Beijing, Xi'an, Shanghai, and Guilin (we had visited the first three on our last trip)—are being transformed at a breakneck pace. The Chinese we met on the streets in restaurants and stores seemed proud of these accomplishments, which led to a noticeable improvement in the standard of living, at least in the major cities. This was especially the case in Shanghai, which is truly breathtaking. Daniel Dennett cajoled us into taking a boat ride around the Pudong part of Shanghai. At night the city is dazzling—almost nothing had been constructed when we were there in 1988. It was as if two new Manhattans had sprung up out of nowhere. There are dramatic plans to continue new construction, we were informed by a director of Shanghai's Urban Planning Exhibition Center where a model city of the future was on display.

We enjoyed royal treatment by our Chinese hosts, first in Beijing, where we were chauffeured by limousine to see the massive preparations for the forthcoming 2008 Olympic Games. It appeared to us that they had a long way to go if they are to complete the Olympic facilities on time. But the construction manager assured us that they were working three shifts around the clock and that it would be finished. We didn't doubt that; China has a vast pool of cheap labor that they can apply to such projects. The rest of the world has discovered the availability of this skilled labor force, transferring vast new industries to China and abandoning their own industrial bases for the allure of Chinese productivity.

Incredibly, the rate of growth of the Gross Domestic Product (GDP) has been 10 to 11 percent over the last four years. In gross terms, it reached $2.7 trillion U.S. dollars in 2006—this is one-fourth that of the U.S., though China has four times the U.S. population. The Chinese hope to quadruple their economy by 2020, despite unforeseen obstacles that may slow it down.

We found the streets of China choked with automobile congestion. Surprisingly, many of the cars in Beijing and Shanghai are four-door, replacing the ubiquitous bicycles that we saw on our earlier trip. As Frazier observed, the air pollution was thick, far worse than Los Angeles on its bad days. One Chinese official told me that a recent public poll asked the Chinese what they most wanted: a huge majority responded that their main interest was to own a large four-door automobile! Given the vast increase in energy consumption, the environmental problems that China faces are awesome. The Chinese government is aware of the need to reach sustainable development without pollution. By all accounts, 85 percent of the streams and rivers are fouled or rancid, depleting fresh water supplies. China produces 70 percent of the world's farmed fish in coastal cities and in the mighty Yangtze River, frequently contaminated by mercury, lead, and other toxic chemicals. Murray Gell-Mann reported that Chinese officials said that China is constructing two new power plants per week, fired by polluting coal, but they cannot get provincial leaders to reduce emissions. Moreover, we did not see any great emphasis on the conservation of energy by producing smaller cars (they seemed to have followed Detroit) or dimming their bright lights (much like Las Vegas and Broadway). In this sense, they seem to be emulating America in wasteful, conspicuous consumption, though the government has recently issued guidelines to radically alter how they grow.

No doubt the chief cause of China's energy/resource/environmental problem is the fact that the population keeps growing. The streets are teeming with pedestrians. Many years ago China instituted a stringent one child per/family policy to restrain population growth. Criticized by the Western world for its restraint on freedom of choice, the Chinese nevertheless felt it was an urgent necessity. This has had unexpected consequences, however, for there may not be enough workers to support their aging parents, the custom in ancient China. The growth of the population is due *primarily to the decline of the death rate* because of better nutrition and sanitary conditions. The average lifespan has risen from thirty-five years to seventy-two years in the past four decades. Were China to catch up with Japan (where the average lifespan is now over eighty), this would place still greater strains on natural resources. Demographic projections indicate that China will add 300,000,000 people by the year 2030—equivalent to the entire U.S. population! The most likely place they can migrate to is Western China—even then, will China have enough resources to feed and satisfy its vast population?

Another urgent problem confronting them is the great disparity in wealth, which could lead to intense internal conflicts. Hence, the Chinese government has focused on *harmony* as a central social goal. "Harmony" is Confucian in origin and a moral norm. Traditional Confucian thought emphasizes the cultivation of a virtuous and happy life. One way to do this is to fulfill your station and its duties; another is to reach personal fulfillment. Presumably, in a socialist society, it is to strive for the common good. In any case, there is now interest in classical China, something spurned by Mao.

Overcoming poverty is now a focus of Chinese leadership. The per-capita income in 2006, according to government statistics (which may or may not be reliable), was approximately $2,042, up nearly 20 percent from the previous year, yet still much lower than other industrial countries of Europe, the U.S., and Japan. In major cities such as Shanghai, the per-capita income is approximately $4,000 per person, but in the countryside (we visited model farms outside of Guilin) the peasants only earn $300 per year, barely enough for food and shelter. They live at a subsistence level and use farming methods that go back millennia. Large numbers of people are leaving rural areas for the cities—but there are not enough jobs for everyone. Hence, rising levels of affluence will no doubt lead to a comparative rise in aspirations. Demands from poorer regions point to an explosive powder keg. There are already reports of tens of thousands of protests throughout the country. Perhaps that is why, although the Chinese leadership is strenuously attempting to expand the GDP, it is now emphasizing the need for distribution of consumer goods in poorer areas to achieve social harmony.

One thing is clear: China is *not* a "Cold War" Communist country. Although its government may be authoritarian, it is not totalitarian; it encourages innovation and enterprise and tolerates some diversity. It has a pluralistic economy with a strong capitalist sector and a great number of privately held stores and restaurants. Former premier Deng Xiaoping's policies are heralded as the salvation of China. The leadership plans to quadruple its GDP by 2020, and thereby increase the per-capita income and standard of living. There is a growing middle class in major industrial centers and cities of perhaps 15 to 20 million people and a large underclass longing to share in the good life. For these reasons, the Chinese continue to keep the throttles on "high" in order to increase production, enabling a wider distribution of consumer goods and services to vast numbers of the indigent population.

China's Political Future

While we were in Beijing, the Seventeenth National Congress of the Chinese Communist Party (73 million members) was in session. Some 2,200 delegates attended. Viewing the meetings on television news each evening (on an English-translation channel) seemed like total anachronism. Two-thousand Communist Party (CPC) officials were shown in the People's Hall—the men were dressed in somber, dark suits or uniforms and the women in staid attire. The Congress opened with a statement of allegiance to Marxism/Leninism. There seemed almost no dissent in the sessions of the Congress, at least none was broadcast. A Central Committee (Politburo) and a standing committee of seven run China. They call it collective leadership. Hu Jinatao, head of the Communist Party, laid out the new party line at the Congress. He pointed out that China had not yet reached socialism and that their goal was to move toward "socialism with Chinese characteristics." The aim, he said, would be to strive for "a moderately prosperous society," which they hoped to reach by 2020. The agenda sounded—at least on paper—worthy: it recognized the need of the people to "exercise democratic rights" and to act only under "the constitution and by the rule of law." According to *China Daily* (Oct. 28, 2007), Chinese democracy will seek "to guarantee freedom, equality, and other rights of citizens." Yu Keping of the CPC Central Committee declared that "universal values serve to bolster political reforms," and these include freedom, justice, democracy, equality, and human rights. Presumably, this will contribute to a harmonious society.

Hu promised to appoint more noncommunists as cabinet ministers to governmental positions. The CPC announced on the eve of the Congress the appointment of two noncommunists, Wan Gang, the new Minister of Science and Technology, and Chen Zu, the new Minster of Health, the first such appointees since the 1970s.

Hu also said that although China will continue its rapid growth, it needs to be balanced and sustainable—the Chinese press hailed this as a new "conservation culture." Reducing the depletion of natural resources and providing environmental protection is the only way to do this. China also plans, he said, to reduce absolute poverty with a reasonable system of income distribution and a growing middle class, guaranteeing everyone a basic standard of living. Thus, they hope to reverse the growing disparity in income. China does not have universal health care, a system of social security, or universal education—services which virtually all of the industrialized democracies of the world have. Compulsory education, where it exists in China, is only for nine years, and large sectors of the country have not even implemented that. One member of the cadre said to me plaintively that the glamour of Beijing and Shanghai do not reflect the massive catch-up that China needs to achieve in the countryside if it is to fulfill its ambitious goals.

The provision of the Communist Party's Congress that I found most surprising is the supremacy it accords science and technology in its future plans. The Party Congress—it is perhaps the only major power in the world to do so—supports as its highest priority the "scientific outlook on development," a goal adopted as an amendment to the CPC Constitution. China is now the fastest-growing sustainer of scientific research and development in the world with a growth rate of 18 percent per year over the past five years. It is now in third place behind the U.S. and Japan and moving up fast. The U.S., Japan, and Europe had an overall growth rate in research and development of only 2.9 percent per year. By all reports, the equipment in its laboratories is equal in quality to the rest of the world. Moreover, the Chinese are seeking to attract the brightest researchers to China, and they are eager for partnerships. (See the lead editorial in *Science*, "Chinese Science on the Move," by Alan I. Leshner and Vaughan Turekian, December 7, 2007.)

Hu, trained as an engineer, was quoted as saying: "Uphold science; don't be ignorant and unenlightened." What a contrast with the current

U.S. administration where "intelligent design" theorists oppose evolution and stem-cell research is effectively thwarted. Traditional Marxist theory emphasizes that the expansion of "the forces of production" is essential to economic growth—the Chinese have recognized that increased expenditures for science and technology are crucial to their effective development.

What role does socialism play in China's future? China is supposed to be in the preliminary stages of socialism. According to Hu, the first aspect is that China should be "people-oriented," and second, its development should be "sustainable and contribute to social harmony." They now recognize that basing policies on economic GDP indexes alone is insufficient. They need to pay attention to wasted resources, social unrest, environmental degradation, and regional imbalances. China has vowed to reduce its per-capita energy consumption 20 percent by 2010 and emission of pollutants by 10 percent in the same period. Are these mere ideological slogans, or will China embrace these challenges as it continues to lunge ahead?

More important perhaps for the future is whether there will be conflict within the "relationships of production" between two powerful forces—the free market/capitalist system and its powerful billionaires and thriving middle class versus the Communist Party cadre. Castrating the private sector could halt Chinese productive power as part of the global economy. On the other hand, if its power grows, would it in time dislodge the Communist bureaucracy and lead to a collapse of the system or the emergence of an outright military dictatorship? Will the diplomatic policies of the current regime be supplanted by hostile confrontations in the future? All of these possible scenarios are disturbing, for it may lead to China's decline, and given the interdependence of the entire global economy, could lead to the unraveling of the world economic political system as we know it.

Prudence suggests that we should continue to work closely with the Chinese and encourage the democratization of the political system, the growth of other parties besides the Communist Party, the right of dissent, a free press, respect for human rights, and widespread participation and grassroots involvement in the policies of the country.

China is perhaps the oldest continuous culture on the planet with strong family traditions, a set of moral virtues with deep roots in its past, and resourceful, intelligent, and hardworking people. Skilled in business, artful in negotiation, we should not push them—backs to the wall—into a classical confrontation of national power-politics. We should continue to welcome them into the new planetary civilization emerging in this age of instantaneous electronic communication where cultural, scientific, philosophical, artistic, and economic exchange is vital for everyone.

Humanism and Atheism in China[2]

No doubt the most significant global developments of the past two decades have been the rise of China (and Asia), the relative decline of Europe and Russia, and the weakening of America's power and influence in the world.

What I found so astonishing in my most recent visit to China was the incredible economic and social progress that China has made. We visited four cities (Beijing, Shanghai, Xi'an, and Guilan) and were able to compare China as it was twenty years ago to China today. The cities have been modernized at a rapid rate, transformed by a building boom of breathtaking proportions.

The dazzling new National Center for the Performing Arts in Beijing, containing an opera house, concert hall, and theater with the most up-to-date acoustics, is touted as the largest in the world. And the more than 2,000 new skyscrapers in Shanghai compete with Manhattan for sheer audacity.

Of special interest is the fact that China is officially an atheist country. China has a long history of disparaging religion and its practitioners, not just under communism but reaching into the ancient Confucian past. As for the Communist Party, it adopted Marxist atheism, viewing religious beliefs and practices as outdated, a form of prescientific superstition. Even today it regards religious monks and gurus as charlatans who bilk a gullible public. Theism has never been a major force in Chinese history; so atheism in the Western sense does not strictly apply. Nonetheless, our Chinese hosts made clear that they reject all gods, the supernatural, and the notion of heaven.

The Chinese Communist government has not suppressed religion (as did the Soviets), provided it remain confined to its own domain. China has never suffered religious warfare as has been experienced in the West. Buddhism and Taoism have many humanistic strains; monotheism or belief in eternal salvation have never been characteristic of Chinese religion. The Chinese are a pragmatic people, and the precepts of Confucianism were based on prudence as tested in practice. It is true that Mao expelled foreign missionaries when he came to power, considering them seditious, and during the Cultural Revolution the Red Guards destroyed many temples and religious artifacts. But the widespread reforms of Deng Xiaoping adopted in 1979 expressed a more tolerant attitude toward religion, so long as it confines itself to private matters and does not seek political power. In addition, many forms of folk religion are apparently practiced in rural areas as in olden days, including ancestor worship. Meanwhile, one can see Buddhist and Taoist monks performing rituals and chants at historic temples; but these are like relics of an ancient past in the bustle of present-day Chinese urban life.

Some tolerance has been extended to Christian bodies. Roman Catholics and Protestant churches are recognized, as is Islam. Western media have made much about a religious revival in China. We did not see much evidence of this on our brief trip, though we did visit a historic Islamic mosque in Xi'an that was open to tourists, and we visited an exotic Muslim business quarter where merchants displayed endless wares.

I met the former editor and founder of *Science and Atheism*, Dr. Du Jiwen, and we conversed extensively with editors and researchers of the Chinese Society for Atheism. Dr. Du delivered an address at the Congress, saying that he believed in religious freedom, and this meant the right to believe or *not* believe. Religious believers, he assured everyone, have the right to practice their beliefs. There even has been talk of a rapprochement of sorts between the Vatican and Beijing. The Communist government had been appointing China's Catholic bishops, a privilege the Vatican reserves to itself, but the government stance seems to be softening at present. Even so, the Chinese have not forgotten the fact that nineteenth- and twentieth-century Western missionaries tried to covert the populace, which they identify with colonial exploitation. Meanwhile, the government has announced that visiting teams to the 2008 Olympic Games in China will be given every encouragement to practice their faiths and hold the religious services they prefer. China's government is attempting to display a positive attitude toward religious freedom before the world.

One group that troubles the authorities is the Falun Gong. This movement sprung up in China in 1992 and has apparently spread worldwide. First introduced by Li Hongzhii as "a method of mind-body cultivation," it is, in part, a form of relaxation that is sometimes called internal *Qigong*. This is naturalistic and can be evaluated empirically. Another form is known as external *Qigong*, the claimed capacity to transmit energy from a master who claims extraordinary powers. This is considered metaphysical and paranormal. The government considers the Falun Gong a cult and a threat to the state. Hence, it was banned in 1999 over protests that members' rights were violated. Some estimates maintain that Falun Gong claims 70 to 100 million devotees in China; that is no doubt an exaggeration. The government still considers Falun Gong a pseudoreligious and superstitious cult that undermines its encouragement of science.

In our many meetings with the Chinese, we have attempted to introduce the principles of *secular humanism*. Like atheism, secular humanism is surely nonreligious, but it emphasizes *humanistic values*. Related to humanism, of course, is its commitment to democracy and human rights and the need for the open society, freedom of conscience, and civil liberties. The ethical aspect of secular humanism emphasizes the cultivation of virtue and personal happiness; considerable interest was expressed in this at the Congress. A principal concern of the Congress was how to raise public appreciation for the scientific method and its naturalistic cosmic perspective. The Chinese are expending a large percentage of the national budget on science and technology, and so they are keenly interested in raising the level of scientific literacy. Support for research is high on their development agenda.

China is governed by the Chinese Communist Party, which holds the preponderance of power, controls the military and police, and dominates the media—indeed, all public sources of information. Yet, China is a mixed economy, and the state has encouraged the emergence of a new class of wealthy entrepreneurs who enjoyed the latitude to set up factories and engage in real estate and stock market speculation. In addition, they have allowed people to open private shops across the country. Thus capitalism is a dominant strand in Chinese life. Today, China is the fourth-largest economy in the world; it expects in less than a decade to become number two, after the United States. Its dynamism is a result of its free-market economy, which was encouraged by Premier Deng Xiaoping, liberating China from the Marxist-Leninist ideology with its central planning.

China's GNP keeps expanding, but with this has come problems of environmental degradation, depletion of natural resources, and pollution of air and water supplies. China's leaders are deeply worried about global warming. Another problem for China is population growth. China has added 250 million people since the year 1980, and it will add 300 million in the next twenty-five years. This is despite the country's one-child policy and other strict efforts to limit births. Population growth has nonetheless continued, driven by the decline of the death rate—longevity has increased from thirty-five years to seventy-two years in the past four decades. Credit the development of public sanitation, improved health care, and an increase in the food supply—the Chinese are very proud of their discovery of a new strain of hybrid rice by Professor Ylan Longfing, which has enabled them to increase food production significantly.

A disquieting development in China today is the disparity in incomes between a still-impoverished peasantry and a new class of very wealthy millionaires and billionaires. Perhaps 150 to 200 million Chinese living in urban centers are involved in manufacturing and construction and have seen their incomes rise, but the leaders recognize that this prosperity needs to be extended to the countryside. This disparity in income is similar to what has been happening in the United States, though much of China is still backward, and per capita income is comparatively low.

The Chinese now talk much about the need to go "green." Development, they agreed, must be sustainable. They also recognize the need to increase supplies of consumer goods and services in the poorer parts of the country. Their goal is to enable all Chinese to lead "a reasonably comfortable life" by 2020—a very ambitious one indeed.

They also say that their hope is to develop a more democratic society in which the universal humanistic values of "freedom, dignity, equality, and justice" will prevail. Whether this goal is achieved remains to be seen. I still remain skeptical until I see concrete evidence of further progress in human rights. We were encouraged by their great economic progress and hope that it will be complimented by political progress in human rights as well.

Notes

1. This article first appeared in *Skeptical Inquirer* 32, no. 2 (March/April 2008), pp. 6–10.
2. This article first appeared in *Free Inquiry* 28, no. 2 (February/March 2008), pp. 41–43.

Section 6

Personal Reflections

XXI

The Convictions of a Secular Humanist[1]

I live what many of my friends think is an unbelievably active life. It is commonly thought that the eighties are a time when people in their right minds should retire. Perhaps I should have my head examined, for I have not. It is also the age when *reflective wisdom* is supposed to develop (if one does not have Alzheimer's). In any case, this is also a good time for me to reflect about humanism.

Being an octogenarian, of course, has its infirmities. I can no longer jog three miles a day—instead I do aerobic trotting for one hour everyday, though at a somewhat slower pace. I cannot get through the day without my spectacles and hearing aids. In the area of libido, George Bernard Shaw was right when he observed that it is a shame that romantic love is wasted on the young!

But octogenarianism also has its surprising virtues. Aristotle said in the *Nichomachean Ethics* that the best time to tell if a person has achieved *eudaemonia* (well-being) in a complete life is when one approaches the end of life. I have lived an exuberant life, fully engaged in the public arena, always busy in writing and lecturing. One advantage of a long life is that I have known many of the world's leading humanists—from Sidney Hook, Ernest Nagel, E.O. Wilson, Francis Crick, Albert Ellis, Andrei Sakharov, B.F. Skinner, Betty Friedan, Antony Flew, and Tom Szasz to Steve Allen and Jayne Meadows, Carl Sagan and Ann Druyan, Isaac and Joan Asimov, Peter Ustinov, James Farmer, Elena Bonner, Vern and Bonnie Bullough, and so many others. I have gained an appreciation for the heroic dimensions of these humanist personalities as we worked on projects, as well as their humor and wit and their exuberant lust for life. All would no doubt make A.H. Maslow's list of creative actualizers, able to savor peak experiences.

It is remarkable to see the shift in attitudes toward humanism in the last half of the twentieth century. I remember well the celebrations of

John Dewey's ninetieth birthday in 1959, which I attended as an impe-
cunious graduate student. On one occasion, Dwight Eisenhower, then
president of Columbia University (and being groomed for a run for the
U.S. presidency), spoke at an event honoring John Dewey. Can you
imagine a presidential candidate doing that today? At that time, no one
wished to be known as "antihuman." Everyone claimed to be a humanist, even the pope and the Marxists. That humanism, more specifically
secular humanism, came under heavy attack from the Moral Majority
and fundamentalist preachers in the late 1970s, '80s, and '90s was a
shock to most of us.

This no doubt was because secular humanism was considered godless
and was identified with atheism. Yet that is not the defining characteristic
of *humanism*, which uniquely expresses a set of ethical values. Religious
conservatives deny that humanists can be moral persons. They ask, "Is
life worth living without God?" or "Can one be good without religious
faith?" *Yes*! I respond. "Life is or can be meaningful on its own terms!"
The refrain that I sing is that "Life can be intrinsically good, overflowing
with value. I have found life wonderful. Every moment is cherished and
counts." That is why I have written so much in praise of exuberance.[2]
The exuberant life is a life of exploration and discovery, adventure
and achievement, creativity and joy, pleasure and satisfaction. The
meaning of life is not found by withdrawing from the world in quest
of mystical transcendence. It is created by each of us as we reach out
to new dimensions of living. In this process emerges the excitement,
drama, and exaltation of living. Life has no prior meaning or purpose;
it is pregnant with opportunities for each person to seize and act upon.
Human beings are creative; they can initiate purposes, plans, and projects and bring them to fruition by their own powers of intelligence and
effort. In my book, *Forbidden Fruit*,[3] I write that humans need to eat
of the fruit of the tree of knowledge of good and evil, but that the *best*
fruit in the Garden of Eden is that of the tree of life. In Genesis 3:22, 23,
we read, "The Lord God said: behold, the man is become as one of us,
to know good and evil; and now, lest he put forth his hand, and take also
of the tree of life, and eat, and live forever"—and thus Jehovah expelled
Adam and Eve from Eden. Good riddance to a life of dependence and
submission!

The chief good for the humanist is *life itself*: pulsating, throbbing, full
of expectations and consummations. It is a life in which moral conduct is
exemplified. We do something not because God commands it but because
our ethical reflections indicate that it is good or right or appropriate.

But "What about the *tragic?*" asks the believer. "Is this not a vale of tears?" Perhaps at times, for we suffer defeats and losses, unrequited loves and disappointments. We may experience severe setbacks that may crush some individuals with their intensity—the twists of outrageous fortune are often unpredictable. There are people who endure lives of desperation, poverty, and disease, or who live in despotic, repressive societies. Yet there is the will to overcome adversity, and, in the place of pain or sorrow, happiness and laughter, delight, and joy can break through. One needs to balance the good with the bad, strive against injustice, and love in the face of duplicity.

We are forever surrounded by naysayers, nihilists, negativists, the pallbearers of guilt, fearful and depressed people. Yet ranged against the killjoys of the world are loving, kind, helpful, inventive, humanitarian, altruistic, affirmative, and positive people who strive to improve the human condition and contribute to human happiness. They are the *optimists* in our midst. They endeavor to live a full life, confronting adversity by taking advantage of new opportunities and willing to take risks and succeed. In my book, *The Fullness of Life,*[4] I said that a person's life is like a *career*; it is a work of art. We are responsible (in part) for who and what we become. We constantly redefine our interests by the schools we attend; the occupations we select; our choice of friends and the people we fall in love with and perhaps marry or divorce; our children and grandchildren; beliefs and convictions; dreams and aspirations; the plans we conceive and unfurl; the beloved causes to which we dedicate our time and talents and sometimes even our lives. These are the Promethean heroic virtues of audacity and our challenge to the rulers or gods on high, and our use of the arts and sciences to better the human situation (see my recent book *Promethean Love*[5] about my philosophy). In my view, humanism first and foremost entails a set of ethical values. These were implicit in the philosophy of ancient Greece and Rome. They were expressed in the efflorescence of the Renaissance; the emergence of modern science; the liberation of humans from bondage by the democratic revolutions of the modern world; the battles for human freedom and human rights; and the defense of freedom of thought and free inquiry.[6]

A mistake often committed today by militant nonbelievers is to simply equate humanism with atheism. The recent books by our esteemed colleagues Dan Dennett, Richard Dawkins, Christopher Hitchens, Sam Harris, and Vic Stenger—now enjoying some well-deserved popularity—point out that belief in God is a "delusion" and that the Abrahamic "God" after all "is not great." But the main thrust of humanism is not to simply espouse the negative—what we do *not* believe in—but what we *do*. We should not begin with atheism or anti-supernaturalism but with humanism. I am a *secular* humanist because I am not religious. I draw my inspiration not from religion or spirituality but from science, ethics, philosophy, and the arts. I call it *eupraxsophy*; that is, the *practice* of wisdom as an alternative to religion. The *convictions* of a humanist involve both the head and the heart, cognition and emotion. These are our rational-passional core beliefs.

What then do I mean by *humanist* ethical values and principles? (1) Ethics is autonomous and not derived from external commands. It is based on human experience and culture and modified by human intelligence in the light of the consequences of our choices. (2) This life here and now, for ourselves, our children's children's children, and the community of humankind, is good for its own sake. (3) Human beings have some power over their own lives and some responsibility for their futures. (4) Humanists have some confidence in our ability to solve our problems by using reason, science, and education and expressing goodwill. (5) We recognize and tolerate pluralistic lifestyles without necessarily agreeing with them. (6) We insist upon the right to privacy. (7) We believe in the open, democratic society. (8) Although we seek our own happiness and well-being, we are deeply concerned with the rights of every person. (9) We are profoundly committed to the well-being of humankind and the planetary community.

May I relate this secular humanist stance to the current public mood in the United States. I am appalled by the apocalyptic scenarios that abound and seem to afflict so many of our fellow citizens. Permit me to focus on two kinds of doomsday scenarios: religious and secular.

First are the scenarios endemic to theistic religiosity from time immemorial, the belief that the City of Man is sinful and corrupt. God destroyed Sodom and Gomorrah and inflicted a worldwide flood in the days of Noah, and, we are warned, He will do so again. "The barbarians are at the gates" scenario today fingers liberals, social democrats, feminists, Satanists, secular humanists, gays, and terrorists. They are said to debauch the social order. The only rescue for us is "the Rapture," the return of Jesus (if you are a Christian), or the hellfires of *jihad* for the enemies of Allah (if you are a Muslim). The way to salvation, say devout Christians, is to entrust your life to Jesus—or the Old Testament for Chassidic Jews, the Koran for Islamists, or the Book of Mormon for Mormons. Many evangelicals predicted that in the year 2000 the end days would finally descend upon us. *Nothing happened.* Hal Lindsey's prophecies in *The Late Great Planet Earth* did not come to pass. We are all too familiar with this form of paranoia and fantasy that is out of cognitive touch with the real world. This scenario is given impetus today by the conflagrations in the Middle East, which allegedly are leading us on the path to Armageddon.

A second class of secular doomsday prophesies also abound today. Although they are grounded in fact and represent real problems that need attention, even many humanists and secularists are caught up in worry over worst-case scenarios—encouraged by sensationalist cable news network program commentators and Internet blogs. I will list only some of them:

- Global warming will raise the level of the seas and wipe out coastal cities from Florida and Manhattan to Bangladesh.
- A virulent form of the Asian flu will spread widely and kill millions.
- The mysterious death of the bees, which pollinate plants and trees, threatens to drastically reduce our food supply.
- There will be a devastating collision with an asteroid, which could destroy all life on Earth.
- Nuclear bombs will come into the hands of Islamic terrorists.
- The survival of humankind is threatened by runaway population in the Third World and ecological devastation of large sections of the planet.
- A right-wing fascist *coup d'état* will seize the American government.
- There will be war with China.
- Drawing on science fiction, Hollywood films and popular novels portray the dystopias of the future, bleak and repressive thought-control.

Now I do not wish to minimize any of these threats. Many pose genuine dangers—such as global warming and the need to reduce carbon emissions, and/or a real financial crisis. What I am concerned about is the pessimism and despair (in reaction, no doubt, to George Bush and the evangelicals in his administration). The fearmongers and pessimists of our time bear down on us daily with their dire forebodings.

During my lifetime, I have been witness to many awesome dislocations and conflicts. I was a four-year-old child when the 1929 stock-market crash occurred, and I lived through the Great Depression of the 1930s. By way of contrast, this was also the time of the Charleston rag, New Orleans jazz, and the talking movies of Jean Harlow, Laurel and Hardy, and The Three Stooges. It was also the beginning of Social Security and other reforms. I visited the 1939 World's Fair at Flushing Meadows and saw the General Motors exhibit, which depicted the superhighways that were to be built after the war—and they were.

I remember vividly the Nazi and Japanese regimes of the 1930s and 1940s. I enlisted in the Army during World War II—I experienced the bombings of London and saw graphic films of the devastation of Rotterdam, Warsaw, and Moscow by Stuka dive-bombers, and later, the destruction by Allied bombers of Dresden and Bremen. We were aghast at the tyranny of the Stalinist Gulag and were horrified by the atomic destruction of Hiroshima and Nagasaki. We were disturbed by the Maoist Cultural Revolution in China, but also pleased by the rebuilding of Europe, the subsequent democratization of Germany and Japan, the creation of the United Nations, and the liberation of the former colonial empires. The Cold War and the fear of thermonuclear destruction was a constant reminder of what we all faced, though fortunately it never transpired. Then came the Korean and Vietnamese wars and the unexpected collapse of the Soviet empire. Today, we are embroiled in wars in Iraq and Afghanistan.

Balance these events with the emergence of a third industrial revolution, first in Japan and South Korea and now in China and India. Many Cassandras of doom in the past had forecast that mass famines would overtake Asia—they have not occurred. In the twentieth century, we were astonished at the great breakthroughs in medicine—antibiotics, surgery, organ transplants. These advances have steadily reduced pain and suffering and extended life spans. New inventions and a plethora of consumer goods have continued to pour forth at a rapid pace—automobiles and airplanes, refrigerators and washing machines, air conditioning and central heating, radio and television, cell phones and computers. The Information Revolution is transforming life in incredible ways. Technology has increased food production enormously. The goal of universal education for all children is gaining wider acceptance throughout the world. The feminist revolution has made great gains. The extension of equal rights to blacks and other minorities, including gays, lesbians, and transgendered persons, continues—not without opposition, but progress is nevertheless seen everywhere.

Especially important is the rapid growth of scientific discovery, which has dramatically enlarged our understanding of the biosphere and the cosmos. The promise of new technologies entices us: nanotechnology, the biogenetics revolution, the emergence of transhumanism and the "new singularity" promise new applications for the continued amelioration of life's problems.

I respond to the scenarios of the doomsday prophets with a *third scenario* of the *progressive improvement of life everywhere on the planet Earth.* I do not deny the need to conquer poverty and disease; the serious problem of diminishing energy resources; the destruction of the natural ecology; and the continued extinction of other species. Nor do I discount the possibility of natural disasters or major wars in the future. But we need to be aware that humankind has managed to survive and persevere in spite of these regressive events.

This third scenario does not project a doomsday future, but is instead hopeful about the ongoing, long-range gradual improvement and enhancement of life for more and more people on the planet Earth. There are no panaceas—only the continued extension of the ideals of the Enlightenment. Secular humanists are calling for a *New* Enlightenment today, drawing on the principles of secularism, naturalism, and *humanism.* It is this last that I especially wish to emphasize. We are living in a period in which scientific discoveries have radically altered our understanding of nature and life and have provided us with new powers to attain our goals. However, the public understanding of the methods and outlook of the sciences and the cultivation of critical thinking are vital if democratic societies are to survive and flourish.

I submit that also essential is some appreciation for a planetary ethics over and beyond the ancient chauvinistic religious, racial, ethnic, national, or gender differences and animosities of the past.

There are two key ethical humanist principles that we now need to promote and defend in *the ethics of the future.* First, we must extend our moral obligations to the broader global community over and beyond nation-states. This means that we should consider *every person anywhere on the planet equal in dignity and value.*

Second, each person is *responsible* for his or her own future and that of society, but in addition we all have a stake in *the future of humankind on the Planet Earth.* This means the application of reason and science *and* the principles of ethical humanism—a concern for improving the lives of everyone on the planet as far as we are capable of doing. Most important is the resolve to work for these goals. Herein are *the convictions of a secular humanist* at the beginning of the twenty-first century.

Secular humanism, I submit, still has great promise for humankind. We need to work together to help create a better world. That has been the beloved cause to which I have devoted my life. I trust that you share many or most of these ideals.

Notes

1. This article first appeared in *Secular Humanist Bulletin* 24, no. 1 (Spring 2008): 1–4.
2. Paul Kurtz, *Exuberance: The Philosophy of Happiness* (Los Angeles: Wilshire Books, 1977).
3. Paul Kurtz, *Forbidden Fruit* (Amherst, N.Y.: Prometheus Books, 1988).
4. Paul Kurtz, *The Fullness of Life* (New York: Horizon Press, 1974)
5. *Promethean Love: Paul Kurtz and the Humanistic Perspective on Love*, ed. by Tim Madigan (Newcastle upon Tyne, U.K.: Cambridge Scholars Press, 2006).
6. See Paul Kurtz, ed., *The Humanist Alternative: Some Definitions of Humanism* (London: Pemberton Books, 1973).

XXII

The Transformation of Universities[1]

I

Universities arguably today are undergoing the most significant transformation in their history. And this is due to a number of converging factors.

One can trace schools of higher education back to Plato's *Academy* and Aristotle's *Lyceum* through the monasteries of the Middle Ages down to the emergence of universities such as Oxford and the Sorbonne, the appearance of institutions of higher learning in North America in the nineteenth century and the development of colleges and universities to train huge numbers of students for the corporate state. I wish to reflect on what is happening, particularly in the United States, by drawing on my own experience. No doubt similar trends are occurring in Canada, but perhaps not to the same extent, for the U.S. always seems more extreme.

I apologize for being autobiographical, but I came of age in the university world in the 1940s and '50s and began teaching in liberal arts colleges and universities right after that. I began my teaching career at a time when the liberal arts curriculum—the "great books" as it was called—seemed particularly relevant and when philosophy was considered to be central to a liberal arts education. Our goal at liberal arts colleges was to expose students to a wide range of fields including the arts, literature, the humanities, the natural-biological-social sciences, history, mathematics, and logic. There were requirements that students had to take in order to receive a BA or BS. I taught at Trinity College in Hartford, Connecticut, an Episcopal school founded in 1823, whose motto was pro *ecclesia et patria*. We called it the "Episcopal Party at Republican Prayer!" Its Board of Trustees was dominated by conservative businessmen. The chairman was Keith Funston, head of the New York Stock Exchange, and the Episcopal bishop of Connecticut sat on the Board. It was an all-male school. Chapel attendance was mandatory every day. The recipients of gentlemen's C's were virtually all members of fraternities; and they quickly learned how to drink their way through school. There were strict quotas limiting Jews and Catholics, and there were almost no blacks. The college bestowed honorary degrees on the senators and governors of the state, but they refused to award one to Governor Abraham Ribicoff for obvious reasons. The senator from Connecticut was Prescott Bush (father of Governor Bush and grandfather of George W.), who was then considered to be representative of the liberal Eastern internationalists.

I taught briefly at Vassar College, a non-sectarian all-women's college in Poughkeepsie, New York. Among my students were Miss Rockefeller and a relative of Irving Berlin. I also was a professor at Union College, a non-sectarian all-male school founded in 1795 and the mother of fraternities. All of these colleges maintained high standards and sought to provide a balanced education for undergraduates. They all eventually changed, became co-ed, and tried to diversify admissions.

The American university seemed to follow the German model because people went on to take advanced degrees, Masters, and PhDs, specializing in specific fields. There were efforts to maintain rigorous standards. I took my PhD at Columbia, which still tried to maintain standards, including rigorous tests in the history of philosophy and four fields (metaphysics, epistemology, logic, and ethics). Students had to take two foreign languages to qualify for a PhD. Columbia required all graduate students to have reading knowledge of German and French. These strict requirements were weakened in subsequent years in graduate schools. Actually my first teaching job was at Queens College in Flushing, New York, which subsequently became a part of the City University of New York.

II

A great assault occurred on the universities in the late '60s and '70s, when the so-called "New Left," drawing upon a kind of Marxist critique, attacked the very framework of colleges and universities. It attempted to change them by demanding participatory democracy. This grew out of the great student uprisings of that time. Both students and faculty were to share in its deliberations; and it used the Vietnam War as a kind of springboard for this major assault. It was a time when violence hit universities worldwide, from Berkeley to the State University of New

York at Buffalo where I taught, all the way to French and European universities. At that time I was involved with Sidney Hook in founding what we called University Centers for Rational Alternatives (UCRA). This organization involved a coalition of liberals and conservatives who wished to defend academic freedom and resisted violence on campus. UCRA attracted under its banner many of the most distinguished public intellectuals in America, including Irving Kristol (later called the "father of neo-conservatism" and his wife, Gertrude Himmelfarb, Oscar Handlin, Jacques Barzan, John Searle, Seymour Lipset, Daniel P. Moynihan, Alan Bloom, Robert H. Bork, Henry Steele Commager, Bruno Bettleheim, Carol Van Alstyne, Fritz Machlup, Nathan Glazer, Kenneth B. Clark, Louise Rosenblatt, Charles Frankel, Thomas Sowell, and others. The campuses were aflame with demands that the entrenched *professoriate* and the great-books curriculum give way, and that the universities and colleges be relevant to the problems of society.[2] I was particularly intrigued by this assault because as a student of John Dewey's followers at Columbia and NYU, I believed that higher education should be relevant to the problems faced by society; and that it could play a key role in democracies in transforming public attitudes and in developing critical thinking, and in particular, attempting to apply the methods of science to ethical values.

I organized a branch of UCRA (probably the largest in the country). This was a statewide faculty organization of several hundred professors. Its purpose was to defend the university from violent protests and to maintain standards of academic excellence at a time when they were under assault by radicals. The provost at my university, Warren Bennis, tried to justify the abandonment of virtually all requirements by declaring that we needed to allow students "to take a streetcar named desire!"

My own institution was under a constant state of siege. I was continually harassed and my life was threatened several times. Mobs burst into my classroom or they attempted to break up public lectures that I gave. At first, the Students for a Democratic Society (SDS), and then the U.S. Labor Party, under Lyndon LaRoche, would leaflet the campus, denouncing me as an upstate CIA agent of Kissinger and Rockefeller.

I can remember a huge rally on my campus in which Herbert Marcuse was the featured speaker. He argued that there were limits to tolerance and that we should not tolerate the intolerable (namely the Right Wing). I was a former student of Marcuse at Columbia; and I responded in kind to his argument in *Dissent*[3] that if we are willing to limit the freedoms of those we disagree with, then right wing militants might some day use the same argument against us: what if right-to-lifers would attempt to ban abortion outright, for they say that it is intolerable to them. This comment was prophetic, given their antics since then. Actually, I experienced this backlash directly about five years ago when Dr. Barnet Slepian, an abortionist in Amherst, New York was murdered. At that time the police had reason to believe that I was also a target and they sought to provide protection.

To graphically illustrate the temper of the times, in the early 1970s I organized an open public meeting at the American Ethical Union in New York City to discuss the violent assaults on free speech on the campuses. I invited Sidney Hook and Albert Schanker (president of the teacher's union) on the one side (he could not make it and sent Jules Kolodney). On the other side were Harold Taylor, president of Sarah Lawrence College and Professor Edgar Friedenberg, guru of the New Left and frequent contributor to the *New York Review of Books*, who defended the radical students, saying that their violence "was trying to tell us something."

As the meeting got underway, the hall was invaded by a group known as "The Crazies," dressed in the colors of the flag. They carried the head of a freshly decapitated pig and placed it on the table before Friedenberg. Corliss Lamont and Charles Frankel were in the packed house shouting to call the police. It took almost an hour before they appeared. We discovered many years later at Senator Frank Church's hearings that "The Crazies" was an FBI front group used to disrupt liberal meetings.

The student demonstrations on campus of course had some positive results. They helped change the governance of colleges and universities somewhat, by taking Herr Professors off their Imperial Thrones. Students now could grade professors and greater choice was given to students to design their own programs. Most colleges became co-ed and there was an effort to open the universities and colleges up to women and minorities, and for some religious schools to become non-denominational.

Interestingly, the period of the late '60s and early '70s had both negative and positive effects. It altered the public's appreciation of intellectuals, and I think that the reputation of the university has suffered ever since. It also marked a basic shift in the focus of higher education, by transforming universities into centers of research conducted by highly specialized faculty; at the same time, it exposed millions of students to the best cultural, scientific, and humanistic knowledge available. Subsequently these universities were transformed still further into institutions whose primary purpose was to contribute to the economic and technological growth of the society. As a consequence, in recent years grantmanship has dominated higher education in America and every great university competes for funds, which are considered an essential component of the economy of a region or state. The former focus of a general liberal arts education, unfortunately, has been supplanted increasingly by an emphasis on training students for careers in the corporate global economy. With this, as we shall see, the creative encouragement of radical new ideas has been de-emphasized.

III

During this entire period, I considered myself to be a defender of Enlightenment values. I thought that there was a corpus of literature that should be read, and that we should introduce students to the best of rational-critical thought, particularly of Western civilization.

Meanwhile, there have been profound intellectual changes that have occurred in the last twenty-five years. First was the emergence of post-modernism, led by philosophers—I'm sorry to say—following Heidegger, Derrida, and French *savants*. They questioned the basic principles and ideals of the Enlightenment, attacked humanism, the objectivity of science, and ethical values; and they also seriously rejected progressive ideals and any notion that there could be a philosophy of emancipation. This became part and parcel of the new conservative outlook that began to develop, in which the free market was taken as the guiding economic-political ideology, not only in the United States but worldwide. On American and other campuses in the world, post-modernists rejected the great books written by dead white males and preferred those written by females and minorities; and they attacked aspects of Western culture as racist and colonial.

At the same time, of course, we witnessed the virtual collapse of Marxism, particularly of any left wing movements of reform. This occurred in France and Western Europe as well, so that the old left-right dichotomy no longer seemed relevant. In controversies about public policy, democratic socialism and Marxism usually had something significant to say; but with the collapse of Soviet communism in Russia and Eastern Europe, and the emergence of the United States as the great superpower, a significant change in the intellectual scene became evident.

Concurrent with these intellectual changes, the impact of the Information Age in the 1990s was becoming apparent. Although we knew about IBM mainframe computers, few people had any inkling of what the development of the PC would mean to office and scholarly work; nor did we foresee how the emerging World Wide Web would have transformed the entire method of acquiring and delivering knowledge. And this not only has had a radical impact on the nature of knowledge and its mode of communication, but on the university itself. It is no doubt a truism to take note of this, but it is *the new technological changes that have had a huge impact on higher education.* These provide new opportunities for knowledge, but also disturbing dangers.

IV

Permit me again to wax autobiographical. In the late '60s and early '70s I was deeply involved in publishing journals. I edited the *Humanist* magazine for eleven years, and in those buoyant days attempted to apply humanist values and principles to modern society and to persuade people about their viability and importance. Indeed, I was able to attract the *Who's Who* of intellectual life. Eventually, I founded the Committee for the Scientific Investigation of Claims of the Paranormal (CSICOP), which published *Skeptical Inquirer* (1976), and I was instrumental in helping to create some one-hundred magazines and newsletters worldwide. I helped to develop the Skeptical movement, resurrected from ancient Rome and Greece. CSICOP focuses primarily on claims of the paranormal and alternative medicine, which were touted to the gullible public by media conglomerates willing to sensationalize and distort scientific objectivity, in order to provide entertainment and such products to consumers.

Secular humanism came under heavy attack from the political right in the late '70s and early '80s. At the same time, conservative religion began to grow by leaps and bounds. In response, I founded the Council for Secular Humanism (CSH) and *Free Inquiry* magazine (1980). Fundamentalist religion was considered to be beyond the pale by most intellectuals, surely those who occupied the ivory towers of the secular universities. When I began in the early '80s to criticize these fringe religious movements, many of my colleagues were appalled that I would even take them seriously. They thought that no one considered them intellectually significant and they insisted that there were other more important things to do. Interestingly, secular humanism became the main enemy of the Religious Right and the Christian Coalition. Tim LaHaye, Pat Robertson, Jerry Falwell, and others thought that we dominated the United States, all of which I thought very amusing, until they seized power during the George W. Bush presidency. *Free Inquiry* was rather prohibitive in predicting that they would be a force to contend with, and that we needed to take them seriously.

I should also point out that I became convinced that secular humanism and skepticism needed a new literature. I was disturbed by the fact that so many publishers did not issue books on free thought, atheism, agnosticism, skepticism, or humanism. Thus in 1969 I founded Prometheus Books. During this period I recognized that small intellectual magazines of opinion could have an impact on public consciousness. There were about eight or ten magazines of influence such as *Partisan Review*, *Commentary*, *The Nation*, *New Republic*, *The New Leader*, *Dissent*, *New York Review of Books*, and later the *National Review*, *The Public Interest*, *The Weekly Standard*, and other conservative publications. The world of books was at that time essential to higher education. Every Ph.D. candidate had to write a master's thesis and a doctoral dissertation, which hopefully would eventuate into some kind of publication. The cultural change that has stunned us ever since is the growth of the information revolution, and the decline of the print media—books, magazines, and newspapers—and the devastating effect that this is having upon university libraries and bookstores, especially the process by which knowledge is being distributed and assimilated.

V

Let me focus first on the decline of the book. Treatises were compiled in Hellenic civilization, written on papyrus, copied and assembled in the Alexandrian libraries, which contained the reflective thought of great thinkers and writers, such as Plato and other great scientific and philosophical authors of ancient Greece and Rome. Books were considered so important that some were even taken as "sacred": the Torah, the Hebrew Bible, the New Testament, and the Koran were worshipped as containing the deliverance of divine wisdom. The production of books was given enormous impetus with the discovery of movable type by Gutenberg. Books could now be distributed beyond the limited coterie of scholars and theologians and they could be read by ordinary people. Thus the great Era of the Book—from the fifteenth through the twentieth centuries—had an impact on higher education. Books defined the university because it was the studying of these great books of literature in the arts and sciences, philosophy, and history that involved scholars. Students were expected to master a specialty, to read the literature within it, and for those who went on for high degrees, to themselves contribute to knowledge.

Of course in the nineteenth and twentieth centuries, scientific research in the laboratory and fieldwork was intensified. The Copernican, Darwinian, and behavioral revolutions were upon us, and so the universities were extended to include the laboratory, the workshop, and the theaters of the performing arts. It's not simply in the cloistered library or seminar room in which books are explicated and critically analyzed, but in the scientific world and the world of the arts. The university was considered to be a vital resource for the discovery and transmission of knowledge. In this process papers are published in journals, read and discussed at conferences.

Where do we stand today? Well, we see the decline of reading, the decline—sadly—of symbolic and cognitive knowledge, and its replacement by imagery, form, and the visual arts. The invention of photography in the nineteenth century was an important discovery, for you could depict without a painting or sculpture, the exact replication of persons or scenes. Subsequently, cinematography and movies appeared, the development of the telephone and radio enabled us to transmit the human voice. The invention of the gramophone could record and playback not only voice, but music and drama. Eventually of course came the invention of network television and cable TV. As the twentieth century progressed, the medium increasingly influenced the message, as Marshall McLuhan pointed out. This was not the cognitive explication of mathematical formulae or languages, the analysis of a Kant or Hegel, Mach or Einstein, Marx or Freud, Sartre or Russell, but the replacement of concepts and symbols by signs and images. These newer forms of communication engulfed us: the sound bite and glance, the process and the scroll have *dramatically* changed how we receive information. The Internet and the web further transform us every day even further. The book is being assaulted on all sides, as are magazines and newspapers; and there is a steady decline in reading per capita.

Libraries are also being transformed. They had been central to universities. They were the repositories of knowledge and experiences, the wisdom of the past, whether fiction or non-fiction. Increasingly today, fewer students use the library; and if they do it is more often the computer that they use. They do not read textbooks as in former years. The demise of the *Encyclopedia Britannica* and *Encyclopedia Americana* as great works assembling and outlining human knowledge is a thing of the past; these were transformed onto computer discs. Today students do not need to go to libraries to pour over reference books. They can go online using *Google, Yahoo!*, or other search engines. Everything you need to know you can find online or by using a cell phone or BlackBerry. I am merely emphasizing what is commonplace. But these technological changes are transforming the university in the sense that traditional scholarly and scientific modes of the transmission and evaluation of knowledge are disappearing. I see this clearly as the founder of Prometheus Books. We have published over 3000 editions over the years. I have seen the decline in scholarly publishing of works of non-fiction and the growth of fiction and fantasy.

VI

Another key fact that has occurred is that traditional departments, limited to specialized fields of expertise, are being bypassed by interdisciplinary work—all to the good, no doubt. My colleague and friend, Irving Louis Horowitz, whose company, Transaction, publishes some thirty journals and about 150 books per-year in the social sciences, observed that thirty years ago there were clearly defined fields in the social sciences, such as economics, political science, sociology, and anthropology.[4] Now there are interdisciplinary fields such as gerontology (on aging), or demography (on population studies). In other words, interdisciplinary investigations often supercede departmental research. These trends are often opposed by intransigent faculty, many of whom still want to defend their entrenched departmental positions and they resist interdisciplinary work. Most of them still wish their students to publish scholarly treatises or if in the sciences, a research project. But increasingly it is difficult to find publishers to do so. Undoubtedly, these trends will continue. One can ask, What is the place of the university library in the future scheme of scholarly work? Is it redundant?—particularly when *Google* completes putting online the entire libraries of Oxford, the Sorbonne, the Library of Congress, and British Museum. At that point publishers will no longer be necessary, at least to the extent that they have been.

The importance of publishers should not be overlooked; to publish a book is not the same thing as to print it, for publishers need to apply the skills of their craft with tender loving care. They need to read manuscripts, edit, fact check, and revise them. Only then are they typeset, packaged, published, announced, and distributed. On top of this are the great efforts expended to get them reviewed. That process is rapidly disappearing. Academic publishing is in dire straits and the number of people who read academic books in any one specialty is declining.

Another key factor on the current scene is the power of the media, particularly of huge media companies—which dominate the publishing industry, movies, radio, television, cable news networks, and the Internet. There is a tendency to squeeze out dissent, unorthodox and unconventional points of view. In the field of publishing, which I am most familiar with, independent publishers have virtually disappeared. They were merged or went out of business. There are today six conglomerates that dominate the media in the United States. Foreign publishing companies, such as Bertelsmann and Springer in Germany, Pearson in England, own or control book publishing in the United States. Publishing is a worldwide phenomenon, no longer explicitly national in character. University presses exist but they only account for a small percentage of the total books published.

Another development is that the contemporary university does not have to be in a physical place where professors assemble, seminars are convened, and students mingle with, for increasingly courses and programs are offered online. The University of Phoenix (a private company owned by the Apollo Group), for example, may be the largest university in the U.S.; for it has a huge existence in cyberspace. The professor of the future does not have to enter the classroom. Many believe that the personal touch is vital for the best education. Mark Hopkins once said, that what we need is a log with a professor on one side and the student on the other. Many have tried to gild the log, with vast buildings, equipment, and university endowment funds. But perhaps the universities of the future will take place in satellite space and as such will be truly galactic in character. These trends are likely to exacerbate. Of course, there will be traditional universities, books, magazines, journals and even faculty members, but on a much smaller scale.

VII

The last point that I wish to make is the decline of universities as bastions of critical and creative dissent. No doubt the Religious Right in the U.S. has targeted secular campuses, insisting that their point of view be given equal time and badgering liberal professors. Unfortunately, many are fearful that the Bush administration has liberal and left wing groups on campus under surveillance.

Now it is true that intellectuals still have some influence, and they are called upon sometimes to provide advice. But the growth of media conglomerates, the transformation of universities primarily into engines of technological and economic growth, means there will be less room for the iconoclast, maverick, or free thinker. What has intrigued me is the collapse of faculty courage and the reluctance to deal with the great social problems of the day. A good illustration of this is the fear of administrations or faculties to provide any critiques of religion, any willingness to step forward and examine critically Christianity, Judaism, or Islam.

As a case in point, we at the Center for Inquiry are actively engaged in probably the most important field of critical Islamic inquiry anywhere; yet we find that although the faculty agree privately with us about the need for this inquiry, they themselves are fearful of being identified with it. That is the primary reason why I created the Center for Inquiry and its multifarious organizations adjacent to but outside of the control of university faculties, administrators, and trustees.

Sidney Hook observed, particularly during the days when the University Centers for Rational Alternatives was in its heyday, that UCRA was virtually alone in its criticism of violence on the campuses. Administrators were fearful to be so identified with radical critics; and they would run for cover at the first whiff of trouble. He observed that there are two great virtues: the first is intellectual—which scholars and scientists have in abundance—and the second is the virtue of courage. Hook said that he was disillusioned by the virtual collapse of courage among faculties who were readily intimidated by the established powers of the American plutocracy. Intellectual thinkers of the past—such as Thorsten Veblen, C. Wright Mills, John Dewey, or Bertrand Russell—played roles as social critics, oracles, and iconoclasts. This is becoming increasingly rare. The assault on the universities today, particularly from conservatives, has not only castrated independent thinkers and activists, but has impeded efforts to present critiques of the unexamined sacred cows of society. If universities and colleges continue to be privatized (as are hospitals and nursing homes), they will then become business schools, pure and simple, focused on training people for the corporate economy, not cultivating a liberal academic agenda.

All of the above point to the fact that in the current age universities are being transformed. They have become indelible parts of the military-industrial-technological complex and the global economy. They are supported, insofar as they are as essential for the corporate state. The preeminent task of faculty is to raise grant money for research. The defining test of how successful the university is is determined by the marketplace—not of ideas—but of funding. Where universities will end up is difficult to say: whether they will survive in the form they have had or whether they will indeed become redundant? Clearly universities and colleges will still exist in the future, if nothing else, to change the diapers of millions of undergraduates who need to be educated and to fuel the global economy with professional cadre. But that they will function as significant centers of dissenting opinion and learning, and in what form, is the great question to ponder for those of us who have spent our lives in the universities.

Notes

1. This article originally appeared as, "The Rapid Transformation of Universities: Personal Reflections on Higher Learning," from *Humanist Perspectives* 159, (Winter 2006/07): 19–23 (including sidebar, references, and notes).
2. Four volumes of the papers delivered at the conferences of UCRA have been published.

    Sidney Hook, Paul Kurtz, Miro Todorovich, eds., *The Idea of a Modern University*, Prometheus Books, Buffalo, N.Y., 1973; Hook, Kurtz, Todorovich, eds., *The Philosophy of the Curriculum*, Prometheus Books, Buffalo, N.Y., 1975; Hook, Kurtz, Todorovich, eds., *The Ethics of Teaching and Scientific Research*, Prometheus Books, Buffalo, N.Y., 1977; Hook, Kurtz, Todorovich: *The University and the State*, Prometheus Books, Buffalo, N.Y., 1978.

    Another account of the efforts of UCRA to defend academic freedom was the book edited by Sidney Hook, ed., *In Defense of Academic Freedom*, Pegasus, N.Y., 1971. This has articles on what transpired on many campuses at that time. It includes an article by Paul Kurtz on "Inside the Buffalo Commune; or How to Destroy a University."
3. Paul Kurtz, "The Misuses of Civil Disobedience," *Dissent* 17, no. 1: (January/February, 1970).
4. See *Transaction*, the social science journal that plays a key role in the social sciences.

XXIII

Final Reflections: Perhaps Facing Death

I

I say "final" since I am in a bed in the intensive cardiac unit at Buffalo General Hospital, awaiting an angiogram this afternoon to determine what is wrong, if anything. And I say "perhaps," since I do not know if I will survive (most likely I will) or what procedures will be done. I have been diagnosed with aortic stenosis, which means that I can drop dead at any time. So if not now, surely some day. So this is my last epitaph on reflections on dying.

I cannot believe that I am more than four-score years (81) and that old age takes its relentless toll. I confirm the aging process every time that I glance at myself in the mirror. "Is that me?" I ask, "for I look older than I feel!" Not that I do not begin to feel the infirmities of decrepitude. But I have been rather healthy and full of energy and exuberance almost every day.

Are these the final reflections? I hope not, and that I have many more years of pluck! Yesterday, as I experienced chest pains, I reread *The Phaedo* of Socrates in which he awaits death in his prison cell. He was 70 years old, or so we believe, awaiting the hemlock to be administered to him by the jailer. The death sentence was imposed by his fellow Athenians in an open trial. The students and followers of Socrates are distraught and they have implored him to flee the unjust sentence (in *The Crito*). He refused to escape, almost playing the role of martyr, and he accepts the verdict with equanimity, rather stoically; though he reflects on the possibility of some form of immortality. The main thing he says is to strive for virtue, the best you can; and this he has done throughout his life. He sent his wife, Xanthippe, and son away; she was crying and beating her breasts, according to Plato. And so Socrates awaits his death with calmness: Plato describes the effects of the potion he drank. Socrates begins to feel numb in his extremities and eventually dies without the expression of fears or tears. Did reason calm his passions or fear of the unknown enable him to die peacefully?

I also read the last days of David Hume, the great skeptic of the Scottish Enlightenment. Medicine was fairly undeveloped in the late eighteenth century, but his doctor confirms after examination that Hume is suffering from some form of growth in his bowels. Hume himself reports to his friends his condition. He apparently suffered from colitis, which was manifested by diarrhea. He grew weaker every day. At one point James Boswell, a theist, visits Hume as he awaits death, prodding him as to whether he will recant and accept religion and salvation. Hume will have none of that. He had been attacked all of his life as an atheist; and indeed he was denied a professorship at the University of Edinburgh by believers who feared his apostasy.

Hume continued editing his writings. By then his repudiation had traveled far and wide. His early philosophical writings were not appreciated in Britain and Scotland—though he made his reputation as a writer—his philosophical writings *were* acclaimed in France, where he was heralded by *Les Philosophs* as a great thinker. At one point he is invited to dinner in Paris at Baron D'Holbach's home where all those present admit to being atheists, and Hume is astonished, because he says that he never met any in Scotland or Britain—deists and skeptics, yes, but atheists? The same fear that was prevalent then, still persists in the world today, especially in America, where disbelief and outright atheism is rejected by the general public. Hume entrusts, his final work, *Dialogues Concerning Religion* to his friend, Adam Smith, the celebrated moral philosopher and economist, to be published posthumously. Similarly his two essays, "On Suicide" and "Immortality," are published after his death.

The account that we have of Hume's final days and death are remarkable. For he remains cheerful until the end, carrying on conversations as best he could, neither tearful nor fearful of his impending demise (at age 65). He knew that he was growing weaker every day, and went about his life as best he could with a touch of stoicism and acceptance of his end. He did make preparation for his body by purchasing a piece of land in the Old Cemetery in Edinburgh, and arranging for a mausoleum to be built. His friend, Adam Smith, in writing about Hume, said that he was a noble man of virtue, as nearly perfect as human beings can be—though he did not believe in the Christian God. The French called him "*le bon David.*"

And so this is a prelude to my own reflections of my possible death, if not today, then at some day. I believe that we should fight against "the dimming of the light," and that we should strive mightily to remain healthy and try to live as long as we can. Rather than *pining* for immortality, which is an illusory myth that so many people swallow; on the contrary I accept the finality of death as a natural fact of human life. If death comes, so be it. I don't want to die. I still have sufficient strength of body and clarity of mind, and I have the stamina and will to continue to exult every day, to enjoy every moment of life, to breathe fully and taste experience richly, and reflect about nature and life. For my interests are ravenous. I read three newspapers every morning (*New York Times, Wall Street Journal, Buffalo News*), read perhaps a dozen books a month, and have project after project that I am willing to embark upon with lust and excitement. Everyone tells me that I need to slow down, take time to savor the succulent moments, smell the fragrance of bouquets and flowers that I purchase every week for my wife. I exercise one hour each day, upper and lower body—I call it aerobic trotting, if outdoors, or jogging on a treadmill, if inside. I cannot sit still a minute. I know that I need to pause sometimes from the hectic pace of life that I set for myself. I realize that I burn out so many around me. The vessel of my life is never full, for it empties quickly and needs to be replenished as a constant pace.

My penchant is the life of activity, for its own sake, the striving after goals, the game of life and the quest for exploration and adventure; there are always new things to discover, new experiences to encounter, new people to meet and relate to. I feel that there are so many things yet to do, and I have so many plans to design and fulfill. I have called my hyperactivity "the fullness of living," and at times I feel as if I am "bursting at the seams," bubbling over with new ideas. I wake up often in the middle of the night with new ideas catapulting me forward—I often get a piece of paper and try to write my thoughts down as they stream forth before I forget them, like the fizz on a newly opened bottle of soda water.

Two attitudes have increasingly come to dominate my outlook. First, a sense of "good will" is essential in life. I do not take this as a stern commandment in the Kantian sense. Immanuel Kant was great philosopher, though he never traveled far from Kowingsberg where he lived; though he had wide interests. Rather, I take a good will to be the mark of a morally committed person. By that I mean, not surely a cognitive predisposition, recognizing our moral obligations and responsibilities to others, but genuine affection for all human beings, an emotional desire to see them prosper. I say that I am a *humanist,* meaning by that, that we should strive as best we can to do good, to try to help where we can, to compliment other persons wherever possible. By this I mean that we should express an affirmative attitude at all time, to try to improve the situation, if we can, to look at the bright side.

The second is to love others—really all individuals, no matter what race or color, ethnicity or nationality, gender or age. Ah, yes, enjoy life and hope that others will as well. I have had an affectionate regard for my wife and family and friends, colleagues and acquaintances, even those that defame me or hate me for my ideas. I meant well, I respond, if perhaps misunderstood.

So, I do not fear death. If it comes, I have no illusions about God or the afterlife; what nonsense. It is *this* life here and now that I appreciate. I appreciate it fully and depart with a tinge of sorrow (perhaps), but in retrospect, life has been wonderful, and I only wish that I can share this exuberance that I have felt throughout, it's not the naysayers who complain, but the yea-sayers that we should herald—those who strive to make life better, as best they can and recognize that joyful creativity is the fountainhead of a meaningful life. Would that all human beings could learn what I have.

Au revoir le monde, bonjour eupraxsophy, the practice of joyful wisdom, based on a *rational-passional* attitude.

—Paul Kurtz
(completed March 6, 2007)

II

It is now Sunday, March 11th. I know that I need open-heart surgery to replace my aortic valve (I am genuinely sorry that some animal had to die, probably a pig, so that I can use its valve and live) and to replace part of the aortic walls and an artery with a bypass. I am awaiting such surgery as soon as possible. Although the survival rate of such procedures is good, given my age, one can never tell what will happen. Given these facts I continue my reflections on what may be my last days.

First, I am *reflection* from beginning to end, always examining all sides of a question or seeking understanding and meaning. My first love is and remains *philosophy*, but philosophy by itself fails us. We need scientific understanding to test and corroborate our theories by testable hypothesis; and we need to untap the full range of the passionate life.

Second, I marvel at the brilliant achievements of modern medicine, able to cut open my chest and repair "this old heart." My father died at

59 (in 1959) because we had not fully developed the science of cardiology. My mother lived until age 95 (she died in 1998) because we did. So we need to marshal the fortitude and ingenuity to break new ground, by exploring the frontiers of knowledge and applying these discoveries for the betterment of humankind. I am convinced that we need to draw on evidence and rational inferences to confirm our hypotheses; that is why I submit that the methods of science (broadly conceived) are the most reliable guide to achieving knowledge and this surely applies to modern-day cardiology, which has made great progress. I agree with Bertrand Russell that to demand evidence for our beliefs is a radical proposal and that large numbers of the species will kill to prevent these methods from being applied to their cherished beliefs.

Third, I am of course an atheist, for I do not think there is sufficient evidence for the existence of God; the later is *the* delusion of humankind, an anthropomorphic rendering of human wants and desires into the womb of Mother Nature. I am especially perplexed that so many humans will deify Jesus and sacrifice their lives for him. Most of what we know about him is poetic fiction (the Bible is a human document, not divinely revealed). The Jesus story has been extrapolated for almost 2000 years by the Gospels and he was ordained by priests and ministers as God. The original message of a dead and risen deity is buried by the sands of time, as is Jesus—if he ever lived. Similarly for Moses and the myth of the "chosen people," a tale told by rabbis to sustain a wandering people. Equally questionable is the mythology of Muhammad, which today captivates large sectors of the human species. Digging into the historic circumstances of the Koran clearly shows that it is unreliable guide for modern humans, a tale contrived by the prophet's companions. We do not have adequate reasons to believe that Muhammad, or Paul, or Moses received revelations from On High. In any case, to derive our essential moral codes from such ancient diktat is folly: it was used to repress women and the poor and keep countless generations of humankind in bondage to fictionalized paranatural tales, indoctrinated in their children, and sustained for the alleged comfort they are supposed to provide. Religious institutions have encrusted these ancient fantasies and made it difficult to overcome them. The transcendental temptation has fed the parables of unknown prophets, and they have outlived their usefulness and relevance.

Fourth, humankind needs to move on to a new stage of life. The perspective of the universe should not be fixated on the creation story repeated over and over again, but a new naturalistic account of nature and the human species as part of an expanding universe. So it is the astronomers and physicists, chemists and biologists, paleontologists and anthropologists, and countless other scientists who can better account for who and what we humans are. We evolved over millions of years by natural selection and other natural causes. And we are part of a vast cosmic scene, a magnificent awe-inspiring universe that we can unravel and comprehend—at least, in part, by the sciences. Much of it is still veiled in mystery; and we need to continue to use our critical intelligence to explore and explain the cosmos: the polarity of chance and contingency, regularity and order, chaos and plurality.

It is evident that each of us contains trillions of particles of recycled matter; the atoms that compose our bodies contain elements that have survived over eons of time. "From star dust we came—and upon our deaths—to star dust we shall return," to paraphrase an ancient metaphor.

Fifth, I can find no evidence for a separable "soul" or "spirit"—another illusion of the infancy of the race; and surely no evidence for personal immortality; and least of all for "salvation" by a theistic being. What an anthropomorphic fantasy read into the universe by our forbearers!

Thus, my reflections of a life long lived is that we need, as best we can, if we can, to break the chains of illusion, and face life and especially death, for what it is: the end of mortal existence. I accept my death when it comes as a natural fact. Of course, I would like to live as long as I can, to extend my days and years, to continue to exult: to love and be loved, to know and understand, to enjoy the pleasures of taste and sensation, to work cooperatively with others in building a better world, to expand ethical appreciation and dedication, to improve and preserve this lovely planet (a blue-green dot as viewed from outer space) upon which we live; and to await each day with expectation and adventure. Surely, I have suffered defeats in my life: I have sometimes been disappointed and I have witnessed the sometimes tragic aspects of life—the contingent accidents, afflictions and misadventures that virtually all people experience. But the negative aspects of human existence in my view needs to be balanced by the laughter and joyful play of children, the passion of romantic love, the satisfaction of learning and discovery, the nobility and excellence that I have found in so many people, the cherished value of individual freedom and creative fulfillment, the satisfaction of shared experience—of music and the arts, and nature itself—and the wondrous discoveries of scientific inquiry. Ah yes, all of these things are essential parts of the full life brimming over with affirmative values.

But then—what is the *meaning* of life? I would say that life presents each person with opportunities, whether we choose to untap them fully depends on each person's choice. Life, my life, your life presents us with challenges, and what we make of them depends on what we do, what I have done, or you have done. We need to learn from experience and modify our behavior, if we can.

But then *how* a person lives depends on *where* he or she lives. Living in America in the twentieth century—an open pluralistic society—has afforded options that I could not have had in other places on the globe. Under whatever sky I live, I am still *me*, but how I have lived depends on the alternatives that a free society makes available; and America has provided me with unlimited horizons, because it is still relatively free. Every generalization about the United States can be countered by a contrasting generalization, and for every good there is an evil, and for every achievement, a default. Yet after all is said and done, it is still an open frontier where people from everywhere came in search of a new life. In this sense it has been the universal culture on the planet—for virtually every racial, religious, ethnic, and national group has been represented here. What I cherish most is its freedom and its sense of decency and generosity—though there are of course notable exceptions, embarrassingly so—self-righteous, self-interested individuals concerned only with greed and their own gain. That is why the older I became the more I realized the need for altruism and empathy, caring and compassion in a person's life, and a genuine concern for others. This entails a positive devotion to social justice, genuinely felt.

I have had the great fortune of visiting over sixty countries of the world many times and I love them equally, La Belle France (what a beautiful land, what cultural enrichment), England and Scotland (the source of our democratic institutions, and my appreciation for empirical philosophy, eloquent literature and poetry), mother Russia (a seasoned culture and people who have suffered so much under Czarism and Stalinism, and now can become democratic and humanist), Germany (I forgive my German friends for Nazism, and I appreciate their music (Beethoven) and philosophy (Kant and Marx)), China (an amazingly rich historic culture of endurance and creativity), Africa (how much they have been oppressed and only now can they flower), India (a vast gentle land in need of a new Enlightenment), Peru, Mexico and Latin America (which needs to break the shackles of repressive religions of the past). I love each an every European (Italian and Serb, French person and Irishman, Englishman and Spaniard, Russian and Pole) and every African and

African-American, Japanese and Vietnamese, Korean and Chinese, Australian and Argentinean, Hispanic and Native American, Jew and Gentile, Eskimo and Congolese.

And I say that we have reached a juncture in human history where every person on the planet Earth should be considered as equal in dignity and value. The new agenda for humankind is to develop a new planetary humanism, where our goal is to make the world a better place for everyone. We need to obliterate poverty, disease, discrimination everywhere. We need to transcend the dogmas of the past. We need to go beyond the dysfunctional archaic religions and build a new morality where every person is entitled to equality of concern, no matter what his or her gender or sexual orientation, race, creed, or ethnicity, where every child will be provided with the opportunities for education and cultural enrichment, where all people on the planet can enjoy the fruits of their labor, where the vast disparities of income and wealth can be reduced, a planet which can progress beyond nation-states and create a new vibrant planetary civilization in which peace, prosperity, cultural enrichment, scientific discovery, and philosophical wisdom can flourish.

There will of course be new problems and crises, new conflicts and disputes in the future. Yet I believe that a secular and democratic world community with new transnational institutions protecting human rights *can* evolve.

In any case, men and women need ideals to live by, and I have always been devoted to ideals—how challenging it is to build a better planetary community—and how much I regret leaving it. I only wish I can add years to my life to engage in this great dream of a better world.

And so, when I depart from this life, I will have no illusion of an afterlife; I will be happy that I took part in the game of life; and hopeful that others will discover the zest and vitality of living fully: I have drawn deeply upon cognition, though this has been supplemented by the courage to persevere and the compassionate caring that I have had for others.

I remain a Stoic, *que sera sera*, though I have done what I could to not submit to the status quo, but to work for a better world. I have lived with intensity and purpose, and have enjoyed every moment. And I will say in parting, *Adieu le monde!*

Index